An Ethological Study
of Children's Behavior

THE CHILD PSYCHOLOGY SERIES
EXPERIMENTAL AND THEORETICAL ANALYSES OF CHILD BEHAVIOR

EDITOR
DAVID S. PALERMO
DEPARTMENT OF PSYCHOLOGY
THE PENNSYLVANIA STATE UNIVERSITY
UNIVERSITY PARK, PENNSYLVANIA

AN ETHOLOGICAL STUDY
OF CHILDREN'S BEHAVIOR

W. C. McGREW
Department of Psychology
University of Edinburgh

 *1972*

ACADEMIC PRESS   New York   San Francisco   London
A Subsidiary of Harcourt Brace Jovanovich, Publishers

ACADEMIC PRESS, INC.
111 Fifth Avenue, New York, New York 10003

United Kingdom Edition published by
ACADEMIC PRESS, INC. (LONDON) LTD.
24/28 Oval Road, London NW1 7DD

LIBRARY OF CONGRESS CATALOG CARD NUMBER: 71-182617

PRINTED IN THE UNITED STATES OF AMERICA

To π

Contents

Contents

Preface

The relationship between ethology (the biological study of animal behavior) and human behavior has been until recently a largely tenuous and speculative one. Many workers, both practicing ethologists as well as social scientists and clinicians, have drawn numerous analogies between nonhuman and human animals, but empirical studies in human ethology remain few. This book presents an attempt at a quantitative, direct investigation of the behavior of a special type of *Homo sapiens*, the preschool child. The book attempts to show that both the rationale and methods of ethology (and these are inextricably linked) can provide a useful and exciting new approach to hitherto neglected aspects of children's behavior, particularly that which is manifested in social interaction in nursery schools.

By the nature of the subject, a study in human ethology must straddle several of the established academic disciplines. It is hoped that workers in these varied fields will find useful ideas and information in this volume. Zoologists studying animal behavior (and ethology has been gradually creeping up the phylogenetic ladder since its early beginnings with invertebrates, fish, and birds) may be interested in this initial attempt at its logical extension into the Hominidae. Psychologists, particularly those in developmental and social psychology, may find useful ideas from alternative approaches to human behavior other than the more current indirect and experimental ones which dominate contemporary research. Anthropologists and sociologists may find potential value in the attempts to deal with social structure and organization and in the obvious need for cross-cultural extension of these studies into diverse human societies. Primatologists, it is hoped, will derive some use from the comparative viewpoint adopted throughout, just as it is hoped that those workers with human behavior who have not familiarized themselves with the exciting findings on nonhuman primates in the past ten years will be encouraged to do so. Finally, if for those individuals whose main concern is with the development of healthy and happy children, whether they be teachers, counselors, pediatricians, therapists, or child health workers, the book sheds any additional light on the young child as an active social being, I will feel more than amply rewarded.

Because human ethology is such a new field of enquiry, the first three chapters of the book are devoted to a review of the literature from the many relevant fields and to a discussion of the theoretical and practical problems involved in applying ethology to man. The lengthy fourth chapter constitutes the first attempt to provide a comprehensive ethogram for the young *Homo sapiens*. This contains descriptions of facial expressions, gestures, postures, and locomotor behavior patterns, and discussion of their significance and function. The succeeding chapters make use of this repertoire of behavioral measures in studies of selected aspects of social behavior: group structure, group formation, introduction into a group, effects of group density, and periodicity in behavior. Finally, a detailed bibliography of references pertinent to human ethology is presented, which I believe to be the most comprehensive yet published.

Only time will tell how successful I have been in presenting a case for human ethology. Like all tentative efforts in newly emerging areas of investigation, it is likely to age quickly. By the same token, it is difficult to compare the book with other published volumes in the field since these are yet so few. (For a recent exemplary exception, see *Ethological Studies of Child Behaviour,* Blurton Jones, 1972.) Rather, the single source which has provided the most stimulation for my work is just now a century old—*The Expression of the Emotions in Man and Animals* by Charles Darwin. Darwin saw much more than even he knew, and we who call ourselves human ethologists are fortunate that he set such an example of descriptive clarity and rich detail.

W. C. McGrew*

Present address: Tulane University, Delta Regional Primate Research Center, Covington, Louisiana

Acknowledgment

I am grateful to the following individuals and institutions without whose generous assistance this volume could not have been produced: Professor L. Weiskrantz and the Institute of Experimental Psychology, Dr. C. Ounsted and The Park Hospital for Children, and Professor D. Vowles and the Department of Psychology, University of Edinburgh for research facilities and equipment; The Rhodes Trust, The Population Council, the National Institute of Mental Health (U.S. Public Health Service), and the Social Science Research Council (U.K.) for financial support; Miss J. Lawrence and the staff of the Slade Nursery School, Miss M. Baker and the staff of the North Oxford Nursery School, and Mrs. L. Bruce and Mrs. E. Smale of the Epworth Halls Nursery School for their patience and valuable advice; Mrs. J. Clarke and Mr. C. Holmes for computer programing and Mrs. M. Smith and Dr. A. Barr of the Oxford Regional Hospital Board for electronic data processing assistance; Mrs. P. Faust (Bedford College, London), Mrs. A. Hentry, Mr. D. Raffaelli, and Miss B. Rowland for IQ testing; Mrs. R. Palmer and Mrs. P. Williams for typing; Miss M. Wicksteed and Miss P. Simon for translations; Mr. J. Rae for assistance with illustrations; Mrs. I. Fay, Miss J. Potter, and Mrs. D. Lloyd for aid in data analysis; Miss C. Tutin for proofreading; Mr. A. Turner, Mr. J. Broad, and Mr. S. Lawson for photographic assistance; Mrs. C. Hutt, Mr. S. J. Hutt, Dr. M. Manning, and Dr. N. Blurton Jones for advice and criticism; Professor D. S. Palermo, Editor of the Child Psychology Series, and the staff of Academic Press for their encouragement and aid.

I am especially grateful to Professor D. M. Vowles and Mrs. P. L. McGrew. The former supervised most of the research and unstintingly provided encouragement and stimulation throughout the course of the study. The latter aided in all aspects of the research mentioned above from its inception to completion.

I am also most grateful to the three- and four- year-olds of Oxford and Edinburgh who so graciously endured my scrutiny while at the same time providing inestimable enjoyment.

I must thank the following publishers for permission to reprint various materials published by them: *Ethological Studies of Child Behaviour*, N. G. Blurton Jones (ed.), Cambridge University Press, London and New York, 1972); *Proceedings of the Second International Congress of Primatology*, Vol. 1, C. R. Carpenter (ed.), and *Proceedings of the Third International Congress of Primatology*, Vol. 3, H. Kummer (ed.), S. Karger Verlag, Basel and New York, 1969 and 1971, respectively; *Direct Observation and Measurement of Behavior*, S. J. Hutt and C. Hutt, Charles C. Thomas, Springfield, Illinois, 1970.

Chapter 1

Introduction: Historical Review

This book is an exploratory study of the problem of applying ethological methods to young children's social and, particularly, agonistic behavior. But because few such studies have been attempted so far, little literature exists in the area of human ethology. Moreover, the nature of this area is necessarily cross-disciplinary, and knowledge from several different and normally separate fields is relevant. For these reasons, the following historical review touches on several sometimes overlapping areas of knowledge outside human ethology: social psychology, developmental psychology, aggression, anthropology, sociology, and primatology.

Developmental Psychology

Developmental psychologists have published hundreds of papers and dozens of books on young children's social behavior, and particularly on young children's aggression. The obvious question that arises is: what new knowledge can be gained by applying ethological methods in this area, and how does the ethological approach differ from the more traditional ones? In replying, one

1

must consider the various research approaches already utilized by developmental psychologists, and the knowledge that results from them. The subcategory of social behavior related to aggression will be separately discussed in the next section.

Developmental psychologists have approached social behavior using a spectrum of measurement varying along a gradient of "directness." At one end are the observational studies of free social interaction in play groups and nursery schools. At the other end are the indirect techniques which do not include observation of ongoing behavior. In the middle are the experimental studies, where selected aspects of behavior or consequences of behavior are recorded in predetermined and controlled situations. A comprehensive review of the studies would require many pages, but a selected survey will be attempted. Unless otherwise stated, the studies listed refer to preschool children (i.e., children usually more than three and less than six years old).

Perhaps the most indirect studies are retrospective ones; for example, Boll (1957) investigated the effects of preschool playmates on social development by interviewing adults about their childhoods. Another indirect approach is to interview children to elicit their verbal comments about certain imaginery social situations, for example, by showing them ambiguous pictures, asking them to finish stories, or simply asking them open-ended questions (Murphy, 1943).

Social relationships and status may be assessed with sociometric techniques, for example, by asking children to state preferences among their playmates in certain situations or on certain criteria. With young children, the process may be facilitated by supplementing the verbal questions with a photographic display of the individuals involved. But adequate validation of this technique came only after considerable results had already been published (McCandless & Marshall, 1957a), and many unresolved difficulties remain. A variant of this is to ask children to name peers who possess certain attributes, for example, "Who is the friendliest?" (Northway, 1952).

Solicited adult judgements of children constitute more direct measures since it is presumed that adult assessment of children is at least partially based on past observed behavior. Adult judges are usually untrained observers, most often teachers, and they generally are asked to rate or rank children on certain attributes or to describe children's overall performance in selected situations. Examples have been teacher ratings of children on an eleven-point scale of dependency (Waldrop & Bell, 1964) and teacher rankings of each child's four best friends (McCandless & Marshall, 1957b).

Another more direct approach is to assess sociability from the results of selected spontaneous behaviors, for example, by examining children's drawings. Lebo (1962) measured the surface area of drawn human figures and used this as an indicator of "expansiveness."

2

Experimental studies in which a child is temporarily placed in a controlled situation, usually alone with an experimenter, take many forms. The doll-play experiment is a common type: a child is asked to play with a standard set of toy figures and accessories while an observer records the resulting "social" behavior (Sears, 1951). Dunnington (1957) gave children a set of 60 toys and recorded such behavior categories as "attacking," "criticism," and "withdrawal" while they played. Another experimental approach is to grade recordings of experimental sessions on certain criteria, for example, Guerney, Burton, Silverberg, and Shapiro (1965) had independent coders grade vocalizations from adult-child play therapy sessions.

Observational studies dealing with ongoing social interactions occur most frequently in the older literature, but what was observed differs greatly from study to study (S. J. Hutt & C. Hutt 1970). Diary studies in which individual behavior is sporadically noted, often on its first appearance, came first, but these often lack systematic consistency. Darwin's (1877) detailed notes on his first-born son from birth to one year set an early example for clarity and precision.

Direct observational studies often have much in common: nursery school or kindergarten setting, subject populations composed of the children of academics, "free-play" periods, observer present in a play room, copious verbal descriptive notes. They vary mainly in the behavioral categories used in recording. Some observers utilize only arbitrarily selected behaviors: for example, attentional shifts (R. W. Washburn, 1932). Others restrict themselves to certain body parts but categorize behavior involving those parts inclusively: for example, differential hand usage in six categories (Brown, 1962).

Some investigators use totally inferential categories: for example, all behavior classified into five motivational categories such as "recognition status" (Rafferty, Tyler, & Tyler, 1960). Others use more behavior categories of a less inferential nature: for example, 33 categories (e.g., "securing negative attention") by Emmerich (1964). Still others use more explicit categories involving the results of behavior: for example, 30 categories such as "gets willing cooperation easily" (Stott & Ball, 1957).

Studies using more objectively defined behavioral schemes sometimes include a few broad, inclusive categories: for example, "solitary play" (Parten & Newhall, 1943). Other workers use graphic recording techniques: for example, children being represented by geometric shapes and "conversations" indicated by connecting lines (Marshall & McCandless, 1957). Still other workers define behavior more specifically (e.g., "threatening gesture"), but lump results into broad groups for analysis: for example, into "physical aggression" (Walters, Pearce, & Dahms, 1957). Finally, a few research workers restrict themselves to selected specific patterns and then examine them in detail: for example, laughing and smiling (Ding & Jersild, 1932). Many studies combine more than one of these approaches and usually correlate results between two methods of measurement or use one to substantiate the other.

Aggression

Aggressive behavior has probably received more research attention than any other class of young children's behavior. Most authors have considered it a subset of social behavior but others take exception to this (e.g., Berkowitz, 1965). Besides receiving empirical attention, aggression has been the subject of considerable theoretical discussion (see, e.g., Kahn & Kirk, 1968). As the previous developmental psychology section was concerned primarily with methods, and the methods discussed there apply to studies of social aggression cited here, problems of theory will be stressed in this section. This will be approached in three ways: (1) definition, (2) origin, and (3) nature of aggression.

In a theoretical discussion, definition of terms is essential. Many authors unfortunately have not defined aggression or aggressive behavior even in their empirical studies; other have purposely avoided it as undefinable (e.g., Kummer, 1967; Vowles, 1970); and considerable disagreement exists among those who *have* defined it (H. Kaufmann, 1965). Besides the question of whether aggression is necessarily *social* behavior or not (and, if it is, destructive behavior directed toward objects becomes "redirected" aggression) there is the question of intent. Berkowitz (1965) considered intention to injure as essential in labeling a behavior as "aggressive." Buss (1961) argued for its exclusion since intentionality is empirically useless in studies of animals and nonverbal humans, and its ascription is questionable in general, whatever its obvious importance. (However, Bower, Broughton, and Moore [1970] recently described research on newborn infants in which it is possible to infer intention to behavior; this involved reaching toward real and apparent objects and differential emotional responses to the two situations.)

Among authors restricting aggression to social situations, some restricted its application to attack (Walters, Pearce, & Dahms, 1957), some to attack plus all other "repelling behavior" (Barnett, 1967), and some included all aspects of interanimal conflict, including predation (S. L. Washburn & Hamburg, 1968). Carthy and Ebling (1964) also included self-inflicted damage, for example, suicide, as aggression.

Additional confusion arises from other similar terms which may be used either without definition, interchangably, or with overlap: agonistic behavior, anger, ascendance, assertive behavior, violence, hostility, animosity, etc. Buss (1961) advocated considering this behavior in three ways: aggression as an instrumental response, anger as an emotional reaction, and hostility as an attitude. Scott (1962) proposed to discard the terms aggression and hostility and include both under the broader label of agonistic behavior. Patterson, Littman, and Bricker (1967) considered aggressive behavior as a subclass of "assertive behavior", that is, behavior denoted by a "demand characteristic." The unfortunate result of the terminological hodgepodge are statements such as: "I have used the term hostility in my title, instead of aggression, in order to direct discussion towards the theme of animosity rather than assertiveness " (de Monchaux, 1964, p. 83).

Definitional problems aside, considerable discussion has appeared on the origins of aggressive behavior. Some authors have proposed that aggressive tendencies are phylogenetically "built-in" to man, that man's biological nature makes human aggression inevitable, at least to the extent that it cannot be prevented or eradicated, only possibly controlled. These fall into three main groups: the classical ethologists, the psychoanalytical theorists, and the popularizers. The first held the predominant position in ethology until about 15 years ago (see Tinbergen, 1951): aggression was thought to result from the activation of some innate aggressive drive. The activating stimuli were specific, usually prominent morphological characteristics presented by conspecifics in behavioral displays. In the absence of these "releasers" the aggressive "energy" accumulated, and the behavior might eventually be performed *in vacuo*. This view of aggression's "spontaneity" was derived from animal studies and is still influential in some popular treatises on human aggressive behavior, for example, Storr's *Human Aggression* (1968) and Lorenz's *On Aggression* (1966). Criticism in the 1950's (e.g., Hinde, 1956; Lehrman, 1953) rendered much of this theoretical position suspect, and modern ethologists have largely abandoned it, with some conspicuous exceptions (Eibl-Eibesfeldt, 1970). The fact remains that no empirical evidence, either physiological or psychological, has ever been presented for the existence of an "aggressive drive" in *Homo sapiens*.

Some writers have attempted to link the classical ethological view with that of thinkers in the field of psychology founded by Freud. Freud paid little attention to aggression in his earlier works except as a by-product of sexual drives, and when he did emphasize its independent existence, he incorporated it into the "death instincts." Then, in 1920, aggression was considered as primarily self-destructive, that is, turned inward. Later followers retained this instinctivist view, for example, Klein's hypothesized struggle of life (or love) and death (or hate) instincts during child development. Fletcher (1968) and Storr (1968) have recently attempted to synthesize findings from the two areas and apply them to human aggression.

Dollard, Doob, Miller, Mowrer, and Sears (1939) proposed another explanation in the "frustration-aggression hypothesis." In it, all aggression was taken as resulting from frustration, and, conversely, all frustration led to an activation of an "instigation to aggression." The latter part was soon modified to include instances in which frustration did not lead to aggression (Miller, 1941). During the succeeding 30 years the hypothesis has generated considerable research and much criticism. For example, preschool children may respond to frustrating circumstances with other than aggressive behavior, for example, regression to more youthful play patterns (Barker, Dembo, & Lewin, 1941). Aggression was displayed by individuals who had not been frustrated but who had learned to behave aggressively through observation and imitation (Bandura & Walters, 1963). Because of its shortcomings, some authors have proposed that the hypothesis be abandoned altogether (e.g., Buss, 1961), but Berkowitz (1965) presented a modified version as being still valid and useful.

The frustration-aggression hypothesis did not specify whether the resultant aggression was "learned" or "innate" or some combination of the two. Many social scientists (particularly American psychologists influenced by Behaviorism) adopted the view that aggressive behavior is individually acquired and can be wholly accounted for in reinforcement theory terms (Bandura & Walters, 1963). Patterson, Littman, & Bricker, (1967) recently discussed young children's assertive behavior in ongoing social interactions, presenting empirical evidence that behavioral consequences could serve as positive or negative reinforcers. Earlier work had already shown that prior experimental training of either "aggressive" or "constructive" types differentially affected children's reactions to frustration (Davitz, 1952). In addition, other early experience factors have been shown to influence aggressive behavior in lower animals, for example, maternal environment, as examined in cross-fostering experiments with different mouse strains (Southwick, 1968).

Physiological evidence relevant to the origins of aggression in primates remains scarce, although it is increasing as practical problems are overcome, for example, by telestimulation techniques (see, e.g., Maurus & Ploog, 1971). Delgado and his associates have conducted extensive studies of brain stimulation and behavior in rhesus macaques and have consistently elicited aggressive behavior from certain areas, notably the thalamus. Because the stimulated aggressive behavior varied according to several situational factors, for example, the presence of other members of a social hierarchy, and did not take the form of stereotyped motor responses, he concluded that a "drive" had been induced (Delgado, 1966). Ullrich (1966) proposed that aggressive behavior can occur as an unconditioned response to aversive stimuli, and Azrin, Hutchinson, and Hake (1963) produced fighting in squirrel monkeys (*Saimiri sciureus*) by inflicting pain through electric shock. Candland (1968) showed that heart-rate change recorded telemetrically can be used to predict the probability of occurrence and outcome of aggressive interactions in squirrel monkeys.

Although the terms "aggression" and "aggressive behavior" have been used interchangeably in this section, it must be remembered that many phenomena are included under these terms. As Buss (1966) stated, "There have been hundreds of studies of aggression . . . but only a few in which a subject aggresses physically against another person." For example, Haner and Brown (1955) claimed to have measured aggression in elementary school children by recording the pressure a child exerted on a plunger which stopped a frustration-associated buzzer. Some authors made no effort to restrict aggression to behavior at all: "Aggression is not always manifested in overt movements but may exist as the content of a phantasy or dream or even a well thought-out plan of revenge" (Dollard *et al.*, 1939, p. 10). Any attempt to synthesize and deal comprehensively with all these phenomena may be doomed to failure, but the problem of aggression is sufficiently vital to merit continued attempts, as Vowles (1970) has argued in his recent systematic survey of its facets.

Most experimental studies of interpersonal aggression have used indirect measures based on behavioral consequences and not behavior patterns themselves. In Ulrich's (1966) study, the "other" child (who was in fact hypothetical) was not present in the room with the subject; aggression was measured as the frequency of button pressing, where button pressing resulted in the destructive vibration of the other individual's table (also hypothetical). Buss (1963, 1966) used strength of electric shock allegedly delivered to compatriots by college students; but the shock was not in fact delivered and the supposed fellow subjects were experimental confederates. Results of aggression directed to other individual's possessions involves more directness, for example, Davitz's (1952) "Break the Ball" game in which the winner was the last child who successfully protected his ping pong ball after all others had been smashed in the melee.

Direct measures of children's aggressive behavior during social encounters vary similarly with those used in other social behavior studies. Davitz (1952) had independent judges rank individual protocols in order of "aggressiveness." McNeil (1962) used behavior check sheets with items like "sulks," "fights to protect self or others," "swears, calls names," that is, items describing overt behavior mixed with those inferring its function. The same relationship seen earlier usually held: the more behavior categories used, the more specific and objective they tended to be.

The doll play situation is a specialized type of observation used in studies of children's aggressive behavior. Children's vocalizations about and manipulations of stick figures and furniture are recorded, and aggression is used in its widest sense to include all violent or destructive referents in the child's actions. Normative data for preschool children was presented by Sears (1951) in terms of age, sex, sibling status, and absent father's influences. As the general conclusion has been that doll play behavior closely parallels free-play behavior, later research workers used the technique as validation in other studies. For example, children showed greater aggression in doll play sessions following periods of social isolation than after periods of social interaction (Hartup & Himeno, 1959).

Aggression, perhaps more than any other aspect of social behavior, has been the subject of considerable recent popular discussion, and literature in the area continues to proliferate. All the works contain references to findings of animal behavior studies which are thought by the authors to be useful in understanding human behavior. In addition to Lorenz's and Storr's books, three volumes by Robert Ardrey: *African Genesis* (1961), *The Territorial Imperative* (1967), and *The Social Contract* (1970), are relevant. All considered the innate, spontaneous nature of human aggression; the first dealt with its evolutionary origins, the second with its expression in territoriality, the third with its crucial importance in social conventions. Another recent addition is *Violence, Monkeys and Man* (Russell & Russell, 1968), which is an attempt to relate human violence to population pressures and primatological studies. Other popular books dealing with the biological background of human behavior, and which include sections on aggression, are *Wild Heritage* (Carrighar, 1965), *Nature and Human Nature* (Comfort, 1966), and Morris's two best sellers, *The Naked Ape* (1967) and *The Human Zoo* (1969). Finally, two semipopular anthologies of papers on human aggression have appeared: *The Natural History of Aggression* (Carthy & Ebling, 1964) and *Man and Aggression* (Montagu, 1968). The first was an attempt to approach the topic of aggression from widely varying viewpoints, for example, psychological, sociological, historical, etc., while the second was a polemical attempt attacking the Lorenz-Ardrey viewpoint. All the books stress speculation and wide-ranging inclusiveness at the expense of specific empirical studies.

Social and Clinical Psychology

Social and clinical psychologists have recently published many studies of specific behavioral elements as used in ongoing human social interaction (e.g., Mehrabian, 1969). The area investigated has been generally labeled "nonverbal communication" (although "extra-verbal" might be more accurate since most elements are performed simultaneously with verbalization). Several comprehensive reviews of this research exist: Argyle (1967, 1969), Argyle and Kendon (1967), Blurton Jones (1971d), Duncan (1969a), Sommer (1969), and Vine (1970). Other studies (e.g., C. Hutt & Coxon, 1965) have described accounts of patient behavior in clinical situations, often as it is related to diagnosis, therapeutic progress, or prognosis.

Most research workers have used the traditional experimental methods of social psychology, the most common being the small group ostensibly assembled for other reasons. Eye contact during adult diadic interactions has been studied in considerable detail, for example, Argyle and Dean (1965), Argyle, Lalljee, and Cook (1968), Kendon (1967), and Kendon and Cook (1969). They have related eye contact to other factors: visibility of interactants, distance between them, and conversational signals. However, recent research developments have emphasized the importance of methodological niceties, particularly in artificial social situations, and have generated some controversy (Argyle, 1970; Stephenson & Rutter, 1970; Vine, 1971; White, Hegarty, & Beasley, 1970).

Kleck, Ono, and Hastorf (1966) examined similar behavior in adolescent diads using a more contrived situation: the confederate was presented as a physically "stigmatized:" (i.e., crippled) individual. In larger groups, more indirect measures of interaction have been used; for example, Hare and Bales (1963) recorded seating position in five-man laboratory groups. All these studies involved bringing people together in specifically assembled groups.

Other experimental studies used more diverse and indirect methods not involving ongoing social interactions. Sommer (1961, 1965, 1968) administered questionnaires measuring seating preferences to students and obtained cross-cultural differences. Norum, Russo, and Sommer (1967) arranged task-play situations with preschool children and problem-solving situations with adults, and recorded preferred seating positions. Competition over food was used in a study of dominance among retarded girls (Hollis & Gunnell, 1965); in one experiment a modified Wisconsin General Test Apparatus was utilized. Faw and Nunally (1968) recorded single children's visual fixations to photographs of faces of differing "affective value." A start has been made toward relating physiological measures to nonverbal communication; McBride, King, and James (1965) found significant changes in GSR with differences in social proximity among adults.

Other workers have modified natural situations for experimental use; such "naturalistic" studies are most easily done with low-status members of institutions. Sommer and his colleagues used hospital cafeterias and university classrooms in which they could manipulate the social situation. In another study (Felipe & Sommer, 1966) the experimenter violated the "personal space" of psychiatric patients and university students in natural surroundings and observed their avoidance responses. Altman and Haythorn (1967) compared social behavior in partially isolated and control groups of sailors on a naval base.

Several workers have conducted observational studies analogous to those of the field ethologist, that is, they recorded specific behavioral elements of spontaneously occurring social interactions without interfering with or modifying them. Many of these dealt with abnormal individuals from a clinical viewpoint (Esser, 1968; S. Wolff & Chess, 1964); the behaviors selected for examination ranged from a specific pattern, for example, the head nod (Birdwhistell, 1962) to general sociability (Raush, Dittmann, & Taylor, 1959). The psychiatric hospital context was "natural" in that it included undirected, free-time periods within the usual hospital routine.

Finally, some research workers noted normal adult social behavior in everyday social contexts. Sommer (1965, 1967) watched students in a university library and recorded seating patterns and "territorial defense" of working space.

Roos (1968) noted social interactions on shipboard, particularly as these related to "jurisdiction," a special case of territoriality applied to temporary priority over space or objects. Mann (1970) recorded the social dynamics (and traditions!) of naturally occurring waiting lines, for example, at bus stops.

Anthropology and Sociology

Anthropological and sociological knowledge is usually of marginal relevance to human ethology; workers in these disciplines are not primarily concerned with individual social behavior. When they do consider it, it is usually in superficial, often anecdotal terms, as their main concern is with larger, more complex institutions. The possibility that an ethological, evolutionary approach to such institutions might yield valuable knowledge was only recently proposed and empirical work remains to be done (Freeman, 1966; Tiger, 1970a, 1970b; Tiger & Fox, 1966). In her recent book, Callan (1970) elaborated on this subject, examining four principal topics: regulation of population size, aggression, greeting behavior, and dominance. But even such minute cultural details as shaving off the eyebrows in mourning (Grinsell, 1950) might find possible functional explanations in the studies by Eibl-Eibesfeldt (1968) of eyebrow flashing in greeting.

For example, the urban male youth gang has been studied for over 40 years by sociologists and social workers, and much knowledge has been compiled (Yablonsky, 1962). Only recently, however, have workers begun to consider the biological implications of this social grouping, and biologically derived concepts such as territory ("turf"), intergroup agonistic interactions ("rumble"), and social hierarchies may prove useful in further analysis (Barnett, 1967; Davis, 1962). Tiger (1969) put forward a theory of the possible evolutionary significance of such "male association patterns" (see also, S. L. Washburn & Lancaster, 1968).

The recent upsurge of anthropological research on the evolution of human social life is pertinent to human ethology. Evidence has accumulated in three fields: (1) archaeological studies of prehistoric living sites, (2) studies of contemporary "primitive" peoples, and (3) studies of nonhuman primate natural history (De Vore, 1965; Jay, 1968). The first now contributes limited numbers of fossils and artifacts. But Dart (1949) presented detailed speculation concerning australopithecine predatory behavior based on fossil concentrations. Brain (1970) has more recently used australopithecine fossil material to infer prehistoric carnivore predation on early man.

Hunting and gathering societies, for example, Australian aborigines and Kalahari bushmen, have been considered the contemporary peoples whose behavior most closely resembles early man's (S. L. Washburn & Lancaster, 1968). Field studies of them sometimes yield descriptions of specific behavior patterns, for example, Sahlins' (1960) description and photograph of grooming among Kung bushmen children, and I. Jones's (1971) study of stereotyped aggression in Australian Western Desert Aborigines, and discussion of social organization, kinship, territory, etc. More popular studies sometimes yield useful information, for example, the bushman's greeting gesture, "raising one's open right hand high above the head," discussed by van der Post (1958). Specific behavioral description sometimes occurs in studies of more advanced human societies, for example, Samoan villagers (Mead, 1928), American plains Indians (Oliver, 1962), etc. Initial efforts have been made to compare certain behavior patterns across cultures, for example, postures (Hewes, 1955) and child rearing (Sorenson & Gajdusek, 1966).

Anthropologists have conducted many studies of the social behavior of free-living nonhuman primates (e.g., DeVore, Jay, Sade, Washburn); this research is reviewed in the next section. Here, consideration of a specific problem, for example, tool use, may be informative. Anthropologists have attached great importance to the evolution of hominid tool-using, particularly as it relates to other significant evolutionary advances, for example, upright posture, group hunting, thumb opposition, cerebral cortex size (Gruber, 1969; Hewes, 1964; Lancaster, 1968; Oakley, 1965; S. L. Washburn & Howell, 1960). Oakley considered the ability to make tools to be the essential difference between man and the other primates, but Goodall's (1964) research on chimpanzees disproved this. Recently, Gruber (1969) redefined the problem, stating that: "Oakley's definition of 'man the tool-maker' holds, if we add the criterion of the modification of a natural object, *using another object or some implement as an aid in manufacture* " (his italics). Animal behaviorists have adopted a more empirical approach in examining tool-usage through laboratory experimentation (Kohler, 1925; Parker, 1969) and field observations (Goodall, 1964; Jones & Sabater Pi, 1969). The ethological emphasis on evolutionary significance and survival value provides ground for synthesis of these views; Kortlandt and Kooij (1963) catalogued and classified known examples of primate tool-using and related it to habitat type and predatory propensities. K. R. L. Hall (1963) related primate tool-using performance to adaptability and presented ways that it could be derived from existing fixed motor patterns. Recently Menzel, Davenport, and Rogers (1970) examined environmental effects on the ontogeny of chimpanzee tool use and found that wild-born animals were much superior to restriction-reared ones. Finally, in her recent comprehensive review of vertebrate tool usage van Lawick-Goodall (1970) placed primate implementation behavior in its phylogenetic context.

Nonhuman Primate Studies

The recent upsurge of primate behavior research has provided much relevant information for human ethology. But because the research workers involved are of such varied backgrounds, for example, zoology, anthropology, psychology, some studies are more relevant than others, and to contain a brief review to a manageable length requires careful selection from the recently-plentiful studies. The findings most relevant here fall into two general classes: (1) information about specific motor patterns and the situations in which they occur (see Chapter 4 for references to specific nonhuman primate behavior patterns), and (2) investigations concerned with broader, conceptual categories of behavior, for example, territoriality, dominance.

All behavioral studies involve categories of description, but the "level" of description, that is, the detail with which the motor patterns are defined and the resulting specificity of operational items, differs considerably. Many workers have used systems of a few broad categories, for example, physical aggression, threat, and play (Bernstein & Mason, 1963b; Hansen, 1966; Harlow, 1959; Southwick, 1967). Other workers have used category systems of greater detail, with a correspondingly larger number of items, for example, grimace, slap, and crouch (Altmann, 1962; Bobbitt, Jensen, & Gordon, 1964; K. R. L. Hall & DeVore, 1965; Kaufman & Rosenblum, 1966; Poirier, 1970; Wilson & Wilson, 1968). Bertrand (1969) used both approaches in studying the stumptail macaque (*Macaca speciosa*); her descriptions are the most detailed yet produced for a single nonhuman primate species. Jensen and Bobbitt (1968) discussed the relative merits of "molar" and "molecular" approaches. The latter approach is most useful to the ethologist, because he is concerned with problems of causation, survival value, and evolution, and it enables him to approach behavior comparatively.

Often zoologists experienced with ethological methods applied to lower vertebrates have conducted the detailed studies (Chance, 1956; Crook, 1967; Hinde & Rowell, 1962). Often these have been field studies rather than laboratory ones (Deag & Crook, 1971; K. R. L. Hall & DeVore, 1965; Kummer, 1968; Schaller, 1963; van Lawick-Goodall, 1968a). Recently other workers, including those with psychological training backgrounds, have begun dealing with objectively described, specific behavior items in studies of captive nonhuman primates (Jensen, Bobbitt, & Gordon, 1969; Kaufman & Rosenblum, 1966; Sackett, 1966, Wilson & Wilson, 1968).

Primatological studies have forced the re-examination of certian broad behavioral topics originally derived from studies of lower animals, for example, dominance hierarchy (see Maslow, 1936). Initially, such conceptual descriptions were usually applied intact to primate behavior, but later careful studies showed these applications to be overly simplistic. (See Gartlan, 1968.) They have since been repeatedly revised to account for the more complex and adaptable nature of primate behavior. It is now debatable whether the unitary concept of "dominance" has any justifiable application to the structure of primate social relations; instead, the many interrelated aspects of behavior associated with priority, deference, and role-playing need to be explored together (see Chapter 5).

Primate studies have also generated "novel" areas of animal behavior study, for example, dominance coalitions, learning sets, cultural transmission, and language acquisition. These new contributions usually reflect the phylogenetically advanced capabilities of the primates. Many such ideas may prove useful in approaching human behavior problems, but empirical investigations remain to be done in many cases. Such findings from nonhuman primate studies cannot be validly transferred in toto to the human condition or vice versa (although some writers still make the attempt; see Kraus, 1970). They can only serve as provoking stimuli for suitable studies of possibly similar phenomena across primate species. Initial results indicate that useful similarities exist, for example, Esser, Chamberlain, Chapple, and Kline (1965) on territoriality in mental patients; W. C. McGrew (1969) on dominance hierarchy in nursery children; and Grant (1965b) on displacement activities in mental patients. Similarly, increasing realization of the complexity and flexibility of nonhuman primate societies has stimulated the application of analytic concepts from sociology and anthropology to nonhuman studies, e.g., role theory (Benedict, 1969; Bernstein & Sharpe, 1966; Reynolds, 1970).

The ontogenetic development of behavior patterns in nonhuman primates has received considerable attention although gaps remain, for example, detailed long-term longitudinal studies in naturalistic situations (only the Cayo Santiago studies approximate this, for example, Sade, 1965). Comparison with corresponding human development is hampered by lack of equivalent chronological and motivational data on different primate species (see Kellogg & Kellogg, 1933). Most longitudinal research has been done with mother-infant interaction, for example, the research groups of Harlow at Wisconsin, Hinde at Cambridge, and Jensen at Washington. Harlow's rhesus macaques (*Macaca mulatta*) have been followed the longest, in some cases through multi-parity, but all have been raised in varying degrees of abnormal deprivation. Hinde's rhesus infants grow up in conditions closely simulating natural groups, and they have been studied at six months (Hinde, Rowell, & Spencer-Booth, 1964) and at two and one half years (Hinde & Spencer-Booth, 1967). Studies of pigtail macaque (*M. nemestrina*) mothers and infants by Jensen's group have produced the most sophisticated analyses of behavioral elements in interactional sequence (Jensen, Bobbitt, & Gordon, 1969; Jensen & Gordon, 1970).

Generalizations about nonhuman primate social behavior have progressively narrowed in scope as findings have accumulated. Until about 10 years ago, authors could still attempt generalizations about the order as a whole (see, e.g., Carpenter, 1942; Chance, 1963; Sahlins, 1960). Following the first wave of modern field studies (and the resulting monographs), the generalizations shrank to the species-specific level, for example, Jay (1963) and Schaller (1963).

Finally, as particular species began to receive second and third looks in different localities, the truly flexible character of primate social organizations became apparent. Different populations of the same species living in different habitat conditions showed radically different social variations; for example, compare Rowell's (1966a) Ugandan forest population of baboons with S. L. Washburn and DeVore's (1961) Kenyan savanna one. Excellent discussions of social organizations related to environmental factors are found in Crook (1970) and Rowell (1967).

Human Ethology

Many research workers have discussed the possible extension of ethological findings and methods to human social behavior (Ambrose, 1968; Barnett, 1955; Berg, 1966; Bowlby, 1957, 1958; Bridger, 1962; Chance, 1967; Eibl-Eibesfeldt, 1970) Freedman, 1967, 1968, 1971; Grant, 1965a; Hamburg, 1968; Hass, 1970; S. J. Hutt & C. Hutt, 1970; Jensen & Bobbitt, 1968; Kaufman, 1960a, 1960b; Klopfer, 1968; Kraus, 1970; Maslow, Rand, & Newman, 1960; Masserman, 1968; Price, 1967; Rule, 1967; Russell & Russell, 1957, 1971; Spitz, 1955; Tinbergen, 1968; Zegans, 1967).

Such papers often follow a strikingly similar pattern: reference to Darwin, description of methods, citation of animal work, justification of its relevance, general speculation, and plea for research. Most have appeared in nonbiological publications, apparently intended to convince "outsiders" (nonbelievers?) of the usefulness of ethology. Regrettably, few of the authors have translated their convictions into empirical investigations or have since described and analyzed recurring fixed-action patterns (i.e., a descriptive term referring to relatively stereotyped, discrete movements capable of reliable, replicable recording by an observer) exhibited by humans in social interaction.

The published studies thus far are so diverse that the only inclusive definition of human ethology seems to be "a biological approach to human behavior" (see Tinbergen's discussion of ethology and related disciplines, 1963). Several investigators have adopted ethological "attitudes" toward behavior seen in experimental conditions, that is, they have used objective descriptions of motor patterns rather than standard instrumental responses or indirect measures. Other investigators have adopted "naturalistic" approaches, that is, they have recorded ongoing behavior in specially designed free-field situations or restricted environments. Still others profess to be using ethological techniques when transferring concepts derived from lower animal studies (e.g., dominance, territoriality) to human social situations.

The description of behavior patterns is the primary problem, and no worker has yet claimed to have produced a definitive list. Although existence of a finite behavioral repertoire is taken for granted since only a finite combination of muscles and joints exist in the human body, this task is laborious because of the large number and variability of motor units. The ethologist is faced with recognizing stereotyped, recurring patterns in a behavioral stream, then abstracting and defining these patterns in an objective, reliable way. Desmond, Franklin, Valbona, Hill, Plumb, Arnold, and Watts (1963) published a detailed repertoire of the newborn human infant, and Prechtl (1956, 1958, 1965) elaborated on certain of these, as well as relating them to intrauterine and birth irregularities. In preliminary studies, Blurton Jones (1967), Grant (1965b), and W. C. McGrew (1969) listed various subsets of the total social behavioral repertoire of preschool children. Grant (1965b, 1968) also published lists of behavioral items for adults in interview situations. More recently, Blurton Jones (1972a) and Grant (1969) have produced expanded glossaries of human behavior patterns.

The above studies used behavioral items of approximately the same descriptive level: those easily recognizable by an observer of ongoing interactions. These might be termed *compound* patterns of behavior. Recently Blurton Jones (1972b) presented findings at a more basic level: specific components described in terms of individual muscles.

The next problem is one of analysis: With what frequency and under what conditions does a behavior pattern occur? How does it relate to the occurrence of other patterns, both those by the actor, and in social situations, by the reactor? How do these phenomena change over time? Ambrose (1961) provided an early detailed example in his analysis of the smiling response in infancy. Freedman (1964) investigated the smiling response and fear of strangers and their relation to heritability. Blurton Jones (1967) presented a valuable descriptive account of children's social interactions in nursery schools, giving particular emphasis to distinctions between agonistic and "rough-and-tumble play" behavior.

Many workers have investigated the biological significance of specific social behavior patterns. This research generally falls into two groups: (1) observations of normal individuals in which the causation, survival value, and communicative function of certain patterns was straightforwardly considered and from which useful normative data was ascertained, and (2) observations of abnormal individuals, in which certain patterns appeared drastically altered in frequency or form, and from which some link with specific disorders and their attendant symptoms was sought. Eye-to-eye contact or gaze fixation is an important early social variable, related to maternal-infant attachment and later social approach/fear (Robson, 1967; Robson, Pederson, & Moss, 1969). In autistic children, however, the avoidance of eye-to-eye contact or gaze aversion prevails and appears to have a significant signaling function related to the disorder (C. Hutt & Ounsted, 1966).

The research group at the Park Hospital in Oxford utilized a modified ethological approach in studies of behaviorally disordered children (C.Hutt & S. J. Hutt, 1965; C. Hutt, S. J. Hutt & Ounsted, 1963, 1965; S. J. Hutt & C. Hutt, 1970; S. J. Hutt, C. Hutt, Lee, & Ounsted, 1965). They used a "free-field" situation, limited subsets of broadly defined items, and a range of specific experimental conditions. Their results, carefully quantified and often related to simultaneous physiological measures (e.g., EEG), presented valuable, immediately applicable knowledge. In another example, Currie and Brannigan (1970) used descriptive ethological techniques to assess the behavioral repertoire of a young autistic girl, whose social behavior they then appropriately modified using operant conditioning techniques. Recently several popular works concerned with human behavior have appeared which refer to the potential usefulness of ethology (Ardrey, 1961, 1967, 1970; Comfort, 1966; Hass, 1970; Lorenz, 1966; Morris, 1967, 1969, 1971; Russell & Russell, 1968; Storr, 1968). While containing stimulating and far-reaching ideas about the origins and functions of human behavior, none of these presented original empirical findings. Such speculation can constitute only a limited contribution, and the popular aspect of human ethology appears to be approaching satiation while the less spectacular, empirical side is still largely unexplored. Callan (1970) discussed such "etholgizing" in detail in her recent book. For another recent example of this extrapolation applied to contemporary human problems, the reader is referred to Lorenz's (1970) provocative analysis of the "generation gap."

Finally, in reviewing important historical influences on human ethology, reference to Darwin must be made. Such reference has become fashionably obligatory for good reason. Darwin produced two publications, *The Expression of the Emotions in Man and Animals* (1872) and *A Biographical Sketch of an Infant* (1877), which unquestionably show him to have been a keen and objective observer of human behavior in natural contexts. His detailed descriptions of human behavior patterns, his attempts at cross-primate comparisons, and his pioneering efforts to obtain cross-cultural knowledge of human affect and expression more than qualify him as the first human ethologist.

Chapter 2

Introduction: Research Problem

Theoretical Considerations

Having reviewed the brief literature of human ethology and surveyed that of related fields, the next step is to pose a question: why choose ethology as a method of approaching human social behavior? What makes ethology a useful tool? These questions can be answered in two ways: first, by isolating those shortcomings in alternative approaches from which ethology does not suffer, and, second, by presenting those novel characteristics of the ethological method which are unique and advantageous. A further question arising from the review is: why choose young children, or more specifically, three- and four-year-old children, as subjects for a study of social behavior?

Developmental psychologists have so far contributed the most to our knowledge of children's social behavior. In fact, judging from the volume of material published by them, one's first impression might be that they have exhausted the subject. But developmental psychologists have limited their examinations of children's social behavior to a few, traditional viewpoints.

For example, in describing behavior they have used categories of description which are often either very *general* (e.g., "bodily attack," Patterson,

17

Littman, & Bricker, 1967), or *inferential* (e.g., "competes for status," Walters, Pearce, & Dahms, 1957) or *both* (e.g., "unfriendly acts," King, 1966). Such categories make replicative attempts difficult because they force other workers to construct supposedly corresponding categories intuitively. They can be especially confusing when translation of terms into other languages is necessary.

However, general or inferential terms may be useful if defined specifically and objectively (e.g., as early ethologists labeled patterns such as "Upright Threat" in other animals). Unfortunately many developmental psychologists have neglected to define their behavioral categories, or, when they did so, the definitions often remained incomplete or dependent on synonyms. Even a lengthy study restricted to two specific behavior patterns, *laugh* and *smile*, gave no definitions of them (Ding & Jersild, 1932), and repetition of their frequency counts is impossible since bout lengths were not given. This unfortunate inadequacy in description applies at two levels of behavioral categorization: (1) to the motor patterns exhibited, and (2) to the functional categories into which the motor patterns were grouped.

Most published research in developmental psychology has been greatly influenced by the Watsonian Behaviorist views put forward early in this century (Burnham, 1968). Following Watson, most research workers held that the origins of behavior could be wholly accounted for by postnatal individual experience. By concentration on "learning," they largely ignored the evolutionary significance of social behavior patterns, although it is fair to say that this viewpoint has yet to be adequately investigated. Many have retained the Behaviorist view (albeit while paying lip service to the obsolescence and sterility of the "innate-acquired" dichotomy) in the face of mounting evidence that phylogenetic factors are more important in explaining behavioral phenomena than previously thought.

Especially within the last decade, research workers investigating nonhuman primate behavior have contributed much useful knowledge of man's closest relatives, but few have extended their research programs to include *Homo sapiens*. Many primatologists have seemed reluctant to attempt the integration of human behavior with that of the other primate species. Many have seemed constrained to stress the differences and not the similarities between the primates, automatically regarding man as the "special case" and therefore above comparison. Some research establishments, for example, the Regional Primate Research Centers in the United States, have incorporated these views into official policy: they conduct only nonhuman primate research (Eyestone, 1966). Speculation by practicing primate investigators about human and nonhuman behavior has recently increased (Jensen & Bobbitt, 1968) but real comparative knowledge remains scarce.

Anthropologists and sociologists have traditionally been concerned with human social behavior at a more gross level (i.e., societal rather than individual) than psychologists. Their reports of specific motor patterns have been only anecdotal and peripheral to their major emphasis on the results of behavior in general, for example, in kinship studies. Also, the literature of these disciplines is so permeated with the concept of "culture" that few workers will consider the possibility of universally human social behavior patterns. Similarities between behavior patterns used in diverse societies are largely ignored, or modifications and variations are stressed. (An ironic turn of events when one considers that one of the initiators of human cross-cultural studies was Darwin.)

Clinical psychologists have contributed many useful descriptions of human social patterns, although this often forms only a minor part of published studies and must be assiduously sought out. Inevitably, clinical studies deal with abnormal individuals, often with those suffering from behavioral disorders. Application of this knowledge to "normal" human behavior requires extrapolation with careful qualification. Clinical workers (with a few conspicuous exceptions, e.g., Scheflen, 1963, 1964, 1965) are primarily interested in description of symptoms, so that the function of behavior in social interaction or its possible derivation is usually left unexamined.

Social psychologists examining extra-verbal communication (sometimes called paralanguage) in human social encounters have conducted the studies closest in content to human ethology. They have investigated certain types of behavior such as eye contact more thoroughly than have any similar attempts by human ethologists. Other research work in this area, for example, Sommer's invasions of "personal space" (see review in Sommer, 1969) might be assigned to either field. Social psychologists have worked only with selected behavior patterns, however, and none have attempted an ethogram for *Homo sapiens*. Most nonverbal communication research has been done in artificial experimental situations, and its applicability to daily life remains to be confirmed. (For example, in experimental situations subjects may be considerably over-attentive, and this may bias results.)

Both practical and theoretical advantages exist for using ethological analysis to investigate young children's behavior. Contemporary ethological label, describe, and define behavior objectively, in terms of body parts and motor patterns. They eschew inferential labels, for example, "threat face," and subjective adverbial descriptions, for example, "frightened" walking. Their definitions refer to specific, recurring fixed-action patterns, free of motivational prejudgments. Ethologists use extensive definitions couched in simple terms, for example, Blurton Jones's (1967) definition of a beat as ". . . an over-arm blow with the palm side of the lightly clenched fist. The arm is sharply bent at the elbow and raised to a vertical position then brought down with great force on the opponent."

Using such behavioral categories, ethologists directly record the behavior of normal individuals as it occurs. There is no need to resort to indirect

19

measures: ratings, tests, questionnaires, projective techniques, interviews. Consequently, ethologists need not speculate about the applicability of doll play results or the validity of test scores to ongoing interpersonal behavior. By recording behavior directly, ethologists see it functioning in real-life situations, and by using sophisticated and inconspicuous recording aids, they attempt to avoid disrupting ongoing behavior. (Which is *not* to say that a flourishing area of experimental ethology does not also exist, some of which has been concerned with human behavior, e.g., Blurton Jones & Konner, 1970; Freedman, 1969; B. T. Gardner & Wallach, 1965.) As potential observer disruption is usually directly proportional to the size of the observed species, children make more difficult subjects than fruit flies, but recently developed technological advances (e.g., portable videotape, telemetrized microphones) minimize this.

Use of discrete behavior patterns enables quantitative analysis. Frequencies, combinations, and sequences of patterns can be derived by recording incidences of behavior over time. (See, e.g., Altmann, 1965; Jensen, Bobbitt, & Gordon, 1969.) Based on this, some ethologists seek to find recurring "constellations" of patterns which occur frequently together. (See, e.g., van Hooff, 1970.) Members of constellations are considered to be more closely related in terms of motivation to each other than to other behavior patterns outside the constellation. Constellations are used as the bases for more general behavior categories, for example, aggressive, maternal, hunting, etc., which can be defined in terms of their consequences.

Ethology deals with theoretical problems often ignored by other research approaches; for example, it emphasizes the evolutionary significance of behavior. To appreciate the phylogeny of human facial expressions, gestures, and postures we must compare notes among those living animals with whom we most recently shared common ancestry, that is, the nonhuman primates. The grounds for inter-primate comparisons exist on several levels: many behavior patterns show *morphological* similarities across primate species; use of similar body parts with similar musculature and innervation, for example, contraction of the facial *occipito-frontalis* muscle, produces an eyebrow raising pattern in many primate species. Many patterns show *operational* similarities between different structures acting together, for example, hair erection, flushing, pelvic thrusting. *Functional* similarities exist; interpersonal sequences of behavior patterns may result in similar social consequences. For example, one individual's staring at another may lead to the latter's averting his gaze; one individual's directed, horizontally-outstretched arms may lead to the other's approach and physical contact. Finally, *situational* similarities abound; for example, pushing and pulling commonly occur in conflicts for the possession of objects; patting and hugging occur when some individuals in a group are agitated. A partial listing of behavior patterns comparable on these grounds between human and nonhuman primates includes: bite, gaze fixate, play face, play crouch, beat, kiss, slap, stamp, kick, hug, pat, etc.

In addition to interspecific comparison with its implications for behavioral evolution, ethologists also compare behavior of different populations of the same species. Such intraspecific comparison provides an indication of the species' adaptability to different ecological situations, which is presumed to be increasingly important at higher phylectic levels. Recent nonhuman primate findings (Crook, 1970; Jay, 1968; Rowell, 1967) have stressed the dangers of generalizing about single primate species on the basis of limited information. Human ethologists regard the question of the variability or universality of human behavior patterns as largely unstudied and therefore unanswerable at present. Crosscultural ethological studies remain few (Eibl-Eibesfeldt, 1968; Eibl-Eibesfeldt & Hass, 1967a, 1967b; Hass, 1970; Konner, 1972), and until more appear any statements about human behavioral "flexibility" or "plasticity" seem premature. It is known that some communicatory gestures, for example, head nodding as affirmation, are culturally bound (LaBarre, 1947), but other behavior patterns, for example, smiling, appear to be used similarly in all cultures so far examined (Darwin, 1872; Ekman, Sorenson, & Frieson, 1969).

The preceding question, of the degree of culturally-imposed modification on human behavior patterns, also constitutes an ontogenetic problem, as acculturation is a gradual process. Early ethologists stressed the importance of ontogeny through *Kasper Hausen* experiments, but later research workers have shown the importance of detailed recording of normal individual development. Some cultural factors exert minimal influence on behavior; for example, infants show visual tracking behavior as soon as three minutes postpartum (Richards, 1970). Later, the same behavior pattern may be inhibited in culturally modified ways, for example, looking straight ahead while in a crowded elevator.

Many of the generalizations about ethology stated here apply only to methods and viewpoints of contemporary ethology (see Hinde, 1966). Early ethologists adopted different and, sometimes what in retrospect seem unfortunate, approaches to behavioral problems. Early attempts at integrating overt behavior with physiological and motivational mechanisms proved premature (Hinde, 1956; Tinbergen, 1951). Considerable time and effort were expended on the essentially sterile innate-learned dichotomy. In their proselytizing enthusiasm, older ethologists used tenuous direct comparisons, for example, between greylag geese and human behavior, or chose to discuss knowledge from areas outside their competence, for example, the social anthrology of the North American Ute Indians (Lorenz, 1966; Montagu, 1968). This should not be confused with the problems of popularization per se, which apply to any technical field with popular appeal. In any scientific field, advances are built on past shortcomings more often than successes, and ethology is no exception to this.

The choice of primarily three- and four-year-old children as subjects of a study of human social behavior was based on both theoretical and practical grounds. The first five years of life have been almost universally acknowledged (from Freud to Gessell) as a period when development is most marked and crucial. Socially abnormal influences during this period, for example, sustained maternal deprivation, may result in maladjustments lasting throughout life (Bowlby, 1965, 1969). At this age children begin to extend social acquaintanceships beyond the family circle and small neighborhood play group. Verbalization as a human supplement to vocalization becomes significantly more important in peer-peer interactions. Young children's behavior is assumed to be less culturally modified than that of older individuals.

Practical considerations were dictated by child-rearing practices in contemporary Western society. Until the age of three, children spend most of their time at home with mother, and their entrance into British state nursery schools is legally prohibited. (The exceptions to this, day nurseries which take younger children, are still relatively uncommon.) Private nursery schools usually adopt similar requirements, and it is only the rarer "creche" that includes two-year-olds. From five or six years of age onwards, children attend primary school during most of the day, and its regimented schedule makes observations of ongoing social interaction difficult. In theory, one could observe children in streets and playgrounds, but such populations may have irregular membership and habits, and few variables in the situation could be controlled.

On this basis the author decided to conduct research in nursery schools since they represent a fairly homogeneous population which is optimally available in a relatively constant environment.

Behavior Categories

Initially the author aimed to examine a subcategory of children's social behavior: agonistic behavior. Accordingly, this was operationally defined as consisting of *aggressive* behavior (i.e., behavior which normally produces injury to or flight by the child to whom it is directed; e.g., attack, threat), *fearful* behavior (i.e., behavior by an aggressed-against child which reduces damage or threatening; e.g., flight, submissive posture), and *defensive* behavior (i.e., behavior by an aggressed-against child which prevents an aggressor's attack from being completed, but without either attacking in return or fleeing or submitting; e.g., retaliatory threat).

But it became obvious that another closely-related behavioral subcategory was relevant to agonistic behavior. This was labeled "quasiagonistic" behavior and has been called "rough-and-tumble play" by some authors. (Although Harlow and Harlow [1965] originally applied the latter term to only one of four types of social contact play seen in young rhesus monkeys.) Quasiagonistic behavior resembles agonistic behavior in commonality of some motor patterns, but the two seem to function almost oppositely. Quasiagonistic behavior was operationally defined as vigorous, gross activity which does not result in separation or injury. The similarities between the two subcategories are great, and inexperienced adult observers may have difficulty differentiating them, although children accomplish this more consistently.

It also became obvious that agonistic behavior is a very special subcategory. Children spend most of the time in social situations interacting "peacefully," and to study agonistic behavior without reference to nonagonistic social behavior invites distortion. So observations were also made of nonagonistic behavior, which can be operationally defined by exclusion.

Within this operational framework, the author aimed to examine the specific behavior patterns exhibited by children during social interactions. (It should be stressed that such behavior patterns were not labeled motivationally a priori; i.e., the author did not begin by labeling "chase" as "aggressive" behavior. Instead he examined the results or consequences of a particular behavior pattern, i.e., the behavior immediately following chasing which enabled its assignment after analysis to one of the operationally-defined categories.) This examination began with an attempt to define a social behavior repertoire, an ethogram for the young *Homo sapiens*.

In constructing the repertoire the author used two sources of information: (1) published knowledge and (2) personal observations. As mentioned earlier,

Fig. 2.1 Nonagonistic interaction between two girls: inspection of a new tooth.

existing knowledge was scanty, and no inclusive attempt had been published. However, the works of Darwin, Blurton Jones, Grant, etc., provided useful descriptions of some patterns. Many other sources included isolated behavior pattern descriptions and items to be kept in mind while observing. Observations initially consisted of sitting or wandering about in the Slade Nursery taking copious notes on social interaction. As certain patterns recurred, their descriptions were refined and checked at the next sighting.

This process of description and distillation produced an expanding tentative list organized in terms of body parts involved. Each behavior pattern was defined as specifically as possible, as far as such specificity seemed meaningful; for example, Beat was divided into four subcategories. Other initial divisions were reunited, for example, Finger and Fumble were recombined into Automanipulate. Table 2.1 lists the most useful current glossary of behavior patterns, and Chapter 4 contains discussion of most of them. However, the repertoire cannot be considered final, and further modification and extension will occur as research proceeds.

Inter-observer reliability testing was important for checking the soundness of behavior categories. Two observers (A and B) viewed the same videotaped social interactions and noted patterns seen. Coefficients were figured from the most stringent standard formula:

$$\frac{\text{No. of agreements } (A \ \& \ B)}{\text{No. of agreements } (A \ \& \ B) + \text{no. seen by } B \text{ only} + \text{no. seen by } A \text{ only}}$$

Chapter 4 gives the results by behavior pattern. Standards for inter-observer reliability are not uniform, but agreement below .70 was regarded as unacceptable. The definitions of low-reliability items were reworked until usable, or treated with caution and noted accordingly.

Having produced an accurate and fairly inclusive repertoire, the author noted the frequencies, combinations, and sequences of its constituent elements. He also examined the occurrence of elements in relation to their specific social contexts, when appropriate. For example, before and after encounters he noted whether the childred involved were *together* or *separated*, or whether the encounter was a *continuation* or undeterminable because of *other* factors. He noted which children *initiated* or *terminated* the interaction, which children were *intruders* or *possessors*, and which children were *winners* or *losers*.

The contextual aspects were defined as:

Together—in close physical proximity and usually engaged in common activity.

Separate—not in close physical proximity (usually further than 10 feet apart) or not engaged in common activity (usually not having interacted in 10 or more seconds).

TABLE 2.1. *Repertoire of Preschool Children's Behavior Patterns, Arranged by Body Parts Involved*

I. Facial	III. Gestures	V. Gross
1. Bared Teeth	1. Automanipulate	1. Arms Akimbo*
2. Blink*	Finger	2. Body Oppose
3. Eyebrow Flash*	Fumble	3. Fall
4. Eyes Closed*	2. Beat	4. Flinch
5. Grin Face	Incomplete	5. Hug
6. Low Frown	Object	6. Jump
7. Mouth Open	Open	7. Lean Back
8. Narrow Eyes*	Up	8. Lean Forward
9. Normal Face	3. Beckon*	9. Physical Contact
10. Nose Wrinkle*	4. Clap Hands*	10. Quick Hop
11. Play Face	5. Digit Suck	11. Rock
12. Pout*	6. Drop*	12. Shoulder Hug
13. Pucker Face	7. Fist*	13. Shrug
14. Red Face	8. Forearm Raise	14. Stretch*
15. Smile	9. Forearm Sweep	15. Turn
16. Wide Eyes	10. Hand Cover*	16. Wrestle
	11. Hand on Back*	VI. Posture
II. Head	12. Hold Hands	
	13. Hold Out*	1. Climb*
1. Bite	14. Knock*	2. Crouch
2. Blow*	15. Pat	3. Immobile
3. Chew Lips*	16. Pinch	4. Kneel*
4. Chin In*	17. Point	5. Lie*
5. Face Thrust	18. Pull	6. Play Crouch*
6. Gaze Fixate	19. Punch	7. Sit*
7. Glance*	Incomplete	8. Slope*
8. Grind Teeth*	Object	9. Stand*
9. Head Nod*	Open	VII. Locomotion
10. Head Shake	Side	
11. Head Tilt*	20. Push	1. Back
12. Kiss*	21. Reach	2. Back Step
13. Laugh	22. Repel*	3. Chase
14. Lick*	23. Scratch	4. Crawl*
15. Look	24. Shake*	5. Flee
16. Mouth*	25. Snatch*	6. Gallop*
17. Spit	26. Throw	7. March*
18. Swallow*	27. Tickle*	8. Miscellaneous
19. Tongue Out*	28. Underarm Throw	Locomotion
20. Verbalize	29. Wave*	9. Run
21. Vocalize	IV. Leg	10. Sidle
22. Weep		11. Sidle Step
23. Yawn	1. Kick	12. Skip*
	Incomplete	13. Step
	Up	14. Walk
* Not recorded in	2. Shuffle*	
original Slade study	3. Stamp*	

25

Continuation—a temporary separation of individuals while both remained in a larger group or engaged with several other children in simultaneous, partly overlapping interactions within a larger group.

Other—intervention by an adult while interaction in progress, or movement by children to outside observer's field of view.

Initiater—individual making the first move oriented to another which was followed by interaction.

Terminater—individual first changing orientation from the other during interaction, usually by moving away or refocusing attention, so that interaction ended.

Intruder—individual approaching another child already engaged in an activity, from a different location; usually a mobile child not attending to own activity.

Possesser—individual engaged in specific activity, usually stationary and attending to it.

Winner—individual gaining or retaining possession of an object or space.

Loser—individual losing or failing to gain possession of an object or space.

Teacher ratings of children have traditionally been used to validate indirect measures or observational results. Ten adults regularly present in the Slade Nursery School (teachers, nursery nurses, student trainees, and the author) were asked to grade 30 children on three attributes: *aggressiveness*, *activity*, and *sociability*. Each attribute was considered in two ways: *ranking* (e.g., each child was given a rank in relation to the other 29 in terms of his habitual aggressiveness), and *rating* (e.g., each child's activity was rated on a five-point scale: "very inactive," "more inactive than average," "average activity," "more active than average," and "very active"). To prevent prejudgement, graders received no definitions of the attributes, and the author asked each to use personal criteria suggested by the attribute. Graders were asked not to discuss their gradings with others until all were completed, and at the time of grading the behavioral results of the study were unknown. All graders accepted the task willingly, and most seemed to find the attributes meaningful and workable.

Earlier human ethological studies often did not rigorously define their research populations. The author collected background information on individual children whenever possible: age, sex, number of siblings (older and younger), I.Q. (Stanford-Binet Intelligence Scale, Revised), socioeconomic background (father's occupation as classified by the General Register Office), height, weight, and time spent in the nursery since entrance. At Epworth Halls Nursery School parents filled in a questionnaire about participation in other peer groups, number and age of usual playmates, and degree of previous acquaintance with other nursery members.

Chapter 3

Methods

This chapter is the shortest in the book: the facilities differ little from those used in observational studies of preschool children since the 1920's. The recording techniques are also identical in some cases, and the others represent only technological advances that are time-saving and more comprehensive, not revolutionary. The preschool population is significantly different in only one respect from its legions of scrutinized predecessors: we specifically avoided drawing our group from offspring of university staff members and graduate students. Such a group is, of course, very nonrepresentative of the general population, but past investigators have subordinated this possible drawback to the obvious convenience of using university children. No effort will be made here to deal with the theoretical aspects of observing children; S. J. Hutt and C. Hutt (1970) have dealt thoroughly with this.

Facilities

Observations of young children (all of whom are referred to by pseudonyms) were made in two nursery schools: Slade Nursery School, Oxford, and Epworth Halls Nursery School, Edinburgh.

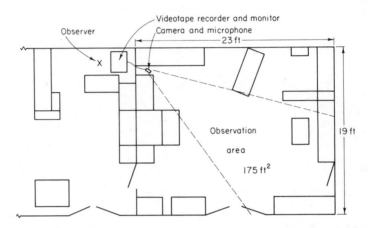

Fig. 3.1. Floor plan of observation play room, Slade Nursery School, Oxford.

The Slade was a state school consisting of three medium-sized, rectangular play rooms (1117 ft^2), a large outdoor play area (11,752 ft^2), and a bathroom and hallway. One play room was used as the observation room for this study; it contained standard nursery equipment traditionally appropriate for either sex (e.g., doll's house, carpentry table) or both (e.g., musical instruments). The space in the room's center remained clear for spontaneous activity, which often involved construction with large blocks or use of toy vehicles. Most social interaction occurred in this area, which the videotape camera's field of view encompassed (Fig. 3.1). The Slade's all-female staff comprised a head teacher, four qualified nursery nurses, and (usually) four student nurses.

Epworth Halls was a private nursery school, financially supported and administered by the Social Science Research Council and the Department of Psychology, University of Edinburgh. It consisted of a carpeted, rectangular play room (22 ft × 36 ft, 792 ft^2), an adjacent outdoor play area (653 ft^2), and a cloakroom and bathroom. The play room contained equipment similar to the Slade's: Wendy House, building blocks, book corner, painting easels, slide, table toys, etc. The small, irregularly-shaped outdoor area contained a large sand pit and surfaced area with see-saw, skipping ropes, etc. Epworth Halls' staff comprised a qualified nursery nurse and assistant, both females. Equipment and activities remained in standard positions, and the videotape camera's field of view included activities comparable to those in the Slade observation room (Fig. 3.2.).

Subjects

Eighty-seven children attended the Slade Nursery School during the study. Most (60%) attended for a half-day, either morning or afternoon, but the rest

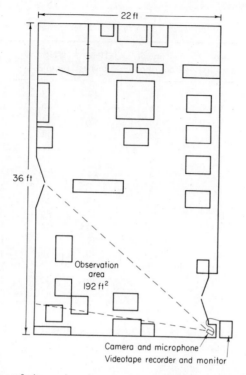

Fig. 3.2. Floor plan of observation play room, Epworth Halls Nursery School, Edinburgh.

remained at the nursery from 9:00 a.m. to 3:00 p.m., including lunch. Total attendance at any one time varied from 55–60.

Thirty children (Ss) "selected" themselves for observation, i.e., appeared most often in the observation room during free play. (See Table 3.1.) They were predominantly of lower-middle socioeconomic backgrounds (86% from Grades III and IV, as determined from father's occupation according to the General Register Office). They had a mean of 3 (± 2.1 S.D.) siblings. Ss's ages during the study averaged 50 (± 7.5) months, and their Stanford-Binet Revised I.Q. scores averaged 106 (± 20.5). Eleven of the 30 Ss had a sibling present with them in the nursery, and their duration of nursery attendance averaged 11 (± 7.4) months. Ss averaged 39 (± 5.6) pounds in weight and 42 (± 2.4) inches in height. All but two Ss (Dustin and Laura, who were of West Indian descent) were Caucasian, native-English speaking, and in good physical condition. Three children were medically classified as "abnormal": Chester was treated for hypo-thyroid imbalance, Everett was treated as behaviorally disordered and hyper-aggressive, and Laura was severely retarded and probably disturbed. All three remained in the nursery past their fifth birthdays because they were judged as incapable of primary schoolwork at the usual entry age.

TABLE 3.1. *Individual Information on Children from Slade Nursery School, Oxford*

Child	Part-/ full-time	Age (months)	Time at school (months)	Height (inches)	Weight (pounds)	Siblings	Social class	I. Q.
Dana[a]	F	54	14	43	43	4	III	110
Patrick	F	53	14	43	40	1	III	105
Tyler	F	50	14	42	42	3	IV	103
Kevin	F	55	23	41	34	4	III	121
Gerald	F	52	7	47	47	1	IV	133
Alvin	F	52	15	42	41	4	II	116
Charles	F	45	14	44	42	2	IV	100
Chester	F	67	19	—	—	2	II	62
Everett	F	62	26	43	47	7	—	77
Dustin	F	56	25	47	56	2	IV	100
Donald	F	40	2	40	34	5	IV	92
Sigmund	P	36	2	39	37	1	III	120
Robert	F	47	15	40	36	4	V	101
Quincey	F	43	2	39	32	7	III	94
Quentin	F	43	2	39	32	7	III	94
Parker	F	47	7	43	41	0	III	155
Gordon	F	43	2	40	37	1	III	129
Ronald	P	45	2	42	41	1	III	113
Noam	F	47	7	42	41	2	III	95
Billy	P	44	7	39	36	1	III	107
Dick	P	40	2	38	40	0	III	124
Karen	F	45	7	42	40	1	IV	105
Vera	F	55	15	42	47	1	III	132
Marilyn	F	51	11	43	37	4	III	—
Jessica	F	52	14	42	37	2	III	133
Tricia	F	54	11	39	36	7	V	101
Sally	F	47	7	41	33	2	III	95
Laura	F	68	27	46	44	2	IV	55
Dinah	P	47	8	37	28	3	IV	107
Anne	F	50	14	43	38	1	III	107

[a]Names are pseudonyms

Because the 30 *S*s formed a "self-selected" sample, it was important to know if they differed from the rest of the Slade's population and, if so, why? The greatest difference ($\chi^2 = 34.2$, $df = 1$, $p < .001$) between the *S*s ($N = 30$) and the non-*S*s ($N = 57$) was in attendance: most *S*s attended the nursery all day (full-time) while most non-*S*s attended the nursery only on mornings or afternoons (part-time). The difference probably resulted from the school's floor plan: the part-time "home room" was located in another wing of the nursery from the observation room, which was one of the two full-time "home rooms." Many of the children's directed activities occurred in their home rooms (e.g., milk drinking, music time, story time), and children often remained there during free play. Although in theory all children had access to all rooms, in practice they tended to stay near their home rooms.

Full-time children were also older than part-time children ($\chi^2 = 7.44$, $df = 1$, $p < .01$), and this explains the other differences between Ss and non-Ss. Ss were older (Mann-Whitney U test, $z = 3.55$, $p < .0002$), had more nursery experience ($z = 3.55$, $p < .0002$), and weighed more ($z = 3.10$, $p < .001$) than non-Ss. Non-Ss height data were not available.

Ss and non-Ss did not differ on variables unrelated to age: I.Q. (Mann-Whitney U test, $z = 1.14$, $p < .13$), sex ($\chi^2 = 1.40$, $df = 1$, $p < 25$), social class ($\chi^2 = .50$, $df = 2$, $p < .80$), and number of siblings (Mann-Whitney U test, $z = 1.42$, $p < .08$).

Thirty-two children, 16 males and 16 females, attended the Epworth Halls Nursery School during the study. (See Table 3.2.) Enrollment never exceeded 20, and changes occurred when older children moved on to primary school and incoming three year-olds replaced them. They were predominately from middle socio-economic backgrounds (69% from Grades II and III), and only two children's parents were connected with the University. They averaged 1 ($\pm .7$) sibling, mostly younger, and 12 of the 32 had a sibling present with them in the nursery. Children's ages at entry averaged 40 (± 4.9) months, and their Stanford-Binet Revised I.Q. scores averaged 111 (± 20.0). All were Caucasian, native English-speaking, in good physical condition, and most were of Scottish national background. One child was probably classifiable as "abnormal": Gary displayed prolonged disturbance at maternal separation, but he was not medically treated for this.

Nursery Routine

Children attended the Slade Nursery School on Mondays to Fridays, from September through June. They arrived with their mothers at 9:00 a.m., then drank a bottle of milk before beginning free play. Fifteen-minute story and music sessions occurred later in the morning, but children attended them voluntarily. At noon the morning part-time children left, and between 12:00 and 12:30 the children ate lunch. The afternoon part-time children arrived at 1:00 while the full-time children napped for an hour. From 1:30 to 3:00 all children engaged in more free play.

Seven adults were usually present in the nursery at any one time, and one staff member always stayed in each play room. The author was the only observer present, but two experimenters conducted short studies in the nursery during the period of observations. Mothers left the nursery soon after bringing their children, most of them only coming to the play room door. When fetching children, mothers sometimes came early and stayed on for several minutes talking to staff members, but observations ended before they arrived.

TABLE 3.2. *Individual Information on Children from Epworth Halls Nursery School, Edinburgh*

Child	Age at entry (months)	Siblings	Social class	I.Q.
Bertha[a]	36	1	IV	127
Carrie	36	1	III	103
Cora	40	1	III	90
Ellen	36	1	I	147
Gladys	56	1	I	—
Hazel	36	1	III	128
Heidi	43	1	II	—
Isabel	39	2	III	111
Karen	49	1	IV	—
Kathie	36	1	II	132
Kristine	36	0	—	—
Marcia	42	1	II	95
Moira	36	1	II	—
Nora	40	3	II	135
Ophelia	40	1	II	109
Teresa	39	1	III	111
Barry	39	1	—	—
Calvin	36	1	I	131
Edward	37	1	II	127
Evan	48	2	I	—
Gary	36	1	III	—
Homer	40	1	III	88
Ian	37	2	IV	96
Ivan	45	2	IV	70
Jack	40	2	II	100
Kenneth	46	0	—	127
Neville	40	2	IV	93
Norman	49	3	II	96
Oliver	42	2	III	118
Sammy	36	3	II	—
Timmy	46	1	III	—
Tommy	36	1	III	117

[a]Names are pseudonyms

Free play periods in both schools were those when all children had access to all nursery facilities (weather permitting) and engaged in activities undirected by adults. During free play adults remained onlookers and did not interfere in the children's activities unless requested to do so by them, or unless a potentially dangerous situation arose, for example, a child attempting to climb a precariously placed ladder. Adults maintained this outlook during children's agonistic encounters unless a child was in danger of injury or sought adult solace. In this atmosphere, children acted largely self-sufficiently, and many procedural rules passed directly from child to child. Physical punishment by adults was rare in the Slade and absent in Epworth Halls, and almost all children performed routine toilet activities without adult aid.

Children attended the Epworth Halls Nursery School on Monday to Friday mornings from August to July. They arrived with their mothers between 9:15 and 9:30 a.m. From 9:30 to 10:15 they engaged in free play. Between 10:15 and 11:00 children heard a story, played organized musical games, and had milk and snacks. From 11:00 to 11:45 they engaged in a second free play period before the mothers arrived to pick them up.

The nursery nurse and assistant remained in the nursery throughout the morning, and male experimenters from an associated cognition study came in and out of the room for short periods. One full-time male observer (the author) and one or two part-time female observers were present in the play room during free play sessions. The nursery nurse's year-old daughter often attended the nursery with her mother. Mothers left soon after bringing their children, most of them only coming to the door. Similarly when fetching children, mothers entered the nursery only after termination of the day's observations. Free play conditions were identical to those in the Slade and the adults behaved similarly.

Observation Procedures

Observations were made from October to December, 1966, and from December, 1967 to March, 1968 in the Slade Nursery School, and from August, 1968 to September, 1969 in the Epworth Halls Nursery School. Three types of data collection were used in the observations: remote audio-videotape, direct audio-tape, and direct written recording.

In both nurseries, a Sony CVC-2000B Video camera (with Kern Paillard 16 mm wideangle lens in the Slade and Sony 25 mm lens in Epworth Halls) and a Sony F-98 cardioid microphone recorded children's activities from an observation room corner. A Sony CV-2000B Videorecorder using ½-inch V-32 magnetic tape and a Sony 9-inch television monitor were connected to them and placed in an adjacent room. In the Slade, the latter equipment sat in an adjacent play room, boxed in by cabinets on three sides, so that it was only partially accessible to the children. Epworth Halls children had no access to the videorecorder and monitor, which sat in an adjacent unused hallway.

Every effort was made to minimize disruptive effects of videotape recording. In both nurseries, the videotape equipment was assembled before the children's morning arrival, and it remained undisturbed until completion of the day's observations. The camera and microphone in the observation room operated silently with no moving parts; children could not know whether it was on or off. Children visually inspected the equipment freely, and they had to be initially restrained from manipulating it. After the initial novelty effect declined (before the beginning of observations), children treated the equipment as just another school fixture. At Slade, some children briefly watched others on the monitor screen over the observer's shoulder, but this did not disrupt ongoing activity in the observation room.

At Slade, the observer made videorecordings over one-hour periods at 9:25 to 10:25 a.m. and 1:30 to 2:30 p.m. He sat at the monitor and videotape recorder taking written notes of the action being recorded. At Epworth Halls, the observer made recordings over 45-minute periods at 9:30 to 10:15 a.m. and 11:00 to 11:45 a.m. He left the equipment after starting it and conducted simultaneous written recording in the observation room.

At Slade, the observer also dictated observations onto a battery-operated Phillips 3302 cassette audiotape recorder while walking among the children. The recorder hung unobtrusively by a shoulder strap under one arm; the microphone was tucked in the observer's breast pocket and the controls hidden in another pocket. The observer verbally described children's behavior into the microphone six inches from his mouth. Because the observer towered above them, spoke quietly, and never visibly manipulated the equipment, children paid little attention to the recording.

In both nurseries, written recording consisted of the observer using pen, clipboard, and sometimes stopwatch to mark standardized check sheets or write out shorthand descriptions of a single child's activities. The observer stood or sat quietly on the room's periphery or moved slowly about avoiding the "traffic flow." He followed simple rules to avoid interfering with children's activities: he maintained the maximum distance from subjects which still allowed accurate recording, avoided facing the subject, never gaze fixated but only glanced at him, and used the physical configuration of the room to best advantage. No child evidenced awareness of "being followed."

As a conspecific, the observer's potential interactional capacities posed special problems, particularly as some observations lasted up to 45 minutes. All adults present interacted with children during some periods and directed some activities (e.g., story time, milk and snack time). Two extremes of observer conduct were rejected: (1) intentional, initiated interaction which would make comprehensive, objective observation impossible, and (2) a totally detached, withdrawn attitude which also might be "unnaturally" wooden. The observer attempted a compromise: he did not initiate interaction with children, but if they initiated interaction with him, he did not refuse, rather, he tried to terminate it as soon as was gracefully possible. Such interactions caused only negligable interruption to the observer's recording, and few such interactions occurred between the observer and subject. The children seemed to conclude early that observers were dull prospects and paid more attention to other adults.

The observer later replayed the videotapes on a large laboratory monitor, then timed and transcribed them into a standardized form. The data were then punched onto eight-hole paper tape for computer input. Vowles and Clarke (1971) describes the computer analysis program.

Similarly, the observer replayed the audiotapes, then timed and transcribed them onto coded sheets. Key punch operators at the Oxford Regional Hospital Board punched data from the sheets onto IBM cards for analysis. Analysis consisted of standard electronic data processing procedures which produced systematic print-out results. Both transcription tasks were tedious: 15 hours of transcription to one hour of videotape recording, five hours of transcription to one hour of audiotape recording. Written description was typed into standardized form.

Chapter 4

Elements of Behavior

Introduction

The problems of ethological description and behavioral elements have already been discussed in Chapter 2. This chapter presents a glossary of behavior patterns exhibited by three- and four-year-old children in social situations during nursery school free play. It is a tentative attempt at defining an ethogram for the young *Homo sapiens*.

The behavioral elements are named using simple, nonmotivational terms which refer either to the body part involved (e.g. Forearm Raise) or to everyday English usage (e.g. Wrestle). Inferential labels, for example, "threat face," or "fearful crouch," might be more evocative, but at this early stage when know-ledge of underlying motivation and consequences is sparse, such labeling would be rash and sometimes confusing. Such knowledge is one of the goals of the research and cannot be predetermined. The number following the pattern's name is its inter-observer reliability coefficient.

When possible, the elements are defined objectively as motor patterns which specifically refer to first-hand observation. Most are not specific enough for electromyographic studies, but definitions in terms of muscle groups, joints, and innervation could be derived for most elements. (For example, Hill [1969] recently presented a detailed account of the gelada's facial anatomy in relation to its unique "lip-flip" expression.) Where orientation is important, especially concerning the other interactant's body-parts, it is given. The elements presented vary in the "level" of descriptive detail used, for example, Blink and Wrestle.

36

Following the description of each element, knowledge from this and other research about the performance, development, and function of the behavior pattern is presented. Particular attention is paid to Grant's (1969) glossary of human behavior patterns, the most comprehensive hitherto published; numerals refer to his numbering scheme. Discussion is not restricted to the preschool age group, nor is it restricted to Western cultures. Speculation about the evolutionary significance and survival value of many of the elements, particularly the directly socially communicative ones, is also presented. Some such speculations may seem trivial or far-fetched, but many lend themselves to experimental examination (see, e.g., Freedman, 1969, 1971). Also, if they provoke more knowledgeable individuals in related fields (e.g., clinicians) to examine behavior from fresh viewpoints, they will have served a useful purpose.

Finally, knowledge of similar behavioral elements in nonhuman primate species is included when pertinent, although a comprehensive review is impossible. This consists of descriptions of movements and their functions in the social life of other primate species, which may shed light on the origins of human behavior patterns (Hamburg, 1968). The most comprehensive quantitative analysis of the behavioral repertoire of a nonhuman primate species is van Hooff's (1970) on the chimpanzee. He carried out component analysis of 53 behavioral elements and found that seven "systems" ("Affinitive," "Play," "Aggressive," "Submissive," "Excitement," "Show," and "Groom") accounted for more than 80 percent of the total variance. Such comparisons do not imply that all human and nonhuman primate behavioral elements are homologously equivalent, although some appear to be, for example, forehead scalp retraction and eyebrow raising, as resulting from contraction of the frontal belly of the *occipito-frontalis* muscle. All comparative speculation should be taken as ideas put forward for empirical investigation or theoretical consideration, and not as proven knowledge.

The author does not attempt to make pronouncements on the extent to which the elements are "built into" the species or "acquired" during individual ontogeny, or any combination of the two. Nor is any attempt made to relate performance to any underlying motivational system or combination of systems. Finally, it should be noted that any generalizations about behavior humans perform is limited to Western culture, more specifically to Anglo-American culture. Where possible, specific reference to other societies are made, but few, if any, generalizations about *Homo sapiens* can be made at this stage. These limitations are necessary because of the tentative nature of this study, but it is hoped that later research will produce more definitive answers.

The behavioral elements are categorized and presented approximately in terms of the body parts involved. (Table 2.1 gives a complete list.) They are organized in six sections of increasing grossness: facial patterns; head patterns; gestures; postures and leg patterns; gross patterns; and locomotion.

Fig. 4.1 constitutes a set of photographs illustrating some of the behavioral elements. The limitations of portraying movements with still photographs are obvious, but this must suffice until a cine-glossary can be constructed. Grant (1969) has provided excellent photos illustrating many human facial expressions.

Inter-observer reliability coefficients were recorded for 80 behavioral elements. These were obtained by having the author and another observer simultaneously or successively record the incidence of elements from identical data sources. The facial behavior patterns were separately recorded from a series of 4-inch X 6-inch black and white still photographs. All other behavior patterns were simultaneously recorded from four videotapes totaling three hours duration. The following formula gave the coefficients:

$$\frac{\text{Agreements (observer } A \text{ and observer } B)}{\text{Agreements + disagreements } (A \text{ only}) + \text{disagreements } (B \text{ only})}$$

Analysis of the 80 patterns showed an overall mean inter-observer reliability coefficient of .84 (S.D. = ± .09). The mean number of recorded instances per behavior patterns used was 21.1 (S.D. = ± 13.0). Thirty patterns could not be assigned coefficients, in most cases because of infrequent occurrence. (An arbitrarily-chosen minimum of seven recorded instances was required for computing a coefficient.)

Facial Patterns

This section includes behavior patterns involving the structures of the face: eyes, nose, mouth, eyebrows, forehead, and cheeks. These are of obvious importance from early infancy onwards; for example, Haaf and Bell (1967) showed that four-month-old infants could successfully discriminate differing degrees of "faceness" over and above stimulus complexity differences. Some behavior patterns include structures acting alone (e.g., Narrow Eyes) and others refer to combinations of the structures acting in conjunction (e.g., Play Face). Some facial expressions are exhibited in isolation, but most occur simultaneously with more gross behavior patterns. The mean overall inter-observer reliability coefficient for facial patterns was .80 (S.D. = ± .07), and the mean number of recorded instances/behavior pattern used in computation was 11.9 (S.D. = ± 3.1).

Bared Teeth

The lips are retracted; the teeth are visible and usually clenched; the mouth corners are usually down; the lower lip may have a squared appearance. Blurton Jones (1972b) described this behavior pattern in detail (including muscu-

Fig. 4.1A. Illustrations of children's behavior patterns: Pucker Face (top left); Laugh (top right); Bared Teeth (center left); Automanipulate, finger (center right); genuine manipulation (bottom left); Automanipulate, fumble (bottom right). **B.** Illustrations of children's behavior patterns: Point (top left; Beat (top right); Beat Up (center left); Object Beat (center right); Pinch (bottom left); dominance interaction (bottom right). **C.** Illustrations of children's behavior patterns: Punch and Flinch (top left); Kick (top right); Hold Hands (center left); Quick Hop (center right); quasiagonistic play group: Jump (bottom left); quasiagonistic play group: Flee and Chase (bottom right).

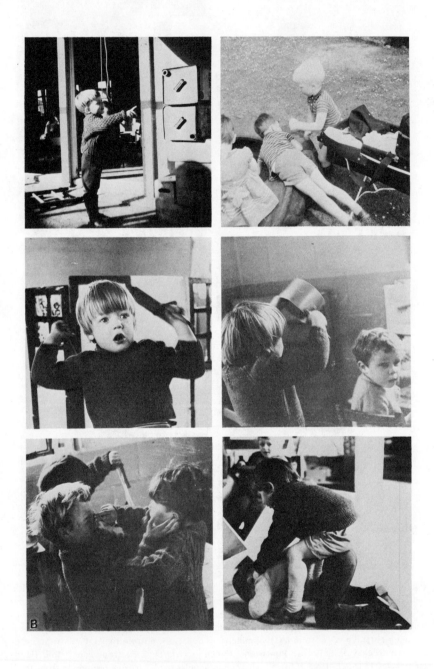

lature) in his "squared lower lip" category. (See Grant's, 1969, No. 39: Intention Bite.)

Bared teeth occurs in agonistic situations, either during physical conflict or in circumstances where it appears that the actor is inhibiting attack (Blurton Jones, 1967). It may occur during physical exertion in social interaction, for example, when two children tug at a box between them. One older child accompanied bared teeth with vigorously shaking his opponents when apparently frustrated by their actions. Bared teeth may also occur in nonsocial situations, for example, while waiting for the loud noise from a toppling pile of blocks, when about to be hit by a falling toy.

Bared teeth may be derived from the mammalian protective response (Andrew, 1963), and the clenched teeth may prevent damage from the jaws banging together during physical conflict or exertion. However, it also resembles the expression exhibited during temper tantrums and may be related to inhibited biting.

The generalized nonhuman primate counterpart of this expression may be the "staring bared-teeth scream face" described by van Hooff (1967). It is exhibited when a tendency, for example, attack, is strongly activated in the actor but is thwarted by the reactor's behavior. Other expressions including visible teeth are noted in Grin Face.

Bared teeth occurred too infrequently to produce a reliability coefficient.

Blink

This is a well-known reflex, consisting of rapid, successive lowering and raising of the eyelids. It may occur singly or in short, repeated series, usually of few than five. (See Grant's No. 9: Blink.)

Blinking commonly occurs when a child is startled, often by some sudden movement near his head, but it may be elicited by an auditory stimulus, for example, a loud bang. It may also occur in non-startling situations, for example, when in close physical proximity to another, threatening child. Such blinks are often "directed" to the threatening child's face, that is, the blinking child does not necessarily display Turn away, Flinch, or Eyes Closed, at least not immediately.

Such blinking may have a communicative function, perhaps signalling that the blinking child is fearful but still unsure enough about the situation to be unwilling to avert his eyes for fear of missing impending action. Also, since Gaze Fixation is likely to occur in this situation, blinking would be an effective cue, particularly if combined with other expressive facial components. Evidence that blinking is linked with communication is established: Condon and Ogston (1967) found that human eye blinks were precisely distributed relative to ongoing verbalization.

Other (probably culturally-dependent) eyelid movements have communicative significance, for example, the acknowledging or reassuring "wink," and the "innocent fluttering" of the eyelids in flirting, but preschool children apparently perform neither. (See Grant's No. 11: Wink). Eibl-Eibesfeldt (1968) discussed various forms of eyelid greeting patterns and their cross-cultural variations.

As a reflex, blinking is well-documented. It is often the first recognizable behavior pattern seen in the infant rhesus macaque, within seconds of the head's emergence from the birth canal (Tinklepaugh & Hartman, 1932). Since rhesus mothers actively participate in delivery, blinking could serve an important communicative function even this early in the infant's life: an indication of its viability, perhaps acting as a stimulus to further maternal care-taking activities. The fact that normal rhesus blinking in response to visual stimulation does not occur till the eighth day may lend support to this idea. Blinking is a threat signal in many nonhuman primates, and many species have eyelids of contrasting color to the rest of the face (van Hooff, 1962). (See also Eyebrow Flash.)

Blink could not be tested using still photographs and ½-inch videotape did not produce a sufficiently sharp image, so no reliability coefficient is given.

Eyebrow Flash

Eibl-Eibesfeldt (1968) defined this behavior as a rapid raising of the eyebrows, which remain elevated for 1/6 sec, followed by a rapid lowering to the normal position. It may occur singly or in short series, and it results from the contraction of the frontal belly of the *occipito-frontalis* muscle. He noted that eyebrow flashing appears to have an attractive function of drawing the other's a head nod. (See Grant's No. 15: Flash.)

Like adults, children appear to use eyebrow flashing in friendly greeting, for example, when glancing up at passing or approaching individuals. It also seems to occur in social surprise situations, for example, "peek-a-boo." Adults' eyebrow flashing appears to have an attractive function of drawing the other's attention to the actor (Grant, 1968). Eibl-Eibesfeldt's paper contains several excellent photographic series of eyebrow flashing in five widely-separated cultures.

The similar behavior pattern found in many nonhuman primate species (see Andrew, 1963) may be homologous to the human one: the same muscles function similarly in both and the innervation is similar.

No reliability coefficient is given for eyebrow flashing as it could not be presented in still photographs and occurred too infrequently in the videotapes.

Eyes Closed (.88)

The eyelids are brought together longer than momentarily (as compared with Blink). (See Grant's No. 8: Eyes Closed.)

Eye closing occurs in agonistic and nonagonistic interactions between children. In the former, it appears to be fearful and is accompanied by *orbicularis oculi* contraction, making the eyes appear screwed up. Children being aggressed-against exhibit it. In non-agonistic situations, eye closing occurs most often in dramatic play, for example, by "Baby" feigning sleep, and in hide-and-seek games. Eyes closed is often supplemented by Hand Cover or burying the face in clothing. It probably evolved from the mammalian protective response (Andrew, 1963).

Grant (1965b) classed Eyes Closed as a "flight element," that is behavior associated with fleeing from another person. Eyes Closed ("Shut") occurred after Flight elements in interview situations and preceded Contact elements, that is, those having an inter-individual attractive function (Grant, 1968). Chance (1962) described "cut-off" postures which reduce incoming visual information, and Eyes Closed may constitute a simple example. The ratio of eye closures to blinks is greater in conversations with strangers than in conversations with friends (Morris, 1967).

Comparable, in nonhuman primates, is the "frowning bared-teeth scream face" which occurs in response to attack and frequently alternates with attack; the eyes are closed or only slightly opened (van Hooff, 1967).

Grin Face (.83)

The lips are spread wide and the mouth corners are retracted; both rows of teeth are visible and usually close together. The expression is reflexive and fleeting in appearance. Blurton Jones (1972b) gave more detail description (including musculature) in discussion of his "lips retracted." This behavior pattern is difficult to relate to Grant's (1969) category scheme; it may correspond to his Nos. 28 and 29: Mouth Corners Back and Oblong Mouth.

Grin face occurs in agonistic or potentially agonistic interactions between preschool children; for example, "It happens when a smile begins to disappear and be replaced with frowns or screams" (Blurton Jones, 1968). It is exhibited most often by subordinates and losers of fights, that is, those individuals often aggressed-against, and seems to function as an appeasement gesture. Children exhibited grin faces after accidently bumping into another, when sitting down to join another child in playing with his toys, when being aggressed-against but seeming unwilling to flee or retaliate, when startled by sudden social stimuli. It seems to involve reassurance as well, and the observer may confuse it with smiling, particularly as the two patterns seem to intergrade.

Andrew (1963) discussed the origin of primate grinning (in the mammalian protective response and the production of high-pitched vocalization) and its function (as a defensive gesture showing friendly intentions).

Several generalized nonhuman primate expressions described by van Hooff (1967) resemble Grin Face: "silent bared-teeth face," "bared-teeth gecker face," "frowning bared-teeth scream face" and possibly "staring bared-teeth scream face." All these are exhibited in agonistic or social stress situations by subordinate, losing, or aggressed-against individuals. Specific examples are the "grimace toward" in rhesus monkeys (Altmann, 1962), "grin" in baboons (K. R. L. Hall & DeVore, 1965), and "grimaces" seen both in mild aggression and submission in common langurs (Jay, 1965). Hansen (1966) reported a similar behavior pattern which is difficult to classify in this motivational frame-work: the "silly grin" used by rhesus mothers to attract their young. No other research worker seems to have confirmed this usage. Perhaps, instead of the mother signalling the infant, both were reacting simultaneously in fear of a frightening stimulus (e.g., the observer?).

Low Frown (.67)

The eyebrows are lowered and brought close together, usually with only a small amount of vertical furrowing; the mouth is normal or the lips may be compressed into a straight line. Blurton Jones (1972b) gave a more detailed description (including musculature involved) and differentiated between "weak" and "strong" frowns. (See Grant's No. 17: Aggressive Frown.)

Low Frown occurs in agonistic situations, and is seen significantly often with beating (Blurton Jones, 1967), often preceding as well as during attack. "Strong" frowns are also seen in agonistic interactions but are usually exhibited by losers (Blurton Jones, 1972b). In threat, low frowns occur with Gaze Fixate and Face Thrust. Non-low frowning occurs in response to bright light and when closely examining an object.

Frowning is an aggressive act among adult schizophrenic patients and may be used in determining social dominance structure on hospital wards (Grant, 1965b). In interview situations, frowning was termed Assertive behavior (Grant, 1968).

Darwin (1872) listed many scattered human societies where frowning occurs as a socially communicative pattern. Several theories have been proposed about its origin (see Blurton Jones, 1972b), but Andrew's (1963) idea that it is derived from the mammalian protective response seems the most reasonable as it can be related to other, simultaneously-occurring behavior patterns.

Low frown is included in two generalized facial expressions seen in nonhuman primate agonistic interactions: "tense-mouth face" by dominants and "frowning bared-teeth scream face" by subordinates (van Hooff, 1967).

Mouth Open (.86)

The lips are separated. Blurton Jones (1972b) scored it in four categories of lip separation: touching, slightly apart, clearly apart, wide apart. (See Grant's No. 44: Open Mouth.)

Mouth opening is important in many facial expressions and vocalizations, but in the child's "normal" face the mouth is closed. For this reason, the author noted cases where mouth opening occurred alone and without sound production. This occurred in several situations: when directing long looks at strange peers or novel situations, when startled, and when breathing heavily after exertion. It appears to result from unconscious relaxation of the musculature which normally keeps the lower jaw raised. In adults it occurs when an individual's mouth suddenly "falls" open in surprise or awe.

Van Hooff (1967) has described two generalized nonhuman primate expressions in which the open mouth is prominent: "staring open-mouth face" in threat and "relaxed open-mouth face" in social play. Mouth opening is seen in rhesus macaque threat, where it often occurs with a direct stare and head-bobbing (Altmann, 1962). Chimpanzee mouth opening is an immediate response to "any sudden disturbance" (Reynolds & Reynolds, 1965).

Narrow Eyes (.83)

The eyelids are brought closer together than normal. (See Grant's No. 10: Narrow Eyes.)

Narrow eyes occurs in agonistic encounters where it appears to function similarly to Low Frown as a threat. The two often occur together, but narrowed eyes seems to occur alone in situations where one individual wants to signal to another without letting on to others also present. At close quarters a frown might be too obvious: Goffman (1959) described this as occurring when a married couple sit opposite each other during a bridge game. Blurton Jones (1972b) examined two degrees of eye narrowness but did not comment on their function.

Eye narrowness is related to gaze direction, for example, individuals looking down their noses are bound to look narrow-eyed. Some other behavior patterns incorporate eye narrowing, for example, Yawn. It is probably derived from the mammalian protective response.

In chimpanzee threat, the eyes are wide open, but during attack they may be "squinted for protection" (Wilson & Wilson, 1968). Eye-narrowing is an important component of the "frowning bared-teeth scream face" performed by losing animals in agonistic situations (van Hooff, 1967).

Normal Face (.71)

The lips are usually together and relaxed; brow and cheeks are smooth and unwrinkled; eyebrows and eyelids are in intermediate positions; general muscle tonus is relaxed. Considerable individual variability exists, however, as some individuals habitually show lowered mouth corners, a "pop-eyed" appearance, etc. This normal variability may result from morphological characteristics, for example, projecting lower teeth, or, in adults, from purposeful alteration, for example, from women's cosmetics. Grant (1968) called this pattern Neutral Face.

Such normal variability must be noted in advance and taken account of when noting facial expression. For example, some mongol children seem to exhibit wide smiles in situations where the Normal Face might be expected. (Is this why mongols are often considered "happy" children?) For economy of recording in our study, normal face was only noted in situations where it might be unexpected.

For nonhuman primates, van Hooff (1967) described a Relaxed Face and an Alert Face. A gradation exists between the former, defined by exclusion as all elements in neutral positions, and the latter, defined as Relaxed Face + fully opened eyes + high muscle tonus. Normal Face seems to correspond to something between the two. Descriptions by most other research workers are brief or absent, apparently on the assumption of self-evidence; for example, Schaller (1963) stated that the undisturbed mountain gorilla's expression "can best be described as placid and peaceful."

Nose Wrinkle (.75)

The skin of the nose is moved upward, producing wrinkling across the bridge of the nose; the nostrils are flared. Blurton Jones (1972b) discussed the musculature involved. (See Grant's No. 51: Wrinkle.)

Children's nose wrinkling occurs in wiping the nose, in sniffing disagreeable odours, and as part of some smiling; but its chief communicatory function is its occurrence in "making faces" (Blurton Jones,1972b). It occurs in many kinds of children's social interactions where it seems to indicate reassurance that the actor does not have aggressive intentions although the situation might warrant it. For example, a little girl tentatively objected to her blocks being used by a group of boys, then when they gaze fixated her, she responded with a nose wrinkle.

Grant (1968) classified "wrinkle" (nose wrinkling) as an assertive behavioral element in adult interview situations. It is probably derived from the mammalian protective response. Darwin (1872) noted that nostril distension may be a sign of anger.

Because the nonhuman primate nose is relatively immobile compared to other facial components, for example, eyes or mouth, and less prominent than in humans, it is rarely mentioned in descriptions of their behavior; van Hooff (1967) did not list it in his detailed description of facial expressions.

Play Face (.83)

The mouth is opened wide and the mouth corners are turned up; the teeth are covered by the lips or only partly visible. Blurton Jones (1967) described it

47

as the expression seen in laughter but without the sound. He described the accompanying posture as being "slightly crouched, side on to the chaser." (See Play Crouch.) The behavior pattern is difficult to relate to Grant's (1969) scheme; his No. 25 (Broad Smile) seems to be closest.

The Play Face is seen in quasiagonistic interactions ("rough-and-tumble play," Blurton Jones, 1967) where it seems to signal the absence of agonistic intention. Both chasing and fleeting individuals display it, particularly in play invitation, which occurs initially and at intervals when the interaction slows down. The exhibition of Play Face often seems to be the only behavioral element distinguishing a playful interaction from an agonistic one.

The corresponding general expression found in nonhuman primate play is the "relaxed open-mouth face," described by van Hooff (1967) as an intention movement of play-biting. It is also associated with "laughing" and "panting" and occurs in all genera of Old World monkeys and apes so far studied. Loizos (1967, 1969) discussed the occurrence of play faces in chimpanzees, where the expression acts as a playful *signal* pattern leading to playful *action* patterns.

Pout (.75)

The lower lip or both lips protrude forward, with the former curling down; the mouth is opened slightly. Blurton Jones (1972b) considered the expression as two separate categories of behavior and discussed the musculature involved. (See Grant's Nos. 33 and 36: Lower Lip Out and Lips Forward.)

Children often display pouting after agonistic encounters, particularly when they have lost a fight over a toy and the winner remains in the group or nearby. Blurton Jones (1972b) stated that "two-lip" pout occurred in arguments and quarrels, and Leach (1972) found that it indicated crossness and unwillingness to do something. In adults, pouting is considered "childish" although it may be considered attractive in females. Darwin (1872) noted that pouting in "sulkiness" is one of few behavior patterns exhibited more plainly by children than adults and pointed out its widespread distribution among many cultures. He considered it to have evolved from the performance of the characteristic nonhuman primate hooing vocalization.

Many nonhuman primates display a "pout face" which "expresses the need to be given body comfort or the opportunity to feed." (van Hooff, 1967.) His later analysis (van Hooff, 1970) classified both silent and vocalized pouting as Affinitive behaviors, and stretched pouting as Affinitive and Submissive. Young chimpanzees display the expression when seeking reunion with the mother and older chimpanzees display it during begging (van Lawick-Goodall, 1968a). Darwin noted this behavior pattern early on (1872, p. 139), and presented an illustration of it in his book on the expression of emotions. Gorillas display a similar expression in mild deprivation situations (Schaller, 1963).

Pucker Face (.89)

The forehead is wrinkled both vertically and horizontally; the brows are brought together and the inner ends raised; the nose is wrinkled; the eyes are closed or partially closed; the mouth is often open. The face in general looks "screwed up." Blurton Jones (1972b) described the musculature involved and his "oblique, slanted eyebrows" (after Darwin, 1872) are included in this pattern. (See Grant's No. 19: Sad Frown.)

Puckering the face occurs significantly often with Red Face and Weep, but it also occurs in children just prior to weeping (Blurton Jones, 1967). Puckering occurs without weeping in children who are losing fights or who appear frustrated without recourse, particularly by social factors. For example, a girl returned to cutting and pasting only to see that another child had taken away her scissors, she then pucker faced. Pucker Face was not seen in nonagonistic and quasiagonistic interactions.

Darwin (1872) described the "oblique eyebrows" expression as indicative of grief and gave numerous examples of its occurrence in other human societies.

Puckering the face seems not to have been recorded in nonhuman primates.

Red Face

Reddening of the facial skin is most apparent on the cheeks and forehead. It results from inhibition of the cervical sympathetic fibres which control the muscle tone of the dermal capillary walls (Goodhart, 1960). (See Grant's No. 116: Blush.)

Darwin (1872) first described face-reddening as an expression of rage in man, but Blurton Jones (1967) refined this description in children. He found that it occurred significantly often with puckered brows in situations resembling temper tantrums where a child seemed highly motivated to attack but did not do so. Red face also occurs in weeping and crying bouts. The redness does not appear around the eyes or mouth, perhaps thereby accentuating their communicatory effect (Goodhart, 1960), but does appear on the ears which, because of their protuding position, enhance the frontal visual effect. Goodhart further stated of face-reddening that "it appears to serve no other purpose than to provide an external sign of anger, embarrassment, or shame."

Face reddening also occurs in sexual situations, for example, blushing in courtship, and it is physiologically similar to agonistic reddening. It commonly occurs in females as a sexual-attractant signal to males. Masters and Johnson (1966) indicated that the "sex flush" is not restricted to the face as was earlier believed but extends over much of the body, and Morris (1967) speculated about its place in the sexual episode as a whole.

Some nonhuman primate species show face reddening during "anger" and excitement: rhesus macaques (Darwin, 1872), red uakari monkeys (*Cacajao rubicundus*) (Eimeryl and DeVore, 1966). However, Hinde and Rowell (1962) did not observe increased reddening during aggression in rhesus macaques.

No reliability coefficient was obtained because both data sources for testing (photographs and videotapes) were in black and white.

Smile (.78)

The mouth is partially opened and the mouth corners turned up; the eyes are partially closed; the teeth are covered by the lips or only partly visible. Blurton Jones (1972b) gave a more detailed definition, including musculature, in discussion of his "mouth corners raised." Grant (1969) described eight different types of smiling. Smiling is easily confused with Grin Face and Play Face, and unresolved difficulties exist about these categories.

Smiling occurs in many types of children's social interactions. In nonagonistic situations it occurs in greetings between friends, upon receiving praise or material reward, during observations of another child "acting silly," during motor activity, in response to "pleasing stimuli" (e.g., music), or as reassurance of friendly intentions towards another. During genuinely agonistic interactions, smiling is less common, but it usually occurs at the beginning of an interaction when one child seems to be trying to prevent its becoming agonistic. In quasiagonistic interactions, smiling accompanies many motor activities as well as functioning to reassure others of noninjurious intentions. Other investigators have pointed out that being knocked down may be acceptable when accompanied by a smile while otherwise it would be treated as aggression. Children also smile while solitary, for example, when watching other children laughing or sometimes when "reading" a book.

In preschool children, Ding and Jersild (1932) found that the greatest amount of smiling occurred in conjunction with motor activity. Smiling occurred about seven times as frequently as laughter, and the two were positively correlated. Walters, Pearce, and Dahms (1957) classified smiling as "physical affection."

Considerable work has been published on infant smiling (Ambrose, 1961; Bowlby, 1958; Darwin, 1877, P. H. Wolff, 1963). Early research workers considered smiling and subsequent maternal attention as an example of a human innate releasing mechanism (IRM), but later work has shown this to be over-simplified. For example, Brackbill (1958) showed that smiling can be "extinguished" in classical conditioning terms. Freedman (1964) showed that smiling is exhibited by blind infants who could not have learned it through visual imitation. Many complications have come from definitional differences and from the equation of different types of smiling, for example, early "reflexive" smiling and later "social" smiling in response to specific individuals.

Darwin (1872) believed that smiling exists in all human cultures and gave several examples; Eibl-Eibesfeldt (1968) recently presented more cross-cultural evidence supporting this. But many cultures "use" smiling differently than Westerners: LaBarre (1947) cited Japan, for example, where smiling is part of a complex, cultivated etiquette system.

Numerous theories on the origin of smiling exist. Holt (1931) believed that the smile developed ontogenetically from the relaxation of the facial muscles in the milk-satiated infant. Andrew (1963) regarded the smile as derived from the grin, which in turn was related to the mammalian protective response and the production of high-pitched vocalization.

Grant (1968) found that smiling often followed "Look At" in interview situations and could lead to elements of any type: Flight, Assertion, Relaxed, Contact. He pointed out that recent research indicated the existence of several kinds of smiling with different functions. An unexpected side-effect of smiling exists in experimental conditions where experimenter smiling may bias subject performance; most past research has ignored this obvious factor (Duncan, 1969; Rosenthal, 1968).

It is difficult to say if smiling occurs in nonhuman primates, largely because of definitional problems. Many workers have applied the term without definition, and Darwin's (1872) descriptions and examples are difficult to distinguish from Play Face and Grin Face. His only illustration (p. 135) appears to be a Grin Face. Research workers have noted that the "relaxed open-mouth face" resembles human smiling (van Hooff, 1967).

Wide Eyes (.86)

The eyebrows are raised and held, producing an arched appearance; the forehead is horizontally wrinkled; the distance between upper and lower eyelids is increased. Blurton Jones (1972b) gave a detailed description of the pattern including musculature in his "raised brows" and "eye openness." Grant (1968) recorded a similar pattern ("Raise" = "eyebrows are raised and kept up for some time") in interviews with adults. (See Grant's Nos. 12 and 16: Eyes Open and Eyebrows Raised.)

Wide eyes occurs in agonistic interactions, usually as fearful behavior during flight or upon meeting an aggressor. It also occurs in defensive behavior, in conjunction with Forearm Raise (Blurton Jones, 1967). It may occur in borderline quasiagonistic-agonistic interactions, in which high-pitched vocalizations alternate with laughing and play faces.

When asking questions in nonagonistic encounters, children frequently raise their brows. In adult interviews, "Raise" appeared to have an attractive function of drawing the other's attention to the actor (Grant, 1968).

51

Darwin (1872) described wide eyes as an expression of surprise and astonishment and gave numerous examples of its use in several human societies. He stated that wide eyes may have originated in the necessity of increasing the field of vision quickly to survey surroundings during times of danger.

Eyebrow raising and eye widening occur in several of the generalized nonhuman primate expressions described by van Hooff (1967): "staring bared-teeth scream face," " staring open-mouth face," "lip smacking face," "lips protruded face." The first behavior pattern functions in nonhuman agonistic situations similarly to its fearful occurrence in children, while the second is an aggressive pattern used threateningly in species with conspicuously colored eyelids. The latter two patterns are approach-tendency expressions.

Head Patterns

This section includes behavior patterns involving structures of the head and neck. Some behavior patterns include structures acting alone (e.g., Tongue Out) and others refer to combinations of structures acting in conjunction (e.g., Head Shake). Most head and neck patterns are exhibited in isolation, but some (e.g., Face Thrust) occur simultaneously with more gross behavior patterns. The mean overall inter-observer reliability coefficient for head patterns was .84 (S.D. = ± .08), and the mean number of recorded instances per behavior pattern used in computation was 19.5 (S.D. = ± 9.8).

Bite

The upper and lower rows of teeth are brought rapidly and forcefully together, usually with the lips retracted. When directed to other individuals, biting is usually oriented to the arms, neck, or upper trunk, and is rarely severe enough to break the skin.

Children's biting is usually aggressive. It usually occurs only once in an interaction, being followed by highly disruptive behavior: crying, flight, teacher intervention. It occurs rarely, probably because of social inhibition: parents and other adults tend to punish without exception offenders in biting incidents. (Is it only coincidental that the teeth are man's most dangerous built-in weapon?) The punishment's effects are evident in the pattern's performance and the immediately following behavior. Bites were sudden and quick, followed by leaning back and quick glancing up with wide eyes to nearby adults. Girls seem to bite more than boys (Blurton Jones, 1967).

Biting intention movements occur commonly in imaginative rough-and-tumble play: these consist of opening the mouth, assuming a "fierce" face, and vocalizing roars and growls. The child usually imitates a carnivore or monster, and the other children respond with fleeing and laughter.

Biting is a commonly observed aggressive pattern in nonhuman primates (Altmann, 1962; Chance, 1956; K. R. L. Hall, 1965; van Lawick-Goodall, 1968b). S. L. Washburn and Hamburg (1968) differentiated between *canine* bites which result in serious damage and *incisor* bites which result in brief pain but not damage. Several authors have mentioned that aggressive biting is directed to certain body areas, e.g., the nape of the neck in baboons (K. R. L. Hall, 1964), and extremities in chimpanzees (Wilson & Wilson, 1968). But biting also occurs in rough-and-tumble play where it is variously labeled: "mock-biting" (K. R. L. Hall, 1965), "inhibited biting" (J. H. Kaufmann, 1967), "play bite" (Bolwig, 1963). Nonagonistic biting is probably a ritualized version of the aggressive pattern, as are many social play patterns. It occurs significantly more often in chimpanzee interactions which end with animals remaining together rather than separating (Loizos, 1967, 1969).

Biting occurred too infrequently for inter-observer reliability testing.

Blow (.80)

Air is expelled from the mouth through the pursed lips; cheeks are puffed. Forceful blowing may produce a recognizable vocalization, and with appropriate buccal adjustment this becomes whistling.

Children sometimes blow at each other in quasiagonistic encounters, particularly at each other's faces or into each other's ears. Blowing appears to be mildly aversive, and the blown-at individuals may Flinch or Lean Back, alternating with bouts of laughter. Only a few older children whistled in the nurseries observed by the author, and those that did could carry a tune.

Blowing as a social behavior pattern seems not to have been recorded in nonhuman primates.

Chew Lips

One or both lips may be rolled into the mouth and the teeth pressed against them. Either the teeth or lips or both may move in opposition to each other, or the expression may be static. Blurton Jones (1972b) divided this into two behavior patterns: "lower lip bitten," and "upper lip bitten." (See Grant's Nos. 35 and 43: Lips In and Bite Lip.)

Children appear to chew their lips in ambivalent or stressful situations, for example, when watching another child being aggressed-against nearby. Leach (1972) noted compression of the lips, sometimes between the teeth, during object possession struggles and in nonsocial situations when a child was concentrating on a task. In adult interview situations, biting the lips occurred in transition between "Flight" and "Contact" behavior elements (Grant, 1968).

Mildly stressed rhesus macaques displayed significantly more frequent noningestive chewing movements than when unstressed (Rowell & Hinde, 1963).

Chewing the lips occurred too infrequently for reliability testing.

Chin In (.88)

The neck is flexed, moving the head forward on the atlas vertebra, so that the chin is moved toward the chest, and the face is kept approximately vertical. (See Grant's No. 53: Chin In.)

Grant (1965b, 1968) included Chin In among Flight elements, that is, those associated with fleeing from another individual. Berg (1966) categorized a similar movement as Shyness behavior where exhibited by young behaviorally disordered children in an interview situation. In our nursery group, Chin In occurred commonly in agonistic social situations. It was exhibited by losers of encounters, children scolded by adults, and children apparently frightened of interacting with strangers or more dominant individuals. Children new to the nursery exhibited it often, even in solitary situations.

Holding the chin close to the chest occurs in other behavior patterns, for example, hanging the head or looking down, in which the facial plane is more horizontal. Chin In's more vertical orientation facilitates the monitoring of other individuals' faces. An extreme stylized form of Chin In accompanied by rigid body erectness ("bracing") is used in the American military by superiors harassing or dressing down subordinates. The subordinate's motivation may supposedly be measured by counting the resulting wrinkles which appear below the chin.

Chin In or an equivalent head movement has not been described in nonhuman primates, but since no species possesses a chin with an angle exceeding 80° (Hershkovitz, 1970) such a movement would be relatively inconspicuous anyway.

Face Thrust (.78)

The head is moved rapidly forward so that the face is vertical and the chin "juts" out and up. (See Grant's Nos. 48, 49, 50: Head Forward, Threat, Chin Out.)

Face thrusting occurs in agonistic interactions among nursery children. Dominant individuals exhibit it toward subordinates in threat, usually accompanied by Verbalize, Low Frown, and Lean Forward. Grant's (1965b) definition of threat included this movement, which, in a later paper (1968), he called "thrust" and included among other assertive elements. Face thrusting occurs early in agonistic encounters before physical attack, but if physical attack does not follow, both individuals sometimes Face Thrust throughout the encounter. The movement may be a ritualized form of a biting intention movement.

Jerking the head forward toward another individual is a threat pattern in several primate species, for example, rhesus macaque (Altmann, 1962; Hinde & Rowell, 1962); baboon (K. R. L. Hall & DeVore, 1965); gorilla (Schaller, 1963). Hinde and Rowell also noted that the lower jaw may protrude slightly.

Hershkovitz (1970) has discussed the evolutionary significance of the primate chin, particularly the human mental protuberance, as a socially communicative structure.

Gaze Fixate (.83)

The eyes are oriented to the eyes of another individual; this usually results in prolonged (more than 3 seconds) eye contact (mutual staring, vis-a-vis). The head is usually slightly lowered and forward, and the face is approximately perpendicular to the line of regard (which is usually horizontal). Gaze fixation also facilitates recognition of pupil size changes, which have been shown to be reliable indicators of attitudes (Hess, 1965). (See Grant's Nos. 1 and 7: Look At and Stare.)

Blurton Jones (1967) found that fixation occurred significantly often with Low Frown and Beat Up in children's agonistic encounters. The aggressor exhibited it, either as threat or preceding attack. In quasiagonistic interactions, gaze fixation was absent, and in nonagonistic interactions it occurred with such elements as Smile and Head Tilt, not with Low Frown or Face Thrust. New children often got gaze fixated during their first day in the nursery.

Robson (1967) stressed the importance of eye-to-eye contact during the first three months of life in maternal-infant attachment. Amount of mother-infant dyadic gazing is related to later infant-stranger gazing and social approach (Robson, Pederson, & Moss, 1969). Gaze fixation as an eliciting stimulus for infant smiling becomes effective by the end of the fourth week (P. H. Wolff, 1963). Schizophrenic children sometimes show abnormal gaze fixation: "looking at the other person's eyes . . . with a persistent, blank, staring gaze" (S. Wolff & Chess, 1964). Gaze fixation between a familiar adult and a young child facilitated approach by normal, autistic, and brain-damaged children (Castell, 1970).

Gaze fixation signifies a readiness for interaction (C. Hutt & Ounsted, 1966), and most studies of normal gaze fixation have used adults. Eye contact was found to increase with physical distance between adults (Argyle & Dean, 1965), but this finding has been questioned (Argyle, 1970; Stephenson & Rutter, 1970; Vine, 1971; White, Hegarty, & Beasley, 1970). Using pupillary response as an indicator of emotional arousal, Coss (1965, 1970) found that paired discoid patterns resembling eyes elicited the greatest response. Nachshon and Wapner (1967) performed detailed experiments on the relation between eye contact and physiognomy in perceiving another's location. Women gaze fixate more than men, and adults gaze fixate more when listening than when speaking. Goffman (1959) discussed the importance of "catching the eye" of another in social interaction; it forces reaction from another even if the response is only rejection.

Staring directed at another individual is used in threat by many nonhuman primates (Altmann, 1962; K. R. L. Hall & DeVore, 1965; Jay, 1965; Schaller, 1963; van Lawick-Goodall, 1968b).

Glance (.93)

A rapid head movement which orients the face is followed by another head movement within three seconds reorienting the face.

Glancing is one of the most common behavior patterns of young children and occurrs in most social contexts. Only eye movements are more common, and these may often substitute for glancing. Glancing serves to monitor visual stimuli or transmit visual signals, as does Look. But glancing differs in that it occurs in situations where visual monitoring or signaling must be speeded up, because behavior patterns are changing rapidly, because attention must be divided between stimuli, because monitoring must be hidden, or because visual signaling must be restricted. Thus children seem to glance more in agonistic situations since such interactions move quickly; they seem to glance more in groups than in dyads because more people's actions require monitoring. Or, in signaling, when looks might be received as threatening, quick glances may be ignored. Besides glancing in almost all social encounters, children glance toward other, nonvisual stimuli, for example, a ringing door bell. While discovering that they are being watched, children initially glance more at the watcher, then avoid glancing or looking at him. Children appear to glance more when "bored" than when "engrossed," more when "excited" than when "relaxed."

Most research on glancing is included in studies of looking, and many studies of looking do not give durations but only cumulative totals (e.g., Argyle & Dean, 1965; Faw & Nunnally, 1968). "Fractional glances" of less than a second occurred in autistic children showing extreme gaze aversion (C. Hutt & Ounsted, 1966).

"Sideways jerking glances" are indicative of "escape-fear-uncertainty" in baboons (K. R. L. Hall & DeVore, 1965). Many other nonhuman primates turn the head away in submission (Jay, 1965; Schaller, 1963) but the authors did not give durations. Glancing as monitoring may occur at unlikely times: Yerkes (1943) saw an infant chimpanzee in the midst of a temper tantrum glance "furtively" at its mother to assess her reaction.

Grind Teeth

The teeth, particularly the molars (side-to-side) and incisors (backward-and forward), are drawn across each other in forceful opposition. This may produce noticeable jaw movements and an audible sound. Similar movements occur when children chew gum.

Teeth grinding in children occurs rarely and its significance is unclear. Zingeser (1969) noted that human "gnashing of the teeth accompanies feelings of aggression, fear, pain, and sorrow" and that pathological grinding is associated with severe anxiety. Blurton Jones (1972b) discussed human teeth grinding and related it to clenching of the molars in stressful situations. Teeth grinding may result from inhibited biting (see also Bared Teeth), but Zingeser considered it a relic behavior which once had survival value in a canine honing mechanism.

Baboon teeth grinding is an aggressive behavior pattern (K. R. L. Hall & DeVore, 1965), and langur canine grinding is associated with tension resolution (Jay, 1965). Rhesus monkeys gnash their teeth (producing an audible noise) when being removed from traps and during copulation (Altmann, 1962). Pig-tailed and bonnet macaques show similar patterns in similar situations (Kaufman & Rosenblum, 1966). Stump-tailed macaque teeth-grinding produces a squeaky noise and conspicuous scalp movements (Blurton Jones & Trollope, 1968).

Teeth grinding occurred too infrequently for reliability testing.

Head Nod (.86)

The head is moved forward and backward on the condyles resting on the atlas vertebra, resulting in the face moving down and up. The down-up sequence may be exhibited once or repeated. (See Grant's No. 54: Nod.)

Among preschool children, the head nod signifies affirmation as it does among adults in Western society. In addition to signifying a simple "yes" in answer to a question, it seems to indicate agreement (e.g., when another child proposes a desirable activity) and reassurance (e.g., in answer to an "uncertain" glance from an individual reluctant to perform an action). It occurs in nonagonistic situations, or in agonistic interactions where it functions in appeasement or submission. Younger children often Head Nod instead of verbalizing, regardless of social context.

Darwin (1872) proposed that the single affirmative head nod was related to the infant's single head movement forward in accepting food. Holt (1931) related it to nursing movements. Eibl-Eibesfeldt (1968) interpreted it as the intention movement of submission. Darwin also described a blind and deaf individual who consistently accompanied a verbal "yes" with a head nod without having been taught this. Nodding in affirmation and greeting, and other similar gestures, occur in many human societies (more than in those where head shaking means negation) but other societies do not use head nodding or use other gestures instead.

Head nodding is an important communicatory pattern throughout the human age-range. Birdwhistell (1962) distinguished five "kinesic stem-forms" of the nod, each performing a different function in dyadic interaction. Grant

57

(1968) found that adult smiling and head nodding occurred together during interviews, and that behavior following the nod was always "Flight" behavior. Certain head nods are abbreviated forms of bowing. Stereotyped head nodding may occur persistently in mental defectives (Berkson & Davenport, 1962).

Head nodding occurs as part of weak threat in chimpanzees, but danger exists of confusion with other similar movements, for example, threatening head bobbing of the rhesus monkey (Altmann, 1962, see illustration, p. 422). Stereotyped rocking (van Lawick-Goodall, 1968b) may resemble head nodding when only the head is moved forward and back.

Head Shake (.88)

The head is rotated upon the axis vertebra, always at least once to one side and then immediately back again in the opposite direction, but often this is repeated several times. The arc covered varies from 180 degress to an almost imperceptible sideways head flick. (See Grant's No. 55: Shake.)

Blurton Jones (1972b) described two signal functions for headshaking: one indicated reassurance (frequently exhibited by adult females to children), and the more common one indicated negation. Head shaking in negation occurs in nonagonistic situations or at times when the actor apparently wishes to prevent an agonistic situation from developing. In the latter case, head shaking is not accompanied by other fearful or defensive patterns, but if a quarrel develops such patterns replace head shaking. Young children often respond to questions with head shaking rather than verbalization, regardless of social context.

Grant (1968) found that adult Head Shake occurred after "Looking At" and was used in two different ways: as "Assertive" denial and as a form of agreement leading to "Flight" behavior patterns. Autistic children may display stereotypic head-shaking, which apparently functions to reduce high "arousal" (C. Hutt & S. J. Hutt, 1965).

Several origins for head shaking have been proposed: Blurton Jones (1972b) suggested that it is related to the reassurance shake. Andrew (1963) suggested that it is derived from the protective response to noxious stimuli. Darwin (1872) suggested that it was derived from early infantile refusal of food. He also pointed out that a blind and deaf girl consistently accompanied a verbal "no" with head shaking without having been taught this. Head shaking in negation and other similar gestures occur in many human societies, but a number of other societies do not use it or they use other gestures instead.

Schaller (1963) noted that gorillas shake their heads in submissiveness in uncertain situations where it indicates "I mean no harm." K. R. L. Hall and DeVore (1965) recorded "sideways jerking glances" in baboons as "escape-fear-uncertainty" behavior.

Head Tilt (.95)

The head is moved sideways to an angle of approximately 45 degrees so that the ear is closer to the shoulder. One side is usually preferred, and it is used so consistently in adults that tilting to the other side may feel unnatural. (See Grant's No. 56: Head to Side.)

Blurton Jones (1972b) noted that children's head tilting occurs with looking and smiling at another child and precedes conversational head shaking. It occurs during nonagonistic social interactions, often directed by older to younger children, apparently when the tilter wants something from the reactor, for example, a toy, compliance. The request is expressed in the form of a question or tentative statement. Sustained head tilting is also oriented to dolls, small animals, and babies, often without verbalization. Head tilting is part of a "head on elbow" posture, in which the forearm is vertical, elbow rests on the table, hand is closed and supports the head through the cheek. Children who look tired or bored exhibit this.

A quick head tilt and then a return to upright head position is an adult greeting gesture. Adult head tilting may be directed to children, especially infants, where it occurs with making faces and baby-talk. Head tilting also occurs in visual investigation, where it appears that the actor is attempting to maintain perspective while examining a nonvertically aligned object. Grant (1968) classed "Head to Side" as an "Assertive" element in adult interview.

Head tilting seems to occur during investigation of objects in nonhuman primates, but this has not been examined in detail.

Kiss

The slightly protruded lips are brought into contact with another person's body surface or an object by moving the head forward (and often leaning forward). The most common targets are lips, face, head, hands. Kissing may also produce a characteristic sound which, as LaBarre (1947) pointed out, may be used in summoning or alerting pets. (See Grant's No. 42: Purse.)

Kissing occurs only in nonagonistic interactions. Only rarely was it directed to objects, and these were usually dolls. Children kissed their mother's but not each other's lips, and the mother's kiss to the child resembled the normal adult-adult affectional "peck": the lips were markedly protruded and held rigid and unmoving, contact was brief. (Such a behavior pattern might be adaptive in that it serves to differentiate sexual and nonsexual affection, thus possible reducing mate-offspring jealousy.) Between children, kissing seemed to be a sign of affection entailing some degree of embarrassment. Kissing was also a comforting pattern, and children and adults both kissed a child's injury site to "make it better." Females kissed more than males. Leach (1972) noted that some children seemed to go through an "experimental" phase of kissing other children.

Kissing is an important affectional pattern in many human societies but is unknown in many others (Darwin, 1872; Ford & Beach, 1952). Absence of kissing in a society must be accepted with reservation, however, since it is known that in several societies kissing only occurs in an intimate sexual context, a situation casual observers might easily miss. Among the South American Tapuya, kissing occurs between men as a "sign of peace" (LaBarre, 1947). Kissing is a common greeting behavior component, for example, the courtly kiss of a lady's hand, or exchange of busses between Eastern European politicians. Eibl-Eibesfeldt (1968) gave numerous cross-cultural examples of kissing customs.

Variations or abbreviations of kissing are widespread. Women may only touch cheeks and not bring the lips into contact when kissing in greeting, perhaps to prevent disturbing each other's make-up. Kissing may be used as a visual signal, for example, blowing kisses across a room. Finally, several other behavioral patterns found in non kissing societies seem to replace it, for example, nose rubbing, blowing on the face (Eibl-Eibesfeldt, 1968).

Chimpanzee kissing occurs in submissive, reassurance, and greeting behavior, and van Lawick-Goodall (1968b) suggested that it may have been derived from infantile suckling. "Mouth-to-mouth" touching occurs in baboon friendly behavior (K. R. L. Hall & DeVore, 1965) and as chimpanzee Affinitive and Excitement behavior (van Hooff, 1970). Eibl-Eibesfeldt (1968) considered kissing to be ritualized mouth-to-mouth feeding.

Kissing between children occurred too infrequently on the videotapes for inter-observer reliability testing.

Laugh (.92)

The characteristic sound is produced by a series of short, rapidly repeated, spasmodic, expiratory movements through the open mouth. This may be stylized into similar verbalizations of "Ha, ha, ha..." It occurs in bouts, and individual elements are difficult if not impossible to define. Weeping and Red Face may accompany prolonged excessive laughter.

Entire books have been written on laughter (e.g., Sully, 1902), and many theories have been proposed about it (see capsule reviews in Ding & Jersild, 1932; Giles & Oxford, 1970). In preschool children laughing occurs often with Run, Jump, Open Beat, and Wrestle, and is probably a specific signal of friendly intention during the hostile-looking behavior of rough-and-tumble play (Blurton Jones, 1967). Ding and Jersild (1932) observed the greatest amount of laughter in connection with motor activity, and those who laughed most were the most active. Laughter did not occur often in response to specific social stimuli or in imitation, although children laughed more with other children than when alone.

Ambrose (1963) stressed the relationship between laughter's ontogeny and the infant's development of ambivalence.

Laughter occurs in nonagonistic and quasiagonistic interactions but not in agonistic ones. Unsympathetic or derisive laughter, for example, in response to another's injury or misfortune, occured only among older nursery children studied by the author, and resembled the stylized verbalization in appearance and usage. In addition to the "spontaneous" laughter of motor play, children laugh in response to peers "acting silly," for example, stuffing a pillow under the shirt and waddling around. Children also laugh while alone and reading books. Tickling may elicit considerable laughter in children.

Laughter is a widespread human behavior pattern (e.g., Darwin, 1872) although LaBarre (1947) pointed out that in some societies it is used in response to nonhumorous situations. The blind and deaf Laura Bridgman laughed normally although she could not have learned it through imitation (Darwin, 1872). In studies of adult interview situations, Grant (1968) included laughter among the "Relaxed" group of behavior patterns, that is, those which indicate lack of emotional arousal.

Early authors believed that only humans laughed, and some went so far as to define man as "the laughing animal." But Darwin described chimpanzee laughter, and later workers elaborated on this (e.g., Loizos, 1967; Schaller, 1963; van Lawick-Goodall, 1968b). Van Hooff (1970) classified chimpanzee panting as Affinitive behavior. Nonhuman primate laughter occurs during rough-and-tumble play, particularly in response to tickling, and may be ritualized from open-mouthed panting occurring after gross body exertion.

Lick

The extended tongue is drawn across the surface of a body part or an object, leaving a trail of saliva. Movements may be single or repeated, and they may range from brief motions using only the tongue's tip to full lapping. (See Grant's No. 30: Lick Lips.)

Children appeared to lick their lips in ambivalent or stressful situations. Children also rarely licked each other in quasiagonistic interactions in what appeared to be imitations of animals; this was responded to with laughter and avoidance. In adult interview situations, licking the lips was considered by Grant (1968) to be a "Flight" element.

Licking is an important allo-grooming pattern in lower primates, but it is primarily restricted to maternal licking of young in higher primates (Sparks, 1967). Lip-smacking, a prominent social signal in nonhuman primates, is probably derived from licking in grooming. Many primate species (including man) show self-directed licking of cuts and other injuries. Mildly stressed rhesus macaques licked their lips significantly more often than when unstressed (Rowell & Hinde, 1963).

Licking occurred too infrequently for reliability testing.

Look (.71)

The head is moved, re-orienting the face, and this orientation is maintained for at least three seconds. Grant (1969) described seven types of looking (Nos. 1–7).

Looking as visual investigation is common in children of nursery age. New children in the nursery spent considerable time looking before beginning manual investigation. Such looks often took the form of "surveys": slow sweeping looks around the room, or visual following of an individual's movements. Children sitting down often looked at active peers across the room, but looks at close range were less common. The children commonly looked at toys while manipulating them, or at other children's hands while they manipulated objects.

The above examples involve looking *toward* something or someone; looking *away* was less common and occurred in social situations. Children often responded to mild threat by looking away, and looking away was part of "giving way" to others, for example, allowing another child to push the subject's toys aside when joining him at table play. Children also looked away from potentially disturbing situations, for example, another child urinating on the lawn about to be discovered by an adult. Looking away may be a "cut-off" posture which reduces disturbing visual input from the other interactant (Chance, 1962), or it may serve to forestall gaze fixation which might provoke the other child. Both explanations could apply to threatening social situations.

Grant (1968) used three categories of looking ("Look At," "Look Away," and "Look Down") in his study of adult nonverbal behavior during interviews. "Look Down" and "Look Away" were closely associated with "Flight" elements, but "Look Down" sometimes led to "Look At." "Look At" was a "Contact" element but was also associated with "Relaxed" and "Assertive" elements. Earlier, Grant (1965b) included direct looking in Threat and Frown, two overtly aggressive patterns displayed by dominant schizophrenic patients.

Some looking behavior takes similar forms across many human cultures, for example, the female looking away in the adolescent flirting ritual (Eibl-Eibesfeldt, 1968). Other simple relationships do not always hold cross-culturally, however; the Witoto and Bororo Indians never look at the person being addressed in conversation, even in groups (LaBarre, 1947).

Looking is an important component of infant development. Home-raised infants receive significantly more looking from caretaking adults and transmitted significantly more looks to them than did institution-raised infants (Rheingold, 1961). Abnormal looking may be manifested in later childhood behavior disorders. Castell (1970) found that durations of looks were three times as long in normal and brain-damaged children as in autistic children.

Looking is obviously important among nonhuman primates, but many authors do not differentiate between gaze fixation, glancing, and looking (see

Gaze Fixate, Glance). Monkeys will quickly learn discriminations or work hard for the reward of looking at another monkey (Butler, 1954). Looking away is a submissive gesture in many primate species (K. R. L. Hall & DeVore, 1965; Jay, 1965; Schaller, 1963; Simonds, 1965); Looking about in a watchful or intimidating manner (often leading to overt aggressive behavior) has been noted in bonnet macaques (Simonds, 1965), but undirected staring with wide-open eyes is a sign of fear in baboons and rhesus monkeys (K. R. L. Hall & DeVore, 1965; Hinde & Rowell, 1962). Looking is part of male patas monkey vigilance behavior (K. R. L. Hall, 1965).

Mouth

The moving lips and gums contact an external object or body part. A small object being mouthed is often held in the hand, but a large object, for example, pram handle, may be mouthed directly.

Mouthing is a prominent exploratory technique in the human infant, probably derived from the initial rooting reflex. The same seems true to a more limited degree in older children as well, for example, with food, where it may become nonsocial play. But mouthing also occurs in social situations similar to those in which Digit Sucking and Automanipulation occur, sometimes in alternation or combination with them. The movements are slow, slight, and patternless, giving an aimless and distracted effect.

A less common type of mouthing is directed to other children's limbs. It resembles biting but no sign of damage results (although considerable saliva may remain). Such mouthing appears to be a quasiagonistic behavior pattern, functioning similarly to mock-biting in nonhuman primates (see Bite). It may be accompanied by growling-grinding vocalizations.

Nonhuman primate mouthing is also exploratory (see protocol in Loizos, 1967), and the motor patterns resemble some feeding movements, for example, mastication. Infant rhesus monkeys spend considerable time mouthing the mother's nipple while clinging to her; this occurs in situations where they seek her solace or protection (Hinde & Spencer-Booth, 1967). Mouthing also occurs in nonhuman primate social play, apparently as ritualized from agonistic biting. For example, van Hooff's (1970) analysis placed gnawing directed to other chimpanzees in the Play system.

Mouthing occurred too infrequently for reliability testing.

Spit

Saliva is propelled from the partially closed mouth by explosively exhaling. A variant, accompanied by a characteristic "raspberry" sound, involves prolonging the exhalation while allowing the lips to vibrate, thus producing a spray of saliva. Both occur simultaneously with face thrust and may be oriented to another individual.

63

Spitting is an aggressive behavior pattern, although the result is not injurious but distasteful. It occurred rarely in nursery schools observed by the author, presumably because it is a pattern (like Bite) which is consistently punished by adults. In each school one boy, a bullying type, did the majority of the spitting; the spitting the other children did was usually in retaliatory imitation. In Western society spitting on another has come to signify contempt (to a humbled opponent) or defiance (from a captive), but it is a sign of affection and benediction among the Masai (LaBarre, 1947).

Spitting has been rarely observed in nonhuman primates. Chimpanzees spit at humans and each other with considerably accuracy up to ten feet, and Wilson and Wilson (1968) regarded its function as intimidation.

Spitting occurred too infrequently for reliability testing.

Swallow

Peristaltic contractions of the esophagous produce movements of the overlying neck muscles, and in males, vertical movements of the laryngeal prominence of the thyroid cartilage (Adam's apple). (See Grant's No. 31: Swallow.)

Children seemed to swallow more in ambivalent or stressful situations, possibly because their mouths are excessively dry. (Cannon [1923] noted that salivary flow may decrease in response to fear.) In adult interview situations, swallowing was considered by Grant (1968) to be a "Flight" behavioral element. The conspicuous movement of the Adam's apple may have signal function in agonistic situations, which may be related to its greater prominence in males.

Swallowing as a social behavior pattern seems not to have been recorded in nonhuman primates.

Videotape records were insufficiently distinct to allow reliability testing of Swallow.

Tongue Out (.75)

The tongue protrudes from between the lips; this may range from only the tip visible between lips pressed together to maximal extension with the lips drawn back and separated. The tongue may point horizontally or be curved up or down over the lips. (See Grant's Nos. 45 and 46: Tongue and Tongue Out.)

Blurton Jones (1972b) described tongue position in four categories (invisible, visible, pushed forward, out of mouth) and found that tongue out was seen during task concentration or during play with a wide open mouth. Stereotyped movements of the tongue in and out were observed and appeared to be "nervous" behavior, but these were sometimes difficult to distinguish from licking the lips. Like school children, some older nursery children used the gesture of maximal tongue extension and face thrust to indicate defiant insult toward adults, and were careful to conceal this from them.

Tongue protrusion has many communicative functions in different societies (although its insulting use in Western society is usually confined to children). Among the Maoris it is thrust out during war dances (Goodhart, 1960), and it signifies anger and shock in Bengali statues. In South China, momentary tongue protrusion expresses embarrassment at a mistake (LaBarre, 1947).

Howler monkey males and females exchange "rhythmic tongue movements with their mouths partly opened" during sexual foreplay (Carpenter, 1965). Common langurs move the tongue in and out of the mouth during mild submission (Jay, 1965). Reynolds and Reynolds (1965) saw tongue protrusion in chimpanzee juvenile play. All these ritualized forms may be derived from the tongue protrusion seen during lip-smacking in many nonhuman primate species (see list in van Hooff, 1967).

Verbalize (.95)

Vocalizations (see Vocalize) whose printed representations occur in dictionaries are verbalizations, and any distinction between verbal and nonverbal sound production on the basis of body movement or sound structure seems impossible. Intermediates occur: the whistled language of the Canary Islands (*silbo*) consists entirely of whistling but is a version of Spanish (Classe, 1957).

Verbalization begins at around one year of age, and by three years the average vocabulary size is about 900 words (M. E. Smith, 1926). In the nursery situation, entering three-year-olds say little for the first few days and, even after 60–70 days of nursery experience, some children verbalize infrequently. Amount of verbalization varies according to social context: nonagonistic situations yield the most and often include long interchanges, particularly in dramatic play. Agonistic and quasiagonistic interactions are less verbal, and some proceed from start to finish without any verbalization, thus indicating the importance of nonverbal communication channels. A few children, usually young and shy, verbalized most when solitarily occupied, usually while "reading" books or playing alone in the Wendy House.

Because of the study's tentative nature and the lack of basic background knowledge of children's nonverbal social behavior patterns, verbalization was treated superficially. To record content of verbalization along with the nonverbal items would have been prohibitive. Only its occurrence was noted, whether it was mono- or polysyllabic, and whether it was a "negative expletive" or not.

All human societies use verbal language (many leaving it up to the anthropologists to supply the printed dictionaries) but to say whether any nonhuman species do or not raises semantic problems. (See Gardner and Gardner [1969] and Premack [1970, 1971] for recent developments in this field.) Hockett (1960) attempted to apply 13 design-features of language to eight animal communication systems ranging from bee-dancing to human language. None of the 13 was unique to human language. Distinction between verbalizations and other vocalizations have tended to be theoretical, for example, "semantic openness" (Bastian, 1965), and not operationally useful.

Nonhuman primates may learn to respond to human verbalization, but instances of nonhuman primate verbalization are few. Viki, a home-reared chimpanzee, learned to say three words (mama, papa, cup) and use them appropriately (Hayes, 1951) but many other attempts have failed. Whether this is a neurological and/or anatomical vocal sound production problem is unclear (Lieberman, Kratt, & Wilson, 1969). It is not one of "intelligence": chimpanzees can send and receive up to 32 learned human sign language patterns (Gardner & Gardner, 1969).

Vocalize (.92)

Air moving through the larynx produces sound which is modified by the buccal anatomy before being emitted through the mouth.

Infants produce vocalizations from birth, and crying is the traditional first sign of life. Vocalizations persist throughout human life although many of their functions are taken over by language. Preschool children vocalize frequently, most often in social situations, and three-year-olds new to the nursery may vocalize more than they verbalize, although this quickly reverses. Many descriptive English terms have been applied to human vocalization (e.g., scream, shriek, growl, etc.), but these and similar attempts to coin descriptive terms have limited use in research investigations. Sophisticated recording and sound spectrograph or sonograph equipment are required.

Vocalization occurs in most mammals, but primate systems of vocal communication are the most complex and varied (e.g., Altmann, 1967; Ploog & Melnechuk, 1969). Mountain gorillas display 22 different vocalizations (Schaller, 1963); Japanese macaques have over 30 (Imanishi, 1963); vervet monkeys have 36 (Struhsaker, 1967). But findings differ in this difficult area: Hinde and Rowell (1962) listed 12 vocalizations for the rhesus macaque whereas Altmann (1962) listed only seven. Species are not restricted to these numbers, however, as many vocal intermediates and gradations exist (Marler, 1965). Field studies have concentrated on the causal and functional aspects of nonhuman primate vocalization, for example, early morning roaring by howler monkeys as a source of inter-troop location and avoidance (Carpenter, 1965). Recent laboratory studies show that environmental influences (e.g., social deprivation) may have drastic effects on the ontogenesis of vocalization in chimpanzees (Randolph & Mason, 1969). Randolph and Brooks (1967) also demonstrated a possible mechanism for this: social conditioning. Masserman, Wechkin, and Woolf (1968) even recently reported the successful training of a rhesus monkey to carry a tune. While many authors have alluded to the functional connection between vocal and nonvocal communication, only Condon and Ogston (1967) appear to have graphically demonstrated the synchrony of chimpanzee body movement and vocal variation.

Weep (.86)

The lacrymal glands secrete excessively so that the eyes become watery and tears spill over the eyelids. In preschool children it usually occurs as part of crying, along with Pucker Face, Red Face, and Vocalize. Weeping may occur without any of these, or with other behavioral elements, for example, excessive laughter or coughing. (See Grant's No. 14: Tears.)

Preschool children rarely weep. Ding and Jersild (1932) saw only 16 instances among 59 Chinese children in 240 hours of observation. Weeping may occur in any type of social or nonsocial situation, as a result of physical or nonphysical painful stimuli. In agonistic interactions, weeping is exhibited by losers of conflicts or by children who have been verbally aggressed against, as well as those injured by attack. In nonagonistic or quasiagonistic interactions, weeping occurs when accidental injury is incurred. New children in the nursery wept after separation from their mothers, and in extreme cases this persisted for several hours throughout the morning or on most mornings for several weeks. Children normally react to physical pain by weeping, but some older four-year-olds make a conscious effort to resist or, failing that, to hide it. Weeping may be mediated by social context; Blurton Jones (1967) noted that crying is often followed by immobility, sitting, thumb sucking, automanipulation, and rocking.

Although the crying vocalization is present from birth, weeping only appears after two or three months. The ductless gland secretion is common to all humans (except, supposedly, witches), but its use is not restricted to negative, painful situations. Western women cry at times of extreme happiness. Among the Wichita Indians, weeping is included in male religious ritual as a tangible representation of helplessness. Weeping functions to lubricate the eyes, and its expression probably becomes associated with painful circumstances so that it occurs even when physical irritation (of the eyes or elsewhere) is absent.

Darwin (1872) noted several examples of nonhuman primate weeping, but modern workers have not described it, even in detailed studies such as Schaller's (1963).

Yawn

The mouth is opened wide, often exposing both rows of teeth, followed by a slow, high-volume inhalation and exhalation. During the yawn the eyes are partially closed, and they may water, resulting immediately afterwards in a "twinkling" effect. Both inhalation and exhalation may produce characteristic sounds. (See Grant's No. 47: Yawn.)

Human yawning occurs in many situations: in response to boredom, drowsiness, and nervousness. Tinbergen (1951) described it as a displacement behavior occurring in mild conflict situations. Yawning has been described as "contagious behavior," but such analysis requires caution; for example, closely associated yawning by several people could be a common reaction to the high CO_2 level, for example, in a stuffy seminar room. Yawning may have an evolutionary significant threatening effect: covering the mouth while yawning may prevent the transmission of arousing signals in nonagonistic situations.

Numerous records exist of yawning in nonhuman primates (Carpenter, 1940; K. R. L. Hall, 1965; van Lawick-Goodall, 1968b). It primarily occurs when individuals are in one of three states: (1) uneasy, (2) aggressive, or (3) recently awakened. The first type were termed "situations of mild stress" by Hinde and Rowell (1962), and here yawning may serve to disengage temporarily sensory receptors, enabling animals to remain in situations advantageous to them in the long term. In aggression, yawning constitutes a threat display of the teeth (especially the canines) which are a primate's chief natural weapons (Darwin, 1872). In baboons the effect is increased by throwing the head back and is accompanied by other social signals, for example, eyelid flashing. (See the excellent figure in Eimerl and DeVore, 1966, p. 117.) Schaller (1963) described yawning upon awakening in gorillas where it closely resembles man's in form.

Gestures

This section presents behavior patterns which involve hand and arm movements. The human evolutionary significance of freeing the forelimbs from locomotory to manipulatory functions is well-known, and this emerges in the rich variety of communicatory gestures exhibited by man. Differential use of gestures is related to socioeconomic status (Michael & Willis, 1968), cultural membership (LaBarre, 1947), subcultural membership (Michael & Willis, 1969) and behavioral disorder (Sainsbury, 1955). Grant's (1969) recently published glossary of human behavior patterns will be referred to when comparable categories exist.

Two types of gestural languages ("letter" signing and "word" signing) exist as substitutes for many spoken languages. An example of the latter, American Sign Language (ASL), has been successfully taught to one nonhuman primate species, the chimpanzee (Gardner & Gardner, 1969), but other related species may possess insuperable limitations; for example, gibbons display marked manipulative limitations because of their highly specialized hand structure (Beck, 1967).

The overall mean inter-observer reliability coefficient for gestures was .83 (S.D. = ± .11), and the mean number of recorded instances per behavior pattern used in computation of the coefficient was 23.7 (S.D. = ± 9.8).

Automanipulate (.85) (Initially divided into *Finger* and *Fumble*).

Fingering is the use of the fingers, particularly thumb and forefinger, to manipulate part of one's body. It usually comprises scratching, rubbing, pinching, or otherwise handling the mouth, nose, ears, or hair. Finger is also oriented to the hands, arms, legs, genitals, or anal region.

Fumbling is similar movements directed to a small object (e.g., a jigsaw puzzle piece) or to a limited aspect of a large object (e.g., a screw on a wagon handle). No difference appears to exist between the movements or functioning of the two patterns, which are now considered in combination. (See Grant's No. 79-86 and 87: Grooming elements and Fumble.)

The movements are slight, repetitive, sometimes stereotyped, and appear to function only superficially: that is, automanipulative scratching appears not to relieve itching, picking appears not to remove objects. Fumbling also appears functionless: no discernable alteration of the object or its stimulus qualities occurs. Automanipulation has two characteristic aspects: (1) it appears "unconnected" to other simultaneous body movement. A child genuinely picking at a loose bit of skin may move his hand, adopt a more comfortable posture, and orient his body to the optimal light; during fingering, the body remains still, and the fingering hand seems to move independently; (2) additional sensory modalities appear "disengaged." For example, the automanipulating child seldom looks at the fingered point, but during "genuine" manipulation, it is visually fixated and the activity concentrated on. Similar characteristics apply in the auditory modality.

The automanipulating child often seems distracted or nervous, gazing off into space or staring blankly ahead. The movement often appears combined with digit sucking and body immobility. Automanipulation seems to appear frequently in "social stress" situations, for example, when a child loses an object struggle, when another child cries, when a stranger enters the room. In extreme cases, a form of withdrawal seems to occur which may function as a submissive signal. One child fingered the opposite-side ear with one hand and sucked the thumb of the other; the result resembled the self-clutching ("huddling") of deprived infant chimpanzees (Mason, 1965).

69

Grant (1968) observed automanipulation (*head groom, scratch, fumble*) during adult interviews; all occurred in ambivalent situations and might be termed "displacement activities." Tinbergen (1951) earlier pointed out that care of the body surface occurs in many mammals in situations where conflict exists between moticational systems. Freud (1960) believed in the importance of automanipulative gestures as indications of unconscious influences in everyday behavior.

Rowell and Hinde (1963) noted significant increases in "scratching" and "other brief skin care" in adult rhesus monkeys during experimentally increased stress conditions. Bernstein and Draper (1964) found increases in "auto" behavior (i.e., "self-directed activity including scratching, self-grooming, etc.") in a rhesus juvenile group after the introduction of an adult male. "Auto" occurred more frequently in a group of all ages than a homogenous juveniles-only group. Schaller (1963) observed displacement grooming and scratching in wild mountain gorillas.

Beat (.72)

Blurton Jones (1967) described this as "...an overarm blow with palm side of the lightly clenched fist. The arm is sharply bent at the elbow and raised to a vertical position then brought down with great force on the opponent, hitting any part of him that gets in the way." Little can be added to the basic description, but this author considered the behavior pattern's more specific components and attempted to refine its description.

a. *Beat Up* is the initial movement of raising the arm to the vertical position, first described by Darwin (1872). It seems to be an intention movement since the complete beating motion does not always follow. (When it does not, the arm is usually lowered more slowly and vertically. Sometimes the hand is then moved to the head and fingering ensues, usually of the hair.) Beat up appears as the least "intensive" form of beat (i.e., the probability of further agonistic interaction is lowest) and functions as a threat. Often the child performing it is far outside striking distance of the beaten-at child.

b. *Incomplete Beat* is the initial movement to the vertical *plus* only partial and sometimes spasmodic overarm movement down. (The complete beat seems to cover almost 180 degrees, judging from situations in which a child beats at another and misses.) Termination of the downward movement before completion seems intentional, perhaps making it "less intense" than the completed movement. Incomplete beat occurred only rarely.

c. *Open Beat* is the complete beat performed with hand open and fingers extended instead of clenched. This "slapping" form appears "less intense" than the "fisted" form. Open beat seems equally as forcefully performed as the orthodox beat.

d. *Object Beat* is the complete beat performed with an object held in the hand. The object's "appropriateness" as a weapon (e.g., a mallet as compared to a ball) seems to be irrelevant, and often the beating movement is not altered to fit the object's qualities. One nursery teacher proposed that object beating occurred spontaneously, that is, only when the beating child already had an object in his hand by chance. Children apparently do not premeditatedly seek a weapon with which to beat. This is obviously related to age (i.e., greater imitative experience) and environment (i.e., availability of weapons). Blurton Jones (1967) stated that weapons are not in the preschool child's "battle repertoire." This difference in results could be due to definitional differences or to differences in adult supervision of the two populations. Grant (1965b) mentioned a nursery school child hitting another with a stick.

Blurton Jones's observation that a beat might strike any part of the opponent's body was confirmed in the author's study. This contrasted with punching, which seemed more "aimed." (See Grant's Nos. 67-69: Beat, Offensive Beating Posture, Defensive Beating Posture, Hand on Neck.)

References to "hitting" behavior by preschool children occur frequently, and many problems of definition and description exist. Walters, Pearce, and Dahms (1957) referred to "hit" and "strike" under *Physical Aggression* but did not define or differentiate them. Patterson, Littman, and Bricker (1967) mentioned "hit" and "punching" under *Bodily Attack* and "hits with a book" under *Attack With an Object*, but gave no definitions.

The development of children's hitting behavior is often referred to but details are usually lacking. Reports are vague and conflicting: Gesell (1940) stated of the 18-month-old child: "He strikes the air rather than the intruding person. When he is more socially mature he will slap the person." But Valentine (1956) observed of his normal infant son that "B even struck his mother several times as early as 1:4."

Tinbergen (1951) described some beating of inanimate objects as "redirected aggression", for example, a man unable to attack an opponent might pound his fist on the table.

Various types of hitting behavior have been noted in nonhuman primates, usually as aggressive patterns (Altmann, 1962; K. R. L. Hall & DeVore, 1965; Sade, 1967; Wilson & Wilson, 1968). Unfortunately, a tendency exists to define such behaviors by using near-synonyms ("bat," "cuff," "slap," "spar," "smack," "swat"), or not at all, making detailed comparison of motor patterns impossible. Only Wilson and Wilson were somewhat specific, and they described chimpanzee hitting patterns which correspond to both Beat and Punch. Hansen (1966) included cuffing and slapping in the category of mother-infant "punishing" behaviors, and Jensen, Bobbitt, and Gordon (1969) analyzed such pig-tailed macaque hitting sequences in detail. Hall and DeVore noted slapping the ground in visual attack-threat and tactilely communicated slapping by adult

71

baboon males. But hitting behavior has also been included among primate social play behavior patterns: Lowther (1940) described simultaneous beating with both arms between young bush babies. Van Hooff's (1970) analysis placed hitting in both the Play and Aggressive systems.

Beckon (.71)

From a position in which the arm is held approximately vertically in front of the body, the arm is flexed at the wrist and elbow, moving it toward the body, palm preceding and fingers together. It may be repeated two or three times in a bout.

Beckoning occurs in nonagonistic social interactions where it functions similarly to the adult gesture inviting approach. Beckoning may be derived from the "gathering in" movement incorporated into hugging or eating and may also serve to direct attention to the performer. The fact that the back of the hand is visible to the receiver and the palm hidden may help to distinguish it from "repelling" behavior patterns: Push, Repel, or Open Beat.

Male chimpanzees beckon to females during courtship, and the movement resembles the maternal beckoning directed to the infant when the mother is about to move off (van Lawick-Goodall, 1968b). The first human sign language movement learned by the chimpanzee Washoe was an abbreviated beckoning motion meaning "Gimme!" (Gardner & Gardner, 1969.)

Clap Hands

The arms are held in front of the body, between waist and shoulder level, and brought rapidly and forcefully together. The repeated movement produces a characteristic sound.

Hand clapping occurs in nonagonistic social situations in nursery-age children. It occurs "spontaneously" with excited behavior like quick-hopping, for example, during pleasurable anticipation, or in response to sudden, novel behavior by another individual. In nonsocial situations, clapping occurs during periods of increased activity, along with skipping, galloping, etc. Preschool children do clap as applause, although this was only observed after adult initiation.

Adult hand clapping as applause is widespread in Western culture, but it has other uses: slow, rhythmic hand clapping may signal an audience's displeasure at delay. Many human societies use hand clapping to accentuate music and dancing, for example, Bushmen (Tobias, 1957). Sharp, single hand claps are sometimes used to frighten or deter children or pets.

Chimpanzees may readily learn hand clapping (cf. any Tarzan film), but naturally-occurring hand clapping has apparently not been observed.

Digit Suck (.88)

The lips are closed around a digit which is inserted into the mouth. (See also Mouth.) This is most often the thumb, probably because of its more accessible anatomical position on the hand. Sucking of objects also occurs: these are usually smooth, relatively hard, rounded objects. (See Grant's No. 74: Finger in Mouth.)

Digit sucking occurs in "social stress" situations, for example, after receiving chastisement from an adult, while watching another child cry, or after losing an object struggle. Children also digit-suck when "uncertain" or "anxious": for example, in the presence of novelty, either of surroundings, people, or objects. P. H. Wolff (1968a, 1968b) has done extensive research on both human and nonhuman infantile sucking patterns.

Isaacs (1933) listed thumb-sucking as a "neurotic trait" in children under six to seven years of age, but Sewell and Mussen (1952) reported that 40% of children between two and seven exhibit it. The apparent contradiction is probably semantic, relating to different research workers' ideas of "normality." Rather than emphasize digit-sucking's frequency, it might be better to consider its *uses* by a child, for example, limb-sucking as a stereotypy in autistic children (C. Hutt & S. J. Hutt, 1965). Freud's (1962) view that thumb-sucking provides "auto-erotic satisfaction" might be empirically tested. The use of inferential descriptive terms ("sensual sucking," "undesirable behavior," "comfort habit," "nervous habit") yields no objective knowledge and may distort data interpretation.

Mead (1928) stated that she did not observe thumb-sucking in "primitive" human societies, but Ainsworth (1963) recorded it in over half the Ganda infants she observed in Uganda.

Sucking is a mammalian reflex necessary for infantile ingestion of the mother's milk. But many mammals, especially primates, exhibit non-nutritive sucking long after infancy. Benjamin (1967) discussed two general theoretical positions on its etiology: the psychoanalyst's "sucking drive" and the learning theorist's "pleasurable association." Little empirical confirmation has been attempted, but Benjamin (1961) earlier showed that bottle-fed rhesus monkeys engage in more non-nutritive sucking than cup-fed ones.

Drop (.92)

By hand and finger extension (with small objects) and arm extension (with larger objects) an object is released without imparting force to it; its movement is solely a consequence of gravity.

Voluntary release of objects is a late-developing pattern: not until around 44 weeks can infants intentionally drop objects through the air (Gesell, 1940). The later bouts of repeated object-dropping which so exasperate mothers are related to object novelty (C. Hutt, 1967). By preschool age, dropping occurs in many types of social and nonsocial situations. Fearful children drop toys (apparently involuntarily in some cases) but such dropping is sometimes oriented toward aggressors and may be related to throwing (see Shovel Throw). In agonistic and quasiagonistic situations, children drop objects onto each other, sometimes with intent to cause pain (as evidenced by concurrent verbalizations). Abrupt object-dropping without looking often occurs when a child's attention is suddenly diverted or captured.

Kortlandt and Kooij (1963) reviewed dropping of objects in agonistic situations by nonhuman primates. They differentiated it from nonagonistic dropping based on the dropper's orientation and threat behavior, and several observers have noted that males most often performed such dropping.

Fist (.60)

The fingers and hand are maximally flexed and the thumb may be inside or outside the clenched fingers. Often the arm is extended vertically downward, sometimes rigidly.

Fist clenching has been described as part of Beat and Punch, but it also occurs in situations where the child appears motivated to attack but is also intensely fearful. This ambivalence may be indicated by the fact that although the fist is clenched (presumably making the hand a more efficient weapon), it is inconspicuously held down and at the side (a nonthreatening, fearful position more similar to Slope). This account agrees with Darwin's (1872) observations of fist clenching in anger. He described many cross-cultural examples of fist-clenching in arguments (not physical conflicts), although he believed that the pattern was restricted to cultures that fight with their fists. Darwin also described alternate hand clenching and opening in fearful situations.

Fictional literature is full of tense situations where enraged but self-restraining individuals clench their fists so tightly that the knuckles go white (another signal?). A clenched fist is a traditional salute of militaristic groups, for example, the Spanish Republican forces, the Black Power movement.

Fist clenching seems not to occur in nonhuman primates except as part of hitting (see Beat section).

The low inter-observer reliability coefficient is probably due to fist-clenching's inconspicuousness and ½-inch videotape's limitations.

Forearm Raise (.71)

The forearm is raised to a horizontal position over or in front of the head; the elbow is partially flexed at approximately 90 degrees. (See Grant's Nos. 70 and 71: Arm over Face, Arm over Head.)

Blurton Jones (1967) stated that Forearm Raise occurred in agonistic interactions where it functioned to protect the head from an opponent's beating and that it was an alternative to fleeing. Darwin (1872) described a fearful individual's arms "being thrown wildly over the head." In nurseries observed by the author, it occurred only in agonistic and quasiagonistic interaction or in situations where the performer was startled and mistakenly perceived danger, for example, a nearby child holding a toy over the performer's head while building a castle. It seemed to occur in situations where the child could not easily flee, where the aggressor was a socially-attractive friend, or where fleeing would take the actor away from a desirable activity. It may signal: "I am afraid of being injured by your aggression but I am not leaving." Berg (1966) categorized "The forearm. . .held up in front of the face" as Shyness behavior when exhibited by young behaviorally disordered children in an interview situation.

Holding the forearm horizontally makes it maximally effective against vertical blows (like Beat), and forearm hair may provide additional protection. (Schaller, [1963] noted the presence of considerably more hair on the male gorilla's forearm than on any other body part.) Forearm raising probably represents a primitive startle response which has evolved social communicative significance. Perhaps the contemporary custom of prisoners of war putting their hands behind or atop their heads while the forearms and elbows project horizontally is related to this.

Van Lawick-Goodall (1968b) described the chimpanzee startle response: to "fling one or both arms across its face or to throw both hands in the air." Van Hooff's (1970) analysis showed parrying movements to occur both in the Submissive and Play systems. Merfield and Miller (in Schaller, 1963) described gorillas being attacked by men with sticks as "putting their arms over their heads to ward off blows, making no attempt at retaliation."

Forearm Sweep (.87)

The arm is extended horizontally or obliquely (hand down) between waist and shoulder level, away from the body. The forearm precedes and the hand is open. The trunk is upright and the feet may be spread further apart than normal. Contact most often occurs with the other individual's trunk or arms.

Forearm sweeping occurred in many kinds of social interaction and seemed to function as a mild aggressive pattern. It functioned to enlarge the space around an individual, and if it occurred at the expense of another child, then conflict might ensue. If not, then no quarrel occurred. Children used forearm sweeping to "brush" others from their path or to squeeze through a crowd. They sometimes used it to prise themselves into a line. Forearm sweeping was rarely reacted to with serious aggression and often went apparently unnoticed. Like underarm throwing, it was relatively inconspicuous, with the hand held far from the Beat Up or Punch Side position. When used in agonistic interactions, it was not to strike a blow but to exert gradual direct force, often in conjunction with Body Oppose. But, unlike Push, the force was indirectly exerted in a glancing, unsustained manner.

The baboon startle reaction (K. R. L. Hall & DeVore, 1965) resembles forearm sweeping in form although it is combined with other elements and is much quicker. Chimpanzee "hitting away," described by van Lawick-Goodall (1968b) as a threat gesture and defensive reaction to startling animals, also resembles Forearm Sweep.

Hand Cover

The open, partially flexed hand moves to the head, where the bunched fingers and palm are held close to or in contact with the eyes, ears, nose, and/or mouth. (See Grant's Nos. 77 and 78: Cover Eyes, Hand on Mouth.)

Hand covering appears in many social situations. A child may cover his ears with both hands in response to loud noises or when another child leans close and verbally threatens. A child may cover his eyes in "playful" fright during group play, for example, when a "monster" approaches. A child may cover the nose as a response to another child's threat to "bash his face." Finally, under physical attack, a child may cover most of his face with upright hands side-by-side.

Hand covering apparently functions to shield sense organs and other important facial features from either transmitting or receiving stimuli. The former case is exemplified in the head-flagging of the black-headed gull, where complete turning away of the frightening black-masked face is essential to pair formation (Tinbergen & Moynihan, 1952). Children's eyes or exposed teeth may function similarly, and hiding them might reduce the face's threatening aspect. The latter is exemplified in the "cut-off" postures described by Chance (1962), in which turning away the visual receptors reduces arousing social input. In children, covering the eyes may enable a frightened child to remain in an attractive location.

Adults in Western culture display hand covering in many situations. The mouth is covered during sneezing to prevent spraying another, to hide yawning (a socially negative behavior), or to indicate regret at having said the wrong thing. While watching horror films, adults may cover their eyes although simply closing them would achieve the same result. The symbolic significance of hand covering is indicated in the world-wide distribution and appreciation of the well-known Japanese monkey triumvirate. Hiding the face with the hand by the female is part of the flirting ritual in many human societies (Eibl-Eibesfeldt, 1968).

Similar movements have been described in nonhuman primates. After being startled, chimpanzees "fling one or both arms across the face" (van Lawick-Goodall, 1968b) and baboons wipe the muzzle with the hand (K. R. L. Hall & DeVore, 1965).

Hand Cover occurred too infrequently for reliability testing.

Hand on Back

The open palm is placed on another child's back, usually at the bottom of the shoulder blades. The actor stands or walks at the reactor's side.

Blurton Jones (1967) said that it occurred only when one child led another to an adult after a mishap. A few exceptions exist in which an adult is not involved. Hand on Back seems to be "comforting" and may lead to Shoulder Hug. It never occurred during agonistic or quasiagonistic interactions.

Amazonian Indians slap one another's backs in greeting, while some Polynesian males rub each other's backs in this situation (LaBarre, 1947) The slang expression "pat on the back" means well-earned praise. All these examples have in common the factor of "reassurance."

Placing the hand on another's back occurs in chimpanzees during situations of surprise or uncertainty, and such behavior was classed as reassurance (van Lawick-Goodall, 1968b, see two photographs on p. 373).

Hand on Back occurred too infrequently for reliability testing.

Hold Hands (1.00)

Two children grasp each other's hand, palm to palm, usually while facing the same direction, holding inside hands (the left hand of the child on the right, the right hand of the child on the left).

Holding hands occurred only in nonagonistic social interactions. It was most often initiated by females, and by older children toward younger. It occurred during locomotion, usually walking, and while sitting beside each other. Children seemed to hold hands more often during uncertainty or uneasiness, and such physical contact presumably provided comfort (see Physical Contact). Holding hands was often seen during dramatic play between "Mummy" and "Baby."

Between adults, holding hands is an affectional pattern, probably derived, like hugging, from mother-infant interactions. Birdwhistell (1962) described its occurrence in the "American adolescent courtship dance," where after taking a girl's hand the boy must await a counter-pressure on his hand before initiating the "finger intertwine." Hand holding commonly occurs in mothers and young children for maintaining contact and steering. It persists into adulthood under frightening or suspenseful conditions (e.g., viewing horror films). A ritualized form exists in hand shaking, a greeting and leave-taking behavior, which may provide reassurance through physical contact and through displaying absence of weapons and lack of bad intentions.

Among nonhuman primates, physical contact is an important aspect of socialization, and in at least one species this includes hand grasping. Chimpanzee hand touching is a reassurance gesture made by dominant individuals toward subordinates, and it also occurs occasionally in greeting (see photographs in van Lawick-Goodall, 1968b, p.353).

Hold Out (.90)

The arm is extended horizontally forward, fingers partially extended and together, and usually clasping an object with the palmar side up. It is often directed toward a person and followed by releasing the extended object.

Holding out objects to other people occurs in nonagonistic social situations. It often comprises the initial social overture to strange adults and sometimes to strange children and, as Blurton Jones (1967) noted, it is often unclear whether one is to respond by reaching toward and grasping it or not. Judging from the consequences when he took the proffered object, it was sometimes only extended for visual inspection.

Holding out also occurs to familiar persons, that is, parents and friends. Giving or showing objects to parents did not occur in greeting encounters where touching the parents occurred (Blurton Jones, 1967). This may be due to conflicting approach-flight motivation. Holding out the hand alone also occurs in greeting situations, for example, the initial movement in adult hand-shaking.

Holding out the hand toward another individual constitutes "reassurance" behavior in chimpanzees, and fearful individuals extend the hand (palm up) toward more dominant individuals (van Lawick-Goodall, 1968b). Holding out the hand palm up is also a chimpanzee food begging gesture, and the food sharing response also incorporates it. Van Hooff's (1970) analysis classified chimpanzee holding out as an Affinitive behavior.

Knock

The knuckles of the fist are brought sharply into contact with an object or person by forward extension of the forearm at the elbow. The movement occurs in short bouts of repeated rapping, and a sharp, characteristic noise results.

Children may knock on objects (e.g., Wendy House door) similarly to adults with definite imitative aspects, but it seems to function generally to attract the other child's attention. Children also knocked on each other's heads in quasiagonistic interactions in the Wendy House.

Nonhuman primate hitting behavior patterns are discussed in the Beat section. Chimpanzees strike objects with their knuckles during investigative behavior, and knuckle-walking was an important facet of pongid (and hominid) evolution (Tuttle, 1967).

Knocking occurred too infrequently for observer reliability testing.

Pat (.88)

The forearm is rapidly and repeatedly flexed and extended so that the hand is moved vertically, palmar side down within a six-inch radius. The wrist flexions and extensions result in light contact onto the surface of an object or another person. Pats are usually delivered to the head, shoulders, back, and upper limbs.

Patting occurs in nonagonistic social interactions. It seems to signal reassurance or comforting in children, and it is often exhibited by older to younger children or between siblings. Patting may be directed to a specific location of injury. Walters, Pearce, and Dahms (1957) classified it as physical affection.

Adult-child patting is also important. Rheingold (1961) listed it among patterns of maternal care and found that home-raised infants received significantly more patting than institution-raised ones. P. H. Wolff (1963) found that patting the infant's hands between his in a game of "pat-a-cake" was the most efficient smile eliciting behavior he could perform.

Chimpanzee patting is identical in form and is exhibited by dominants toward agitated subordinates and by adults toward small infants (van Lawick-Goodall, 1968b).

Pinch

The thumb and index finger are forcibly opposed with an object or part of another's body in between. (See Grant's No. 73: Pinch Nose.)

Pinching is an aggressive behavior pattern in children's social interactions. Recording it is difficult because of the minimal movement involved and because children use it surreptitiously. It occurs most often in crowded group conditions where it is directed to appendages and the lower trunk, but it also occurs in dyadic encounters where it is directed to the nose, ears, etc.

Adults may use pinching to punish children, and male-female pinching (as a test for firmness?) is meant to be sexually provocative in some southern European countries.

Pinching's form is identical to a basic mode of social grooming in nonhuman primates (Sparks, 1967), and through grooming experience individuals may learn that misdirected or overly-forceful grooming causes pain. The behavior pattern may then be generalized to agonistic situations.

Point (.82)

The arm is fully extended, usually horizontally, and oriented to a stimulus, with palm inward and vertical, or downward and horizontal. The index finger is extended and the other digits partially flexed, but less commonly the entire hand may be extended. The favored hand is usually used, and an object, for example, stick, may function as a "pointer." Palm orientation is useful for distinguishing pointing from reaching or holding out. Pointing to physical contact with the object ("poking") also occurs.

When directed toward inanimate objects, pointing seems unrelated to the type of social encounter. However, pointing toward other children seems to have special threatening significance in agonistic encounters. This probably results from its capacity to force and focus attention on a particular spot (cf. "Uncle Sam Wants You" recruiting posters). A difference in gaze direction exists between the two situations: when pointing toward an object in a social situation, the pointer's gaze is usually directed to the other person. When pointing toward a person in the same situation, the pointer's gaze follows the point (and increases its intimidating power?).

Pointing has rarely been observed in nonhuman primates. Poking at other chimpanzees with the index finger was described as mild threat by Wilson and Wilson (1968) but as playful by van Hooff (1970).

Pull (.86)

The arms are flexed toward the body, usually the chest, thus drawing an object or person toward the body or vice versa. Pull is usually preceded by reaching and grasping.

Pulling is exhibited by children in most types of social interactions. In agonistic interactions, it is most often directed toward specific body parts of the opponent, for example, hair, ears, appendages, or his clothes. It also occurs in property disputes when both parties attempt to pull a small object away from the other and toward themselves. Children also may attempt to pull opponents from larger toys (e.g., rocking horse) or out of desirable spaces (e.g., inside a box).

In quasiagonistic interactions, pulling is part of rough-and-tumble play and a component of wrestling. Participants attempting to flee or get up from the ground are often pulled back into the melee. Such pulling is most often directed to the trunk or appendages and never to the hair. Finally, pulling is seen in "friendly" interactions which include physical contact, for example, two children holding hands may pull each other about without resistance, in dramatic play the "Mummy" may pull the "Baby" in appropriate situations.

Loizos (1967) listed pulling as a primary feature of nonhuman primate social play. Pulling also occurs in attack, and mature males may pull small individuals completely off the ground or pull victims under them to be stamped upon. Van Lawick-Goodall (1968b) listed hair-pulling separately and states that handfuls of hair may be pulled out during chimpanzee fights. Mother-infant pulling occurs in several contexts: drawing the infant into the ventral clasping position, or restraining the infant's locomotion away from the mother. Chimpanzee infant-mother hair-pulling acts as a tactile signal of clinging sufficiency (van Lawick-Goodall, 1967). The tail offers an additional object for pulling in many species.

Punch (.71)

The arm is moved rapidly from an approximately horizontal position at the side, forward approximately 180 degrees (or until contact) in a sidearm motion. The arm is held partially flexed; the fist is tightly clenched; and the knuckle side of the hand precedes. The movement varies in form more than Beat, and its specific components follow.

a. *Punch Side* is the initial movement of swinging the arm to the side, so that the hand is approximately in the body's median coronal plane. The arm may be briefly held in this position before the punch is carried out, or it may be slowly lowered or brought toward the body if not carried out. It functions as a threat (see Beat Up), and the probability of complete Punch is probably indicated by simultaneously emitted facial expression and posture. Low Frown and Lean Forward seem to indicate high likelihood of attack; Wide Eyes and Lean Backward seem to indicate low likelihood.

b. *Incomplete Punch* is the initial movement to the side plus only partial sidearm movement forward. The complete punch seems to cover a horizontal arc of 180 degrees, and termination before completion appears intentional. Like Beat Incomplete, it appeared to be "less intense" than the full Punch, and it occurred infrequently.

c. *Open Punch* is the complete punch performed with hand open (fingers extended and together). The result is a "slap," a stereotyped movement used by adults in situations where hitting with a clenched fist is socially unacceptable, for example, man to woman, mother to child. Open punch is the movement normally used in "spanking." The body part contacted seems important. Slaps to the head in children's interactions appear to be received as aggressive, whereas slaps to the buttocks appear to be treated as "playful." This seems to be true even in the absence of other agonistic or quasiagonistic cues: pilot tests with adults indicate that ability exists to differentiate beating and open punching on tactile cues alone.

d. *Object Punch* is the complete punch performed with an object in hand. It appears more awkward than Object Beat and is less common. Sometimes both hands move simultaneously forward to strike the reactor from both sides, for example, like a cymbalists' motion. Object punching also occurs when sticks are brandished horizontally in a stick-fight between children.

Blurton Jones (1967) stated that "punching" did not exist in the repertoire of three- to five-year-old children, but this appears to be wrong. Relative frequency of Punching compared to Beat seems to increase with age (it is less conspicuous to supervising adults!), but even three-year-olds in groups observed by the author were adequate "punchers."

General discussion and hitting in nonhuman primates were included under Beat.

Push (.92)

The arms are extended forward, usually in parallel and horizontal, with the wrists flexed and the vertical palms preceding. Force is directly applied to an object or person. Pushing most commonly occurs when the trunk leans forward while standing or sitting, but it may also be combined in forward upright locomotion.

Pushing is a common aggressive pattern in children (Blurton Jones, 1967; Walters, Pearce, & Dahms, 1957) and appears early in infancy, for example, the infant pushing away the unwanted bottle or breast. In nursery schools, pushing was used in forcibly moving other children away from desirable large objects or out of desirable spaces. Such pushing was often directed to the offender's trunk and shoulders and to his possessions, for example, a large block in front of the Wendy House door. Pushing may be used in social destruction, for example, pushing down another's pile of blocks or sand castle.

Pushing also occurs in quasiagonistic social play. It is an important component of wrestling and occurs in jostling when lining up for desired objects like the slide. In jumping games children may repeatedly push each other off heights with no sign of anger resulting. Children also push at each other through intermediate objects, for example, on either side of the Wendy House door.

Among older humans, pushing occurs in the preliminary stages of diadic fights, especially among adolescents, and such provocative "shoving matches" may be the source of the adjective "pushy." In mass agonistic encounters, for example, protest demonstrations, group pushing between lines of demonstrators and police may be quite common and acceptable, whereas as soon as a blow is struck the situation is distinctly altered and escalated.

Loizos (1967) listed pushing as an obvious feature of nonhuman primate social play. Aggressive pushing also occurs, and, in chimpanzees, the form is similar to human pushing except the knuckles or back of the hand make contact with the opponent (Wilson & Wilson, 1968). It is directed to the back, front, or side, and follows weak threat. It constitutes the least intensive form of attack in rhesus monkeys (Sade, 1967). Pushing by adult males to estrous females occurs in baboon sexual behavior (K. R. L. Hall & DeVore, 1965).

Reach (.78)

The arm is extended horizontally, fingers partially extended and separated with the palmar side usually down. It is often directed to an object or person and followed by grasping and picking up. An incomplete reaching intention movement, in which the arm is held partially flexed with grasping hand (palm vertical) oriented toward the object or person also occurs.

Reaching is important in all social and nonsocial behavior from infancy onwards. Some early research workers observed incipient reaching movements no earlier than 8–12 weeks (Gesell, 1940), but Bower, Broughton, and Moore (1970) ingeniously demonstrated intentional reaching in neonates as young as eight days old. In friendly social interactions, the reactor may respond by holding out the object or body part (often the hand), or displaying nonresistance. In agonistic and quasiagonistic interactions, reaching may lead to the reactor's leaning back, turning away, or fleeing, or it may lead to reciprocal reaching and grappling. Its signal function is best explained as a movement indicating intention to grasp. Children use this in "monster" games, in which the monster adopts the incomplete reaching pose with both hands oriented toward the victims.

Reaching fulfills similar functions in nonhuman primates. It serves as a specific gestural signal in chimpanzee mother-juvenile interactions, leading to the juvenile's climbing onto the mother (Reynolds & Reynolds, 1965). Grasping of other individuals is an Affinitive behavior pattern in chimpanzees (van Hooff, 1970).

Repel

The arms are spasmodically extended away from and in front of the body, not necessarily horizontally, hands open and palm-first. The movements are usually rapidly repeated and accompanied by negative expletives. The movements somewhat resemble pushing intention movements or lowered incomplete open beating. (See Grant's No. 65: Push Gesture.)

Repelling movements occur in children's agonistic interactions. They seem to mean "Get away!" and are exhibited by aggressed-against children along with Lean Back, Flinch, and Wide Eyes. Similar movements occur during highly excited imaginative play, for example, by intended victims of a child acting as a "monster."

For possible comparative behavior patterns in nonhuman primates, see Forearm Raise and Forearm Sweep.

Repelling occurred too infrequently for observer reliability testing.

Scratch

The finger nails are raked across a surface, usually another child's skin; the fingers are locked in partial flexion and usually separated. Scratching occurs infrequently (because children's nails are soft and kept trimmed by mothers?), but seems to be directed to the face and arms. (Scratching differs from self-maintenance or displacement activities. See Auto-manipulation; also Grant's No. 81: Scratch.)

Van Lawick-Goodall (1968b) classed this pattern as attack in chimpanzees and stated that only females exhibited it. Inadequate frequencies in the author's data preclude conclusions about sex differences, but it is an aggressive pattern in children. In Western society, adult scratching is considered feminine and related to maintenance of long, sometimes pointed fingernails.

Scratching occurred too infrequently for reliability testing.

Shake (.92)

The arms are flexed and extended in rapid alternation while the hands grasp a large object or another person. *Or* the forearm moves rapidly up and down or back and forth while holding a small object. In the former, the trunk is upright, usually in a standing or sitting posture, and the other child is held by the clothing or upper arms. In the latter, the arm is partially flexed and held with hands above waist level.

Shaking another child occurs in agonistic interactions where it serves to threaten another individual without injuring him. The shaker often stands facing the victim and shakes him forward and backward while exhibiting Face Thrust and Bared Teeth. It seems to occur in ambivalent situations, where, for some reason, the aggressor will not push or pull the victim down but instead rapidly alternates between the two intention movements. Similar ambivalence may exist in shaking the fist at another individual, which consists of a rapid series of short, incomplete beats not leading to completed beats. The same applies to "brandishing" of weapons. The "dominant" male in the Epworth Halls nursery group often shook other children who "crossed" him, and such interactions rarely led to crying or adult intervention.

Chimpanzees shake their bodies in threat (Reynolds & Reynolds, 1965), but shaking of the opponent has only been recorded as part of "punitive deterrence" during weaning by macaque mothers toward infants (Kaufman and Rosenblum, 1966). Shaking of objects, particularly branches, occurs in many primate species (see list in van Lawick-Goodall, 1968b) in situations of "uncertainty" or "frustration," as well as situations where it seems to be threatening.

Male macaques perform the branch-shaking display in a stereotyped form from certain favored locations (Hinde & Rowell, 1962). Convulsive jerking and body shaking is a "disturbance behavior" in young socially-deprived rhesus infants, but it rarely occurs past the age of three months (Hansen, 1966)

Snatch

After grasping a small object, the arm is suddenly flexed, thereby pulling the object away from another individual and toward the actor's body or above the head. Turning away often accompanies the snatch.

Snatching of objects is a common cause of agonistic interactions among nursery-age children. (In fights over larger objects it is replaced by mutual pulling bouts.) Older nursery children nearing five years of age develop more indirect, less obvious ways of obtaining desired objects from others, presumably because this reduces the probability of adult intervention.

Snatching also leads to antagonism in nonhuman primates. Chimpanzees may use a "rush in and snatch" technique to obtain food from fellows, and the nature of the subsequent agonistic behavior is determined by the relative rankings of those involved (Wilson & Wilson, 1968).

Throw

The forearm is extended forward, hand with palm down, above shoulder-level and usually overhead, imparting force to a released object.

Gesell (1940) studied in detail the maturation of children's throwing and found significant sex differences by three-and-one-half years. During the pre-school years, body movement and orientation are incorporated into throwing, and this facilitates judging the direction of throw. Children threw at each other only part of the time. Most throws seemed undirected and solely for the enjoyment of throwing. Children carefully watched the thrown object. Such throwing occured when the child was "excited" or had recently been "frustrated," for example, refused entry into a playing group. Directed throwing sometimes appeared in social groups, for example, boys throwing wet sand high on the wall. Throws varied between three to fifteen feet.

Socially-directed throwing (so that the object became a weapon) occurred in both agonistic and quasiagonistic social interactions. They looked identical, and the two were distinguishable only from other cues, for example, facial expressions. No object bigger than a ball of six-inch diameter was thrown overarm, and smaller objects, for example, handfuls of sand, were more common. Boys threw more than girls. Accuracy was good at less than five feet, and children seldom attempted longer throws at each other. In addition to inflicting pain, throwing functioned to obtain another's attention or provoke him into action.

85

Lorenz (1966) noted the importance of weapon throwing in human aggression: as distance between antagonists increases, the efficiency of visually communicated threatening and submissive responses decreases. Throwing's importance in hunting as a factor in human evolution is obvious. Throwing in contemporary Western adult life occurs commonly in games and sports, perhaps as sublimation of evolved aggressive patterns.

Kortlandt and Kooij (1963) comprehensively reviewed nonhuman primate throwing. According to their findings, all throwing seen in the wild (with one exception) has been agonistic, and males throw more accurately and frequently. They concluded that although aiming is individually learned, agonistic throwing is a partly "instinctive" primate reaction to large carnivores.

Throwing occurred too infrequently for reliability testing.

Tickle

The separated fingers are moved in a repeated, rapid wiggling motion against another child's body surface. It may be directed to any part of the body but most often to the lateral trunk, axilla, and soles of the feet.

Tickling produces pleasurable irritation, at least in moderation, and the tickled child responds with laughter, writhing, and struggling to escape. Recognizable tickling rarely occurred in the nursery but was seen in nonagonistic and quasiagonistic interactions. The tickled individual usually sat or lay on the ground, and tickling sometimes occurred in group "rough-and-tumble play." Adults frequently tickle children, particularly infants, and children seem to imitate this. Tickling appears to be necessarily social, at least in humans, as experimentally self-administered tickling is virtually ineffective (Weiskrantz, Elliot, & Darlington, 1971).

Adult male chimpanzees initiate play with juveniles by tickling (van Lawick-Goodall, 1968a) and infant chimpanzees respond to maternal tickling by "laughing" (van Lawick-Goodall, 1967). Loizos (1967) pointed out that many social play patterns are derived from agonistic behavior, and tickling may have been adapted from manipulatory patterns such as Pinch or Scratch.

Underarm Throw

The forearm is extended forward, hand with palm up below shoulder level (and usually below the waist), imparting force to a released object.

The early development of throwing is similar for underarm or overarm throwing, but the former drops in frequency with increasing age. Underarm throwing is used by nursery children similarly to throwing (see Throw). The differential use appears when the thrower is a subordinate individual or concurrently exhibits other fearful behavior patterns. Here underarm throwing is more common and gradates into merely dropping the object in the direction of the target individual. Underarm throwing involves much less movement and is less obvious (and therefore less provocative?) than overarm throwing. It is very different from the beating motion which overarm throwing resembles closely. In one instance, a child who lost a property dispute fled from the winner. Then he paused, picked up a small object, turned abruptly and ran toward the winner. About halfway back to the winner, the loser paused, dropped/underarm threw the object toward the winner then turned and fled again.

Kortlandt and Kooij (1963) described "agonistic flinging down and drop-ping of objects" in many arboreal primate species and "agonistic stone rolling" in some terrestrial species.

Underarm throwing occurred too infrequently for reliability testing.

Wave

The arm is held away from and in front of the body, forearm approxi-mately vertical and palm forward, and is moved repeatedly from side to side.

Waving as leave-taking behavior occurs during the first year when it is associated with words like "Bye-Bye." This persists in nursery-age children, at least toward adults, and on through adulthood. Older children more rarely exhibited waving in another social situation where it appeared to function as an attention-getting movement when children were some distance apart. It occurred simultaneously with loud verbalizations; the further the distance, the higher the ambient noise and distraction level, and the more unavailable the other child, the higher the waving arm was held and the greater the movement's arc. Such behavior may derive from infantile flailing, which presumably brings reinforcing attention and caretaking from adults more often than remaining still.

Arm waving included in the chimpanzee's threat display (labeled "bipedal arm waving and running") occurred in situations where attention was called to the performer (van Lawick-Goodall, 1968b).

Wave occurred too infrequently for reliability testing.

Posture and Leg Patterns

This section describes behavior patterns which involve leg movements and static body positions or movements which change the body's position. Leg movements without simultaneous gross body movements are rare, because the legs, unlike the arms, are usually engaged in supporting the body's weight. Posture is usually discussed as part of motor development, but its socially communicative significance, though more subtle than facial expression or ges-tures, is less commonly realized (Hewes, 1957; James, 1932; Scheflen, 1964).

The overall mean inter-observer reliability coefficient for postures and leg patterns was .85 (S.D. = ± .12), and the mean number of recorded instances per behavior pattern used in computation of the coefficients was 23.6 (S.D. = ± 13.0).

Climb (.78)

The four limbs are alternately extended and flexed, resulting in approximately vertical gross body movement on an object or surface. The legs usually push while the arms pull, but in descending, the arms may also push against the surface.

Early climbing is related to the grasping reflex, and a human neonate can temporarily hang by its hands unsupported (see photographs in Eibl-Eibesfeldt, 1970). The almost total lack of pedal grasping ability makes early climbing difficult, however, and an infant does not demonstrate marked climbing abilities until about 18 months (Gesell, 1940). Preschool children will climb on any large object, indoors or out, unless forbidden. Children may construct deliberately difficult climbing situations, or if faced with a choice, appear to select the most challenging routes. Social climbing occurs when groups line up to climb along a selected path again and again. Different-aged children react differently to the same physical surroundings: three-year-olds often climb steps which four-year-olds walk up. Ascent occurs head first and descent usually feet first, except on inclined surfaces such as slides. Young children often climb into chairs as part of sitting down.

Evidence exists that nonhuman primate neonates actually "climb" into the world: as soon as the arms are free of the birth canal, rhesus infants extend them and seize any graspable object; the subsequent limb flexions help to deliver the rest of the body (Tinklepaugh & Hartman, 1932). The same workers found that by 8–10 days, rhesus infants climbed on and off their mothers during exploratory behavior, but the primary tendency to climb upward appeared earlier under experimental conditions at 1–4 days. Climbing in wild-living infant chimpanzees occurs much later: van Lawick-Goodall (1967) did not observe it until 24 weeks in one individual. Climbing rapidly becomes incorporated into the social and nonsocial play of many primate species: gray langurs (Ripley, 1967); gorillas (Schaller, 1963); baboons (S. L. Washburn & DeVore, 1961).

Crouch (.89)

The knees are flexed so that the trunk and head are lowered from a standing posture and/or the back is flexed with the same result from a sitting posture. In extreme crouching, the chest and upper legs are brought together, so that the head approaches the knees. The arms may be flexed around the trunk, or in extreme cases, flexed over and around the head and neck. The neck may be flexed with the face horizontal and down. Crouching may also be combined with locomotion. (See Grant's No. 92 and 93: Hunch, Crouch.)

Children display crouching in social situations in which other fearful behaviors simultaneously occur, for example, Forearm Raise, Flinch. Grant (1965b, 1968) described crouching as high intensity submissive- or flight-motivated behavior in nursery school children and adult mental patients. He found that crouching was associated with Chin In and Mouth Corners Back. Crouching may be considered a sign of fear in everyday life (e.g., "cowering," "cringing"), and it has been ritualized in the customs of certain societies, for example, among the Nyakyusa of Tanzania, women normally crouch when greeting men. Darwin (1872) described fearful crouching as an instictive attempt to escape observation.

Among nonhuman primates, crouching is a fearful or submissive behavior pattern. Recently-persecuted rhesus subordinates exhibit it, often combined with running (Hinde & Rowell, 1962); Altmann (1962) labeled the same behavior pattern when immobile as "fear paralysis." Crouching occurs very frequently in emotionally-disturbed, surrogate-mothered rhesus infants (Harlow, 1959). Submissive crouching occurs in many species: chimpanzee (Wilson & Wilson, 1968), baboons (K. R. L. Hall & DeVore, 1965), gorilla (Schaller, 1963), but not in the patas monkey (K. R. L. Hall, 1965). Chimpanzees display it during approach to a more dominant individual or as appeasement behavior after having been aggressed-against (van Lawick-Goodall, 1968b). Harlow (1959) used crouching as one of his "fear indices" and found that emotionality scores of socially deprived rhesus infants increased significantly in strange situations.

Immobile (.83)

Gross movement of the trunk, limbs, and head ceases for at least three seconds. Often the gaze is fixed. The fingers may continue to move, often in automanipulation, but the movements are restrained and inconspicuous. Immobility may occur in any posture but most commonly while standing or sitting. (See Grant's No. 101: Still.)

Blurton Jones (1967) observed immobility in children who lost possession of toys or were aggressed-against. Such children sat down and thumb-sucked or automanipulated. Immobility also occurs often during group formation and during the first few days of nursery attendance. Children often exhibit it in "socially stressful" situations not directly involving themselves, for example, when another child cries, when other children fight nearby, when strange adults or children enter the room, or when an adult reprimands a nearby child. Children also exhibit brief immobility while "stalking" other children in social play; this may be combined with Wide Eyes and Smile.

"Freezing" is a common fearful behavior pattern in vertebrates, and it often signifies submission and functions as appeasement, that is, prevents further attack from the aggressor. Such displays may have a common explanation: immobility is the antithesis of aggression since no injury can be delivered when no movements occur. In nonhuman primates, fearful individuals sometimes show immobility in specific postures, but they more commonly flee. Rhesus monkeys crouch in "fear paralysis" in response to threat (Altmann, 1962), as may

89

chimpanzees (Wilson & Wilson, 1968) and Nilgiri langurs (Poirier, 1970). The patas monkey shows no fearful immobility; this is probably related to its specialized social organization (K. R. L. Hall, 1965). Immobility also occurs in nonagonistic social contexts, that is, by the groomee during social grooming interactions.

Kick (.94)

The leg is flexed and then rapidly extended at the knee and hip so that the foot moves forward toe-first; it is usually oriented toward an object or person. In a standing posture, the other leg remains upright, supporting the body; while sitting both legs may be kicked simultaneously or alternately. In addition to the complete motion, two specific components exist which may be less "intensive" forms of the behavior pattern:

a. *Kick Up* is the initial leg movement to the maximally flexed position. Instead of the kick being carried out, the foot is slowly lowered sole-first to the ground and the body weight is reshifted onto it. This appears to be an intention movement that has been ritualized to a threat gesture (see Beat Up).

b. *Kick Incomplete* is partial leg extension without completing the movement or without making physical contact. The halted foot is re-flexed to the starting position or moved backwards and lowered to the ground. Incomplete kicking may occur in ambivalent situations, for example, where the victim's retaliatory potential may "inhibit" the aggressive pattern's completion.

Kicking occurs in agonistic and quasiagonistic interactions between children. During property fights, it is often directed to the other's shins, but striking with the arms occurs more commonly. Children knocked down onto their backs often adopt a Kick Up position which prevents their being further attacked. This behavior pattern also resembles Stamp, as the soles, and not the toes, are directed toward the attacker. Children being socially obstructed during climbing often kicked out at the obstructors.

In quasiagonistic play, incomplete kicking occurs when children playfully threaten each other, and it often produces laughter and doubling up by the reactor. Complete kicking also occurs, especially by standing individuals toward the trunks of children lying down. The reactor often grabs at the kicker's foot and pulls him down as well.

Kicking of objects by individuals occurs after losing property fights or suffering other "frustrations." Such kicks are forceful and close to the ground and directed toward large stationary objects, for example, table legs, wooden boxes, etc. It resembles the "re-directed aggression" described by Darwin (1872), and children exhibit such kicking more commonly than striking with the hands, probably because the shoes protect the feet, allowing them to be used with greater force and less pain. Kicking is also common in temper tantrums.

Agonistic and quasiagonistic kicking also occurs in nonhuman primates. Chimpanzees use two kinds of kicking attacks, which depend on the use of bipedal or quadrupedal locomotion (Wilson & Wilson, 1968). Kicking in juvenile rough-and-tumble play occurs in chimpanzees (Reynolds & Reynolds, 1965) and gorillas (Schaller, 1963). In frustration situations, chimpanzees apparently kick at objects, but as some authors use Kick, Stamp, and other undefined terms ("drum," "thump") interchangably, the exact situation is unclear.

Kneel (1.00)

The trunk is lowered and tilted forward by hip and knee flexion, resulting in its resting on the knees (one or both) and feet (both). After assuming the posture, the trunk may be upright or maximally flexed at the hips with the head vertical and facing forward, or horizontal and facing down. When used as a resting position, the buttocks rest on the heels while hip flexion is 45 degrees or less. The forelimbs need not perform any supportive function. Kneeling is common in preschool children but nothing has been reported about its occurrence in social situations. Among adults, kneeling appears to have widespread submissive connotations, whether in the Islamic prayer position or by the vanquished warrior (see Eibl-Eibesfeldt, 1970; Lorenz, 1952). Hewes (1955) pointed out that, across cultures, sitting on the heels while kneeling is mainly a female posture, while squatting on one knee (the "cowboy squat") is primarily a male posture. The former posture is also a Tibetan outdoor sleeping posture which functions to conserve heat (Peter, 1953).

Kneeling occurs only rarely in nonhuman primates; most submissive postures are forms of crouching which may incorporate kneeling. One-knee kneeling may occur as early as nine weeks in the gorilla (Kirchshofer, Weisse, Berentz, Klose, & Klose, 1968). Schaller (1963) observed an adult male gorilla kneel during copulation.

Lie (1.00)

The legs are fully flexed at the knees, then the arms are extended toward the ground and the trunk is tilted sideways; from the resulting seated position the trunk is further tilted, resulting in a sideways reclining posture with the main body axis horizontal to the ground. Alternatively, the legs are fully flexed, then the trunk is tilted forward into a kneeling position, then the trunk and arms are extended further forward into a prone reclining posture. From a seated position, the trunk is extended at the waist either sideways (preceded by extended arms), or backwards (not so preceded).

While the horizontal posture is the basic one that infants exhibit, it is unclear when lying down enters the motor repertoire. At 44 weeks, the child can go from seated to prone and back to seated unaided (Gesell, 1940). Reclining persists throughout life as the most common human sleeping posture, but few research workers have studied it in waking social situations. Grant (1965b) described the occurrence of "sleeping postures" in adult mental patients as "cut-off postures" in response to indirect aggression. Nursery school children rarely display the posture. During agonistic and nonagonistic interactions, an attacked individual may lie on his back with arms extended and legs flexed. This constitutes an effective defensive posture, as the arms can be used to fend off further blows and the legs can be powerfully extended to deliver stamping blows. During wrestling bouts, the two individuals often temporarily lie while in physical contact and rolling about. It appears that each seeks to be crouching or kneeling over the other lying down.

Gorillas lie in prone, supine, or sideways postures during sleeping, and females may lie similarly during copulation (Schaller, 1963). Other nonhuman primates adopt similar postures: baboons (K. R. L. Hall & DeVore, 1965) gray langurs (Ripley, 1967), patas monkeys (K. R. L. Hall, 1965). (See photograph of an especially relaxed male howler in DeVore, 1965, p. 257.) Lying rigidly prone on the ground is an intense baboon fear response (K. R. L. Hall & DeVore, 1965).

Play Crouch (.75)

A specialized version of crouch exists: head and trunk are erect, the legs are slightly flexed, the feet are wider apart than shoulders-width, the arms are partially flexed and held out from the trunk, the shoulders may be hunched. The posture is accompanied by Play Face and/or Laugh. The actor may be oriented side on to another child who subsequently becomes his pursuer (Blurton Jones, 1967).

Play crouching occurs during bouts of quasiagonistic social behavior, often interspersed between bouts of locomotion. It appears to function as a "play invitation" as well as providing an opportunity for the actor to monitor the other participants' behavior while maintaining readiness to move quickly. It may be a ritualized version of agonistic crouching (Loizos, 1967).

Play invitation is a common nonhuman primate phenomenon, and a play crouch posture apparently exists in chimpanzees (Loizos, 1969). It resembles several locomotory behavior patterns seen in play which function as invitations, for example, "play walk" in chimpanzees (van Lawick-Goodall, 1968b), and "play bounce" in patas monkeys (K. R. L. Hall, 1965).

Shuffle (.62)

While the trunk is upright, the feet are moved repetitively in various patterns: together and apart again, from heel to toe and back, from inside to outside edge of the foot, pivoting on heel or toe, onto tip-toes and down again.

No locomotion occurs and no function is apparent, for example, other simultaneous behavior appears unaffected whether the feet are together or apart.

Shuffling occurs in social situations where the child seems "uncertain" or "nervous," for example, waiting to show the teacher a broken toy, surveying the room after giving way to another child. The leg movements may be intention movements of locomotion or gross body activity; the general "mood" communicated in such movements is "fidgety" or "restless." Adults display similar behavior when bored.

Similar behavior is rare in nonhuman primates, judging from the literature. Baboons make "rotating movements of the hands on ground" in threat (K. R. L. Hall & DeVore, 1965).

The low inter-observer reliability coefficient is probably due to the behavior pattern's variable form as here defined.

Sit (.86)

The trunk is lowered by hip and knee flexion; the result is that the body rests primarily on the buttocks. While seated the legs may be extended horizontally, partially flexed with only the feet on the ground, or dangled. The neck is held extended with the head upright. Sitting may be maintained during locomotion, for example, when the buttocks are scooted along the ground. (See Grant's No. 98: Up, Down.)

By 36 weeks the human infant is usually capable of sitting erect and unaided (Gesell, 1940). Children's sitting has not been studied in ongoing social interactions. During free play, children observed by the author tended to sit only on raised objects (chairs, boxes, etc.), probably a culturally related practice (Hewes, 1955). When sitting on the floor, for example, during story time, the legs were usually extended fully forward, and some sitting postures, for example, crossed legs, did not occur. Considerable social psychological research has been done on adult seating patterns in social interaction (see, e.g., Sommer, 1969).

A posture combining sitting and crouching is the common resting position of nonhuman primates, and it has been suggested that the ischial callosities (thickened, hairless areas of skin covering the ischial tuberosities in Cercopithecoids) are an adaptation for ground-living and sitting primates (S. L. Washburn, 1957). Certain sitting postures also have socially communicative significance, for example, Hinde and Rowell (1962) defined four sitting postures which were differentially exhibited according to social status and degree of alertness. Similar behavior patterns occur in baboons (K. R. L. Hall & DeVore, 1965) and patas monkeys (K. R. L. Hall, 1965). Sitting postures also exist in communal sleeping, and several individuals may sit in physical contact. Gorilla infants may sit erect and unaided by 18 weeks (Schaller, 1963), and by 4–6 months baboon and chimpanzee infants begin to sit erect ("jockey style") on their mother's backs when she ambulates (K. R. L. Hall & Devore, 1965; van Lawick-Goodall, 1967).

Slope (.87)

"The actor is standing facing another person, his body is leaning back from the hips, his chin is tucked in and he is looking at the other person, and his hands are frequently clasped behind his back." (Grant, 1965b.) The hands may also be clasped in front of the body, usually at waist level.

Grant observed this posture in children and adults, and he described the behavior as "simultaneous expression of ambivalence." Sloping children seemed in conflict between fleeing and complying with a dominant individual's wishes (usually an adult) by approaching. Adults exhibit a similar posture in situations which may contain ambivalent flight-approach tendencies, for example, at funerals.

The slope posture has not been described in nonhuman primates, perhaps because bipedal postures are difficult to sustain due to morphological characteristics.

Stamp

The leg is rapidly extended, forcefully moving the foot down and usually vertically, sole first, onto an object; the other leg remains as body support. This follows an initial leg flexing at the knee which vertically raises the foot. Stamping is often directed to the floor, or to objects on the floor (e.g., an insect), but it may be directed toward another individual. The resulting noise may be loud (and of signal value?).

Stamping appears to be an agonistic pattern, but it is combined in rough-and-tumble play patterns, for example, jumping, and in nonagonistic appearing patterns, for example, quick hop. Eibl-Eibesfeldt stated that a child stamps his foot to indicate intention to attack (Barnett, 1967). Stamping by adults has several uses: among the native Tasmanians rapid stamping on the ground signalled surprise or pleasure; similar behavior occurs in Western culture to supplement handclapping applause (LaBarre, 1947). The sound of the men's stamping is important in Bushmen dancing (Tobias, 1957).

Among nonhuman primates, stamping (or "stomping") is an attack pattern, preceded by approach and leaping onto the reactor. Van Lawick-Goodall (1968b) and Wilson and Wilson (1968) described similar chimpanzee patterns in which both feet are brought down onto the victim's back. Van Hooff's (1970) component analysis of stamping, stamp-walking, and trampling confirmed this. Van Lawick-Goodall also observed stamping in a frustration situation in the form of rhythmic drumming.

Stand (.88)

The trunk is raised by extension of the hips, knees, and back; the resulting posture is upright with both feet supporting the body's weight, about a shoulder's width apart. The arms usually hang free and the head is erect. Standing is incorporated into most bipedal locomotory patterns. (See Grant's No. 98: Up, Down.)

By 15 months, most children can independently stand up, although they can maintain a supported standing posture much earlier (Gesell, 1940). Social aspects of children's standing are unstudied, but incidental descriptions of unorthodox standing postures, e.g., the one-legged resting position (*Nilotenstellung*), show that small children may exhibit them (Elkin, 1953). Certain subtle postural changes (e.g., muscle tonus, distance between feet, variance from the vertical) seem to have expressive importance, and certain postures seem to have consistently associated gestures, but little is known about this (Scheflen, 1964).

Nonhuman primates are quadrupedal, but bipedal standing occurs in many species under certain conditions. Gorilla infants first exhibit it with support at about 14 weeks (Schaller, 1963). Standing is incorporated into the patas monkey's "alert posture" (giving maximum height for viewing in a tall-grass habitat), as well as into feeding and locomotion (K. R. L. Hall, 1965). It occurs similarly in baboons (K. R. L. Hall & DeVore, 1965), chimpanzees (van Lawick-Goodall, 1968b), and gray langurs (Ripley, 1967). Standing up is part of "bipedal arm waving and running" in threat, and "bipedal swagger" in threat and courtship in chimpanzees (van Lawick-Goodall, 1968b), bipedal attack in chimpanzees (Wilson and Wilson, 1968) and friendly "standing on hind legs in front of another" in baboons (K. R. L. Hall & DeVore, 1965). Bipedal standing by a normally quadrupedal animal makes it conspicuous, and social displays incorporating it usually function accordingly.

Gross Patterns

This section describes behavior patterns which include simultaneous trunk, limb, and head movements. Although not as well-known, their social communicative significance resembles that of facial expression and gestures. Gross body movements have long been studied: Warner (1889) sought to relate evolutionary and neurological aspects of movements to cognitive processes.

The overall mean inter-observer reliability coefficient for gross behavior patterns was .86 (S.D. = ± .07), and the overall mean number of recorded instances per behavior pattern used in computation of the coefficients was 15.6 (S.D. = ± 7.4).

95

Arms Akimbo (1.00)

The arms are flexed at approximately a 90 degree angle with the palms (fingers forward) resting on the hips. The trunk is upright and the legs are spread wider than shoulder's width.

Arms akimbo occurred rarely in preschool children, and its significance was unclear. Children displaying it sometimes seemed "exasperated," for example, after a carefully-constructed column of blocks had tumbled down. Children also imitated their mother's use of the pattern, combined with appropriately inflected verbalizations, in scolding other children. Adults (especially females) display a more "aggressive" variation in which the knuckles (and not the palms) rest on the hips, and the head is thrust forward. Stage parodies of male homosexuals often include Arms Akimbo, but the legs are kept together and not spread.

The nonhuman primate equivalent of Arms Akimbo has not been recorded. The apes most often assume upright postures, but their arms are proportionally much longer than man's, which would make the behavior pattern's performance more difficult. Monkeys have proportionally shorter arms but they less commonly assume upright postures.

Body Oppose

The trunk is forcefully inclined into contact with another individual's trunk; the body is upright and the feet are spread wide (giving a more solid supporting base). It resembles pushing or shoving except that the arms do not exert force; instead they are usually held away from the body, to its side. Common orientations of individuals are chest-to-chest, side-to-side, back-to-chest, chest-to-back.

Body opposition resembles pushing in its effect, and both behavior patterns may appear in agonistic or quasiagonistic interactions, but differences exist. First, body opposition occurs when hand pushing is impossible or undesirable, for example, for using back-to-chest body opposition a child can move an opponent without having to face (and look at) him. Also, the arms not being used makes Body Oppose less conspicuous, and it often occurs in situations like lining up for the slide. Finally, it can be used when the hands are otherwise occupied, for example, in maintaining possession of the "driver's seat" of a toy car while the hands hold onto the steering wheel. But Body Oppose and Push may also occur together.

Body opposition has not been specifically described in nonhuman primates, but from Hansen's (1966) general definitions, it is probably part of "rough-and-tumble" play or "nonspecific contact" in rhesus monkeys.

Body Oppose occurred too infrequently for observer reliability testing.

Fall (.93)

The body suddenly and violently moves down from an upright position to a horizontal one, usually onto the ground. During falling, the body usually twists and the limbs flail without pattern, but usually landing on the buttocks or hands and knees. The hands often move ahead or in front of the head when falling forward. Involuntary or voluntary falls occur, and the latter sometimes consists of actively "throwing" the body toward another individual.

Involuntary falling occurs frequently during the mastery of upright postures in human infancy, but it is unclear when voluntary falling begins to occur. Falling is part of human "rough-and-tumble" play, and groups of nursery-age children incorporate it into repetitive "games," particularly if there is something soft to land on (Blurton Jones, 1967). During group wrestling, children often fall onto each other, or follow repetitive jumping with exaggerated falls accompanied by vocalizations. During dramatic play (e.g., soldier games) falling is a response to being "shot" and is often followed by "playing dead."

Among nonhuman primates, falling occurs commonly in group social play where it is interspersed with locomotion and wrestling, or takes the form of "king of the castle" in gorillas (Schaller, 1963) and gray langurs (Ripley, 1967). Infant chimpanzees may drop onto their mother's backs from vegetation (van Lawick-Goodall, 1968b).

Flinch (.91)

The shoulders are flexed, the face moves partially down and back, the arms are flexed toward the shoulders, the trunk leans away. Flinching may be accompanied by Turn, Blink, or Pucker Face. (See Grant's Nos. 91 and 92: Shoulders Forward, Hunch.)

Grant (1965b) described a high intensity flight posture (Hunch) which consisted of "raising the shoulders and lower the head"; in his example of preschool children, it occurred in response to immediate aggression. The author also noted flinching in children who had been startled, particularly by social threats. Grant pointed out that adults also flinch in response to nonsocial stimuli (e.g., "shudder," "duck"). Like several facial expressions such as the Grin Face, Flinching may have evolved from the mammalian protective startle response (see description by Andrew, 1963). Lorenz (1966) noted that in human rage, the muscles along the shoulders and back contract (originally functioning as hair-erectors) and the shoulders roll in to produce a chimpanzee-like threat posture. If flinching is defensive, both conflicting motivational tendencies connected with the above behavior patterns might contribute to the resulting ritualized behavior pattern. Different durations may be important, as the startle response is reflexive, while shoulder contraction can be prolonged.

97

In chimpanzees, ducking the head (which usually involves shoulder flexion) is an alarm response to sudden stimuli, but shoulder hunching with the head bent and slightly pulled back is also included in two threatening postures: Sitting Hunch and Quadrupedal Hunch (van Lawick-Goodall, 1968b). Van Hooff (1970) found chimpanzee shrinking and flinching to be Submissive behaviors. Similar ducking to nonsocial stimuli occurs in gorillas (Schaller, 1963).

Hug (.89)

The arms are moved horizontally forward from a widespread position toward each other and around an object, thereby encircling it. During the movement the arms are partially flexed, and the hands and fingers are extended. The movement is usually directed toward another individual's trunk in a peer-peer interaction, or toward an adult's upper leg, if both are standing. When held in an adult's arms, the child tends to hug the adult's neck. Hugging may be directed toward inanimate objects, for example, furniture, large toy animals.

The initial arm spreading (extension) is an intention movement having intrinsic signal value when directed to another individual or chimpanzee (see Reynolds & Reynolds, 1965). If the other is some distance away, the performer pauses while approach ensues. Bowlby (1958) considered that the hugging intention movement acts as a social releaser from infant to adult, activating a response to pick up the baby.

Hugging is a nonagonistic behavior pattern. Older children often exhibit it toward young children in "mothering-like" interactions immediately before lifting them up in the arms. (The hugging hands may be locked in a mutual grasp lending extra support.) Actor-reactor orientation may be ventral-dorsal, ventral-lateral, or most commonly ventral-ventral. Mutual hugging occurs, either when one individual responds to another or when two hug simultaneously, for example, following mutual approach of mother and child.

Hugging also occurs in quasiagonistic encounters, where, by encircling both the other's trunk *and* arms, he is rendered helpless ("bear-hug"). The preferred actor-reactor orientation seems to be ventral-dorsal, presumably because the actor is less vulnerable to counter-resistance.

Hugging is a crucial early behavior pattern in primate maternal-infant behavior, appearing in the infant as early as three minutes postpartum and soon after in the mother (Tinklepaugh & Hartman, 1932). During infant development, hugging is an important component of growing attachment, for example, rhesus mother and infant normally sleep in a ventral-ventral, mutual hugging position, and clinging has a "stress-reducing" effect (Mason, 1964). Sex differences in infant hugging have been found; infant male langurs engage in mutual hugging with adult males while female infants do not (Jay, 1965). In human infancy, a comparable exchange of hugging exists between mother and baby, which usually persists throughout the individual's lifetime.

Hugging or embracing is also an important adult afectional pattern, possibly a generalization from the mother-infant interaction (see Kummer, 1967). Mutual hugging is frequent in chimpanzee social play where it is described as the practising of adult behavior patterns (Reynolds and Reynolds, 1965). Van Hooff (1970) found both clinging and embracing by adult chimpanzees to be Affinitive behaviors. Finally, in Nilgiri langurs, it occurs as a direct result of a threat sequence, where it functions "to soothe either one or both participants" (Poirier, 1970).

Jump (.88)

The legs and feet are rapidly extended, launching the body into the air so that it lands approximately upright with both feet together and with partial leg and feet flexion. The arms are usually held out from the body.

Blurton Jones (1967) described this behavior as a specific signal indicating friendly "rough-and-tumble play" in nursery school children; it occurred significantly often with Laugh, Run, Open Beat, and Wrestle. This author recorded similar behavior, and group jumping appeared in rapid bursts and repetitive sequences (e.g., walk-climb-jump-fall-stand-walk...). Children sometimes jumped onto their play partners in mass pile-ups. The three- to five-year-old children observed by the author demonstrated well-developed jumping ability, in contrast in Gutteridge's (1939) low success figures for this age group. The goal of rapid jumping bursts often seemed to be loud noise production from the foot-soles striking the ground. Height of jumps attempted increased with age, as did its incorporation into dramatic play, for example, jumping into "water," "parachute" jumping, etc.

Social play jumping begins at 4–6 months in baboons (K. R. L. Hall & DeVore, 1965), and similar play-jumping occurs in rhesus monkeys (Southwick, Beg, & Siddiqi, 1965), common langurs (Jay, 1965), and gray langurs (Ripley, 1967). Ripley provided detailed descriptions of langur play jumping as related to physical surroundings, ontogeny, and "games."

Jumping is also ritualized for communication in nonhuman primates. Ripley related the "display jump" to vegetative types, supporting structures, and socialization. Nilgiri langurs show a similar display (Poirier, 1970). Jumping from branch to branch is a chimpanzee display occurring during group excitement which may indicate threat (Reynolds & Reynolds, 1965).

Jumping is also used agonistically. It is included in the chimpanzee's "stomp" attack in which the attacker lands forcibly on the victim's back (Wilson & Wilson, 1968). "Stomp" jumping is performed by males and preceded by hair-pulling (van Lawick-Goodall, 1968b). In gray langurs, jumping is important in arboreal chase and flight (Ripley, 1967).

Lean Back (.68)

The trunk is extended at the hips so that the head and shoulders move backward. It results in the trunk being moved from a flexed forward position to upright or on to maximal flexion with the trunk tilting backward. It is usually oriented away from another person. (See Grant's No. 95: Lean Back.)

Leaning back is common in social encounters, and it seems to indicate intention to withdraw from interaction. Aggressed-against children exhibited it as an immediate reaction to aggression (often combined with Chin In). It was conspicuously absent in aggression but occurred with many defensive behavior patterns (e.g., Forearm Raise). It seemed to indicate termination of friendly interactions or surprise at sudden behavior by another, for example, an unexpected ourburst of laughter. Nonsocial leaning back occurs commonly, for example, in sitting down, after reaching forward to pick up an object.

In Scheflen's (1964) study of psychotherapy sessions, the therapist's leaning back signalled "clinical inactivity" which elicited the patient's free associations. Using figures in drawings, Machotka (1965) recorded leaning back ("receiving") as a primary definitive characteristic, and subjects rated "receiving" figure drawings as "cold, impassive, and unaggressive," among other things. Grant's (1965b) behavioral element, Evade ("head and forebody movement away from the other person"), may be an equivalent pattern.

Leaning back is the terminal component of rhesus monkey threat behavior (Hinde & Rowell, 1962) where it probably represents a flight intention movement.

Lean Forward (.89)

The upright trunk is flexed at the hips so that the head and shoulders are moved forward. It is usually directed toward another individual. (See Grant's Nos. 76 and 94: Lean on Hand, Lean Forward.)

Leaning forward occurs commonly in social encounters, and when directed toward another individual seems to indicate an intention to interact which may be aggressive or friendly. Aggressive children displayed it during threat (often combined with Face Trust) and incorporated it into attacking behavior patterns. It was conspicuously absent in defensive behavior patterns, although other simultaneously exhibited patterns such as Low Frown were exhibited either aggressively or defensively. Friendly leaning forward seemed to facilitate communication, for example, to allow easier verbal exchange during noise, and it was also incorporated into certain nonagonistic behavior patterns, for example, kissing. Leaning forward is also directed away from others, for example, in response to attack from behind. Leaning forward also occurs commonly in nonsocial situations, for example, reaching toward an object.

Grant (1968) recorded leaning forward in adult interviews and classified it in the "Relaxed" group of behaviors that frequently led to "Assertion." Leaning forward by the psychotherapist toward the patient signals the beginning of active interaction (Scheflen, 1964). Machotka (1965) used drawings of figures to show that leaning forward ("advancing") was an important variable in subjects' judgements of drawings along various emotional dimensions.

Leaning forward is the initial component of rhesus monkey threat behavior (Hinde & Rowell, 1962) where it probably represents an attack intention movement. The mountain gorilla's aggressive "forward lunge of body" incorporates leaning forward (Schaller, 1963).

Physical Contact

This category includes any amorphous, unstereotyped, unstructured tactile contact between children. It ranges from finger-tip touching to standing surrounded by jostling peers in a line.

Physical contact is more common among children than adults (at least among Britains and North Americans), and E. T. Hall (1966) noted that such contact-avoidance is culturally acquired. Jourard (1966) empirically examined inter-individual contact by defining 22 body zones and considering their "accessibility" to various classes of people. Physical contact between nursery children occurred when passing each other in crowded locomotion, grouping around a person or object, or engaging in group static activity. Such contacts usually went unnoticed or evoked only passing glances. Children seemed to seek physical contact in other situations, for example, children hearing a story sat in contact although the available space was abundant. Frank (1957) noted that in intense emotional situations, tactile contact with another sympathetic person may aid recovery of "physiological equilibrium." Scheflen (1963) described regulatory physical contact's use in a therapist-patient relationship. Children during their first nursery day sought to maintain physical contact with their mothers. This behaviors recalls Bowlby's (1958) discussion of Primary Object Clinging theory: "there is in infants an in-built need to be in touch with and to cling to a human being."

Harlow (1959, 1970) stressed contact comfort's importance in infant rhesus development, and he conducted empirical investigations of the variables involved: food, warmth, motion, clinging surface. Later workers made quantitative records of nonhuman primate mother-infant physical contact from birth onwards (Hinde, Rowell, & Spencer-Booth, 1964; Hinde & Spencer-Booth, 1967; Rowell, Din, & Omar, 1968). Seeking of "reassurance contact" occurs when wild chimpanzees are afraid, agitated, or intensely stimulated (van Lawick-Goodall, 1968b). Van Hooff's (1970) analysis classified chimpanzee touching as Affinitive behavior. The dominant male's "placing the hand" on a subordinate common langur signifies the interaction's end (Jay, 1965).

Because of its extreme variability, physical contacts were not tested by inter-observer comparisons.

101

Quick Hop (.75)

The legs and feet are rapidly extended in alternation, repeatedly launching the body into the air so that it lands approximately upright on alternating feet. The landing involves minimal leg and foot flexion. The hopping is rapidly repeated in bursts, sometimes being almost indistinguishable from fast high-stepping. The arms may be flailed up and down out of synchrony with the leg extensions, or alternately raised and lowered simultaneously with the same-side leg.

Children exhibited quick hopping during periods of "excitement," often in anticipation. For example, children quick-hopped while lining up to look out of the playroom window at falling snowflakes. It also occurred in "rough-and-tumble" play sequences during pauses, for example, when the chaser was due to appear around a corner. Before children fled from a "monster," quick-hopping was common. When children "acted silly" or "showed off," quick hopping was often combined with peculiar vocalizations. It seemed to function socially as an indicator of a highly "aroused" state, perhaps in play invitation.

Similar behavior may occur during chimpanzee group excitement when individuals rapidly stamp, drum, shake branches, etc., producing a noisy uproar, but motor details of this display are not described. It occurs when groups meet, split, move, or prepare to move, and acts as a source of social attraction (Reynolds & Reynolds, 1965). Van Lawick-Goodall (1968b) attributed this behavior to frustration (an explanation compatible with the Reynolds' observations). Quick hopping also resembles nonhuman primate play invitation movements, for example, the patas monkey's "bouncing on the same spot, quickly from hands to feet to hands. . ." (K. R. L. Hall, 1965).

Rock (.80)

The trunk is moved backward and forward (hips extension and flexion) or sideways (hip adduction and abduction) with repetitive, rhythmic movement. The trunk is approximately upright in sitting or standing postures. (See Grant's Nos. 60, 99, 100: Head Rock, Rock, Side Rock.)

Normal preschool children rock after losing conflicts with peers (Blurton Jones, 1967), as do individuals appearing "nervous" or "uncertain," for example, during introduction into the nursery school. Rocking seems most common when a child is sitting still and not socially interacting. Stereotypic rocking occurs in mental defectives (Berkson & Davenport, 1962) and autistic children (C. Hutt & S. J. Hutt, 1965). In the latter, it increases with environmental complexity and probably indicates high "arousal." Adult schizophrenics display rocking in ambivalent situations where it appears to represent alternating intention movements (Grant, 1965b). Children's rocking could represent "regression" in an attempt to emulate the comforting maternal rocking of infancy.

Harlow (1959) included rocking in his "fear indices" in studies of infant rhesus monkeys. Its occurrence increased dramatically in strange, frightening situations. Stereotyped rocking frequently occurs in captive primates raised in isolation, and it increases when the animals are upset, possibly to mitigate emotional stress (Mason, 1964). Wild chimpanzees exhibit similar rocking when "frustrated" or "uneasy" (van Lawick-Goodall, 1968b).

Shoulder Hug (.80)

The partially flexed arm is draped on and around another child's shoulders. The hand usually rests on the other child's far shoulder and may grasp it lightly. The actor's upright body is oriented similarly to the reactor's, usually side-by-side. During arm flexion, the two children may tilt their heads toward each other, and the actor may press against the other's neck with the flexing forearm to facilitate this.

Shoulder hugging occurs in nonagonistic social interactions, often by older to younger children and by siblings. The actor often verbalizes while the two children walk together. In this context, it may function as contact comfort, stimulated by the reactor's prior indications of distress, for example, accidental fall, or loss of toy. It also occurs in dramatic or "rough-and-tumble" contact play. This shoulder hugging is more likely to occur among age-peers and to be of shorter duration. It seems to be a sign of mutual affection and/or a means of directing another child's attention or movements. Adults commonly perform shoulder hugging toward children, and posters and illustrations use it to signify friendship and guidance (e.g., Scouting advertisements). It is also a preliminary boy-to-girl stage of the Western adolescent courtship ritual.

One-arm embracing occurs in several chimpanzee social situations: reassurance from dominant to subordinate, reassurance contact between any individuals, greeting behavior (van Lawick-Goodall, 1968b). Mason (1964) hypothesized that it is derived from mother-infant interaction, in which the infantile hugging response has generalized to other social situations and partners.

Shrug (.90)

The shoulders are quickly flexed and extended in rapid succession. The body is upright and often in locomotion. The pattern is incorporated into flinching. (See Grant's No. 90: Shrug.)

Shrugging rarely occurs in preschool children and its significance is unknown, but it seems to occur in non-stressful situations. It occurs as a stereotypy, however, in autistic children, and apparently functions to reduce high "arousal" levels (C. Hutt & S. J. Hutt, 1965). The adult behavior pattern is socially communicative, often occurring with raised eyebrows, and has several meanings: "Don't ask me!", "It's all the same to me!", or "Who knows?". Grant

(1968) used Shrug as an element in describing adults' behavior in interviews, but the results were unclear: in students it was associated with Flight elements; in neurotic patients it was associated with Assertive elements.

Shrugging has not been described in nonhuman primates, but "twitching of shoulders" occurs in young baboons during maternal separation and as a sign of insecurity (K. R. L. Hall & DeVore, 1965).

Stretch (.75)

The trunk, limbs, and head are maximally extended, either in isolation or combinations. The resulting postures may be prolonged and appear distorted.

Children rarely stretched during nursery school, probably because they were almost continuously active, and stretching seems to occur after periods of inactivity or cramped confinement. Children did appear to imitate adult stretching, for example, in imaginative play, they would yawn and stretch after "sleeping" in the Wendy House bed.

Nonhuman primate stretching is rarely discussed as other than a body maintenance activity. Mountain gorillas stretch upon arising in the morning similarly to man (Schaller, 1963).

Turn (.91)

The trunk is partially rotated, usually in a single, continuous motion. When seated, the child's shoulders are rotated although the buttocks may remain unmoved. While standing, the child's shoulders, and buttocks, and (usually) feet are rotated. In social turning, the ventral side is usually oriented with reference to another child. (See Grant's No. 52: Evade.)

Turning to another child occurs during many types of agonistic interactions: a threatening individual often turns to face the opponent; in defensive behavior, the aggressed-against individual often turns to face the aggressor; or the aggressed-against individual may combine turning toward the aggressor with a flight pattern (e.g., Back). Turning away from another child also occurs in agonistic interactions: a fearful individual often turns away (combined with Flinch, or Forearm Raise); after repulsing a foe or rendering him unwilling to retaliate, an aggressor may turn away, effectively terminating the interaction. Turning is a common nonagonistic social pattern for reorienting the body to another child.

Turning usually occurs simultaneously with looking, and the two seem to function similarly, that is, in orienting the primary human communicative systems (visual, auditory) for maximally efficient sending and receiving. Some indication exists that turning is more "intense" than looking, for example, looking orients only the face with its expressive components, but turning orients the body in readiness for action as well. A facial expression transmitting a threatening intention is not the same as a bodily movement allowing immediate attack. Also, a frontal view displays an individual's size more impressively than a side view. In fearful behavior, similar functions exist: looking away (a head movement) may indicate submission, but the body is still in position to resist. Turning the body away removes the possibility of immediate resistance, as well as making the turning individual less threatening by exposing the back of the head and neck. This turning may function as appeasement. Turning also occurs in social situations where communication is apparently not intended, for example, a child watching a fight may turn away if the combatants approach, although they are unaware of his presence.

Turning and looking away may also function to shut off overly-arousing stimuli from the visual receptors; Chance (1962) called these "cut-off postures." Autistic children apparently turn away more frequently under high group density conditions (C. Hutt & Vaizey, 1966). Adults at a party may indicate unwillingness to interact by turning to talk to other people (Argyle & Kendon, 1967). Grant's (1965b) behavioral element, Evade ("head and forebody movement away from the other person") may be equivalent to Turn Away.

"Presenting" or turning the rump toward another is a submissive posture common to many nonhuman primates (see Altmann, 1962; K. R. L. Hall, 1962; Jay, 1965; van Lawick-Goodall, 1968b). Although variable, many such patterns resemble quadrupedal versions of human turning away, and sometimes (see Jay, 1968, p. 344) the area oriented to the aggressor is the back more than the buttocks. Turning three-quarters away and looking back over the shoulder (plus other factors) is a rhesus monkey aggressive behavior pattern (Hinde & Rowell, 1962). After an ambivalent rhesus threat, continuation of a backward head jerk may lead to the threatener's turning away.

Wrestle (.80)

The behavior pattern is difficult to define because of its complex combination of motor patterns and extreme variability. In general, wrestling is gross body movement by two or more children while grappled in physical contact. More specifically, behavior patterns such as Push, Pull, Fall, Lean, and Body Oppose may be incorporated into wrestling bouts. Each individual apparently tries to "control" the other, that is, limit the other's movements, move the other's body, or keep the other on the bottom while remaining atop him.

Blurton Jones (1967) described wrestling as a rough-and-tumble play pattern and found that it occurred significantly in conjunction with Laugh, Run, Jump, and Open Beat. The author also observed it in genuine agonistic interactions, for example, two children struggling over a desirable position on a large box. Wrestling seemed more common in conflicts over large than small toys. Groups of children exhibited quasiagonistic wrestling; sometimes two or more "ganged up" on a single individual, and they tended to roll in a tangled mass on the floor. Such wrestling was often accompanied by pants, grunts, and other expirations of exertion which agonistic wrestling lacked.

Wrestling is a common behavior pattern seen in social play throughout the primate order: bush baby (Lowther, 1940); howler monkey (Carpenter, 1965); white-faced monkey (Oppenheimer, 1969); rhesus macaque (Southwick, Beg, & Siddiqi, 1965); bonnet macaque (Simonds, 1965); common langur (Jay, 1965); gray langur (Ripley, 1967); Nilgiri langur (Poirier, 1970); patas monkey (K. R. L. Hall, 1965); baboon (S. L. Washburn & DeVore, 1961); gibbon (Carpenter, 1940); gorilla (Schaller, 1963); chimpanzee (van Lawick-Goodall, 1968a).

Agonistic wrestling occurs less frequently. In chimpanzees and baboons, it occurs with biting (Wilson & Wilson, 1968; K. R. L. Hall & DeVore, 1965); patas monkeys show "attempts at grappling" during agonistic interactions (K. R. L. Hall, 1965). Gorilla wrestling was the "most intensive" aggressive response but never resulted in injury (Schaller, 1963).

Locomotion

Locomotion consists of gross body movements propelling the body from point to point in space. Definitions of specific locomotory patterns may seem obvious, but they are presented in the interests of careful description.

Locomotion, per se, is not social behavior in the same sense as Smile or Forearm Raise. But relative frequencies of different locomotory patterns are related to amount of social experience (see Chapter 7). Certain locomotory patterns are important components of social behavior constellations, for example, running as part of "rough-and-tumble" play (Blurton Jones, 1967). Some locomotory patterns, for example, Chase, and Flee, are social behavior items of equal status with Smile or Forearm Raise.

The mean overall inter-observer reliability coefficient for locomotory behavior patterns was .83 (S.D. = ± .10), and the overall mean number of recorded instances per behavior pattern used in computation of coefficients was 32.1 (S.D. = ± 20.9).

Back, Back Step (.93, .75)

The body moves bipedally backward at a moderate rate, alternating legs during each stride, so that one foot is placed firmly on the ground before lifting the other. The trunk may be upright or tilted backward. Back Step is one unit of Back. The leg is moved backward once, placed on the ground, and part of the body weight is shifted onto it.

Backing enters the child's repertoire by 18 months (Gesell, 1940). It is relatively less common than walking, and backing bouts are of short duration. It has been largely ignored by developmental psychologists, although it seems to be an important fearful behavior pattern. It is elicited by an opponent's aggression that is insufficient to precipitate fleeing. Backing has advantages over walking away in this situation, viz., the backing child can "keep his eyes" on the aggressor and need not turn his back, thereby leaving himself vulnerable. Back Step also occurs commonly in agonistic situations, apparently functioning as a defensive pattern. It moves an aggressed-against individual sufficient distance to recover or to initiate retaliation, but not out of range of further attack (and therefore becoming, by definition, fearful). Back Step often functions in regaining balance, for example, immediately after receiving a heavy blow.

Backing by nonhuman primates is rarely mentioned. Hinde and Rowell (1962) described a compound category called "Backing Threat" in rhesus monkeys which seemed to function similarly to some backing by children; they also mentioned that backing was used by subordinate individuals to approach superiors. In the Bristol Zoo rhesus colony, the most subordinate female continually walked backwards around the periphery, anxiously watching other animals (Virgo & Waterhouse, 1969).

Chase (.77)

The child runs with sudden direction changes and veering, frequent speed changes, arms flailing, quick head-orienting movements. It is always directed to others, and the reactor usually flees simultaneously from the chaser. The trunk usually tilts forward. (See Grant's Nos. 108 and 109: Chase, Follow.)

Young children chase in agonistic and quasiagonistic social contexts. The latter occurs more frequently, and Blurton Jones (1967) included it only among "rough-and-tumble play" patterns, but a child may also "seriously" pursue another who has just snatched his toy. The author could not distinguish between agonistic and quasiagonistic chasing from motor patterns alone, but the latter bouts seemed much longer. Agonistic chases are usually diadic but nonagonistic chases involve several individuals. Behavior patterns accompanying Chase, for example, vocalizations and facial expressions, *do* differ, and the fleeing individual monitors his pursuer's mood by glancing over the shoulder. During a bout, agonistic chasing usually changes to nonagonistic chasing and not vice versa. Role reversals between pursuer and pursued occur frequently in nonagonistic interactions.

Most nonhuman primate species chase in both agonistic and nonagonistic social situations. Agonistic chasing usually culminates in physical conflict or threat. Chimpanzee facial expressions during aggressive chasing resemble those during attack (Wilson & Wilson, 1968). Aggressive chasing is probably equivalent to the baboon's "attacking run" (K. R. L. Hall & DeVore, 1965) and the chimpanzee's "bipedal arm waving and running at" (van Lawick-Goodall,

1968b); both occur in situations where simultaneous fleeing by the reactor is absent.

Chasing is an essential element of quasiagonistic social interactions, for example "approach-withdrawal" and "mixed" play in rhesus macaques (Hansen, 1966). It usually culminates in non-injurious physical contact. It is probably derived from agonistic chasing, and Loizos (1967) described the differences between the two in chimpanzees, based on a variety of cues: facial expressions, vocalization, and head and gross body movements. Southwick (1967) found differentiation more difficult in rhesus monkeys, as he did not use the movements themselves but interpretations of them. Arboreal play chases by gray langurs follow particular conventionalized routes (Ripley, 1967). Young animals characteristically display playful chasing, which apparently contributes to the socialization process.

Crawl (1.00)

The body moves quadrupedally, usually forward, with the ventral surface off the ground. Various combinations of the limbs may touch the ground: palms, forearms, knees and toes, soles.

Crawling is the first locomotory pattern displayed by human infants (at about 32 weeks), but by 12–18 months walking replaces it (Gesell, 1940). Nursery children exhibit it nonsocially only in certain situations: for getting under low-hanging obstacles or into small openings, for moving on high or unsteady surfaces. It appears socially in extreme fearful situations as a form of crouching flight; this may appear "regressive." Imaginative play may involve crawling, for example, imitation of a lion, horse, frog.

Nonhuman primate locomotion is generally quadrupedal. Gorillas exhibit the same limb sequence as dogs and human infants (Schaller, 1963). Locomotion away from mother begins by the eighth to tenth day in young macaques (Tinklepaugh & Hartman, 1932). The social situation is important in locomotor development: group-reared rhesus infants appear to develop locomotor skills earlier than those reared in isolation with their mothers (Hinde & Spencer-Booth, 1967). In arboreal species, for example, gibbons, quadrupedal locomotion may be more efficient than brachiation in moving long distances through the forest (Ellefson, 1968). "Creeping" occurs in chimpanzees when aggressed-against individuals leave the aggressor (van Lawick-Goodall, 1968b).

Flee

The child runs with sudden direction changes, veering, frequent speed changes, arms flailing, quick glances over the shoulders. It is usually oriented to others, often occurring simultaneously with another's chasing. The trunk is usually tilted forward. (See Grant's Nos. 106 and 107: Retreat, Flee.)

Like chasing, fleeing occurs in agonistic and quasiagonistic social inter- actions. The two behavior patterns have much in common: Blurton Jones (1967) included both in the constellation of "rough-and-tumble play" behavior pat- terns. Agonistic fleeing may change to quasiagonistic, and the movements involved appear indistinguishable: other simultaneously occurring behavior pat- terns seem necessary for differentiation. The fleeing individual probably indi- cates his motivational state through vocalizations (laugh or high, shrill scream) and facial expressions (which are visible to the pursuer when the fleeing child glances back). Fleeing also occurs without being chased, for example, in response to non-locomotory threat or attack. The loser of a fight over a stationary object may flee while the winner remains in possession of the object.

All nonhuman primates exhibit fleeing, both in response to predators and to conspecifics. In agonistic interactions, it is a response to aggression or to a situation likely to become aggressive. Such fleeing has been categorized as "sub- mission" (Southwick, 1967; Wilson & Wilson, 1968), "escape-fear" (K. R. L. Hall & DeVore, 1965), "flight" (Sade, 1967), and "subordination" (Poirier, 1970).

Quasiagonistic fleeing occurs in social play groups, and it is sometimes difficult to distinguish between running with other individuals and from them. It often occurs simultaneously with chasing, preceded by an "invitation" display to another individual, for example, "inviting play" in the patas monkey (K. R. L. Hall, 1965). Quasiagonistic fleeing is apparently derived from agonistic fleeing (Loizos, 1967). In gray langur play chases, the fleeing individual may institute a "conventionalized pause" by jumping from the ground to a low branch (Rip- ley, 1967).

Gallop (.78)

The body moves rapidly forward, alternating legs during each stride, so that both feet are momentarily off the ground during each stride; in contrast to running, the intervals between consecutive foot-ground contacts differ. The result is an irregular, rhythmic quality. The trunk is upright or tilted forward.

Galloping is uncommon in children, apparently being interchangeable with (and less efficient than) running. Disagreement exists in the literature about its maturation. Cratty (1964) stated that "galloping is usually not seen in three- year-olds but is engaged in proficiently by four- and five-year-olds." But Gesell (1940) states that it is usually developed by 30 months. Since neither defined the behavior pattern, the contradiction cannot be resolved. In the groups the author observed, galloping seemed equally frequent in three- and four-year-olds. Social galloping was completely absent in agonistic interactions (due to its inefficiency?). It seemed to occur most commonly solitarily.

Quadrupedal galloping during social play occurs in young gorillas (Schaller, 1963), and rhesus monkeys (Hinde & Spencer-Booth, 1967). Patas monkey

109

galloping is part of the "play bounce": the animals jump against springy vegetation and catapult off again between bouts of galloping (K. R. L. Hall, 1965). Loizos's (1967) description of "a slow lolloping pace" in chimpanzee play interactions probably referred to galloping, as van Hooff (1970) also showed galloping to be primarily a chimpanzee Play behavior.

March

The body moves bipedally forward at a moderate rate, alternating legs each stride, so that one foot is placed firmly on the ground before lifting the other; the stride is even and short; heel and toe contact the ground simultaneously (cf. the walking sequence of heel, then toe); both legs and arms are raised higher than in walking. The trunk is upright. The net effect is a brisk, stereotyped, and slightly exaggerated manner. Marching in place also occurs.

Marching is relatively rare in nursery children. Children exhibiting it were usually in groups, often engaged in imaginative play. It never occurred in agonistic encounters. Marching seemed to be engaged in for "its own sake," that is, it did not seem to function as approach or avoidance relative to other individuals.

Marching has been recorded in nonhuman primates, but it is unclear from accounts whether this referred to a motor pattern or to the spacing and speed of the moving group. For example, Anthoney (1969) described baboon troop marching in the Chicago Zoo. Certain characteristics of marching, for example, exaggeration and repetition, resemble those Loizos (1967) described for play behavior evolved from patterns functioning in other motivational contexts.

March occurred too infrequently for reliability testing.

Miscellaneous Locomotion

This category includes extremely uncommon or atypical locomotory behavior patterns, for example, locomotion which need not involve any muscular movement (sliding down an inclined plane). Children may "scoot" in locomotion with their buttocks, bellies, or back in continuous contact with the floor while propelling themselves by leg flexion and extension. Children may "tiptoe hop" while upright with only ankle flexion and extension providing propulsion. They may also dance, roll, twirl, somersault, "swim," "leapfrog," etc.

Nonhuman primates display a variety of bipedal, tripedal, and quadrupedal locomotory patterns not mentioned in other categories. The variety is enriched by their wide range of habitats, for example, arboreal as well as terrestrial, and, in the New World monkeys, by a fifth locomotor appendage: the tail.

Because no specific behavior pattern exists for this category, interobserver reliability testing was not performed.

Run (.94)

The body moves rapidly forward, alternating legs during each stride, so that both feet are momentarily off the ground during each stride. The trunk is upright or tilted forward. Running movements may occur in play, that is, without locomotion, and these grade into Quick Hop.

Social running functions as approach or avoidance oriented to other individuals. It is a component of rough-and-tumble play, occurring significantly often in combination with Laugh, Jump, Wrestle, and Open Beat. Boys run and laugh more than girls (Blurton Jones, 1967). (Blurton Jones used running as an overall category including chasing and fleeing.) Frequency of running increased with nursery social experience, although children run skillfully long before nursery entry (beginning at about 21 months: Gesell, 1940).

Nonhuman primate running is mainly quadrupedal but may be bipedal. Compound "attack" patterns often include running (K. R. L. Hall & DeVore, 1965; Hinde & Rowell, 1962; van Lawick-Goodall, 1968b), and these workers did not differentiate it from nonagonistic running. Running also occurs in "threat" display (Wilson & Wilson, 1968). Running is also an important play element (see examples in Loizos, 1967). Running's form may be adapted to special habitat conditions: gorilla running in dense vegetation (Schaller, 1963), gray langur running in different types of trees (Ripley, 1967).

Sidle, Sidle Step (.73, .75)

The body moves laterally at a moderate rate by alternating leg movements, two per stride. One foot is place firmly to the side before lifting the other foot to be placed nearer it. The trunk is upright or tilted to the side. Sidle step is one unit of Sidle. The leg is moved laterally once, placed onto the ground, and part of the body weight is shifted onto it.

Sidling enters a child's motor repertoire by 18 months (Gesell, 1940). It is relatively uncommon and rarely consists of more than two or three strides. It is often used to move around an object, or between two closely positioned objects. Social sidling is a surreptitious way of moving away from or toward a frightening individual. Sidling away often precedes being attacked, apparently in response to threatening cues. Children also sidle from agonistic situations that may potentially involve them, e.g., two individuals fighting nearby. An aggressed-against child who apparently wants to continue playing nearby may sidle; e.g., after losing his shovel to another, he may sidle along the sand trough and continue sand play. Sidle Step seems to be low "intensity" sidling. Sidling and backing have similar advantages over walking: the sidling child can visually monitor nearby action without directly facing it (which might be threatening), and he remains ready to adopt easily defensive actions, for example, Forearm Raise.

Sidling has been rarely noted in nonhuman primates. When a subordinate rhesus macaque approaches a superior "it often edges toward it sideways" (Hinde & Rowell, 1962).

Skip (.78)

The body moves forward, alternating legs during each stride, by placing one foot on the ground and hopping slightly on it before shifting the body weight onto the other foot to repeat the same movement. It is essentially a syncopated combination of hopping and walking/running, and rhythmic arm-swinging increases proportionally to increased rate of progression.

According to Cratty (1964), children's skipping follows galloping onto-genetically and appears relatively late: at approximately 5½ to 6 years. Children observed by the author exhibited it much earlier: fairly often in the fourth year but commonly by the fifth birthday. Though often performed solitarily, skipping in groups also occurred in protracted bouts. Social skipping contrasted with locomotory patterns always appearing solitarily, for example, Sidle.

Skipping has not been recorded in nonhuman primates, probably because it is a skilled bipedal movement.

Walk, Step (.94, .75)

The body moves bipedally forward at a moderate rate, alternating legs during each stride so that one foot is place firmly on the ground before the other leaves the ground. The trunk is upright, and the arms swing forward and backward in unison with the opposite legs. A Step is one unit of Walk. The leg is moved forward once, placed on the ground, and part of the body weight is shifted onto it. The other leg may be brought forward and placed beside the other.

Walking is the most common locomotory pattern of nursery children; by nursery entry at three, children have been walking for almost two years (Hindley, Filliozat, Klackenberg, Nicolet-Meisler, & Sand, 1966). Its expressive significance is well-known: observers' judgements of walking as an indicator of "dominance-feeling" in adult women were accurate at above chance levels (Eisenberg & Reichline, 1939).

Nonhuman primates usually walk quadrupedally. Although capable of bipedal walking, they are morphologically unadapted for it, and for some species, for example, mountain gorilla, bipedal locomotion would probably be selectively disadvantageous (Schaller, 1963). Frisch (1968) indicated that Japanese monkey bipedal walking increased due to "cultural" influences, that is, as a by-product of inventive food-washing habits which increased bipedal walking while carrying foodstuffs. [Hewes's (1964) views on hominid evolution stress the importance of food carrying and concomitant bipedal locomotion.] Walking style is related to social status in baboons (K. R. L. Hall & DeVore, 1965) and Nilgiri langurs (Poirier, 1970) and differs recognizably according to age and sex in gray langurs (Rigley, 1967).

Chapter 5

Social Organization of the Nursery Group

Introduction

The significance of social behavior can only be fully understood in the context of ongoing social interaction, and this necessarily requires a group. In this study, the groups consisted of daily assembled three- and four-year-old children. Most interactions involved smaller subgroupings and not the entire group, but all interactions took place with reference to it. Group members, differentiated along age, sex, social experience, height, weight, and home background lines, constituted an array of possible playmates, and engagement between them was nonrandom. Subsequent chapters will deal with more specific problems in social behavior, but this chapter attempts to present a general picture of the social interaction and the social structure in which it occurs.

Theoretically, a social interaction may be defined as the performance by two or more children of behavior patterns which mutually influence each other's behavior. However, ascription of *influence* to a motor pattern involves an inference by the observer, so social interaction must also be defined operationally: the performance by two or more children of specifically defined, relatively fixed-form motor patterns while in close spatial and temporal proximity. (Many motor patterns performed by children in close proximity may, upon further analysis, turn out to be socially insignificant, e.g., chewing gum, but these cannot be excluded a priori.) These motor patterns occur in consistent and recognizable combinations and sequences.

When possible, comparisons with nonhuman primate social behavior are included, as many similarities exist between the nursery school group in Western society and the infant play grouping in nonhuman primate troops. Both constitute groups of young primates experiencing initial age-peer contact. Although of mixed sex composition, both types of groups include same-sex subgroupings displaying different behavior types, for example, rough-and-tumble play primarily by males. Like nonhuman primate play groups, the Slade and Epworth Halls nursery groups spend the majority of time in free social play. In both cases this is monitored and sometimes interfered with by adult females of the species, either the nonhuman primate mothers and relations or the nursery nurses. Some young nonhuman primates even use the same area daily for social play, for example, the "arena" of young free-living patas monkeys, *Erythrocebus patas* (K. R. L. Hall, 1965). In both cases play group members spend part of the day together and the rest with parents, siblings, and other individuals engaged with them in eating, sleeping, traveling, etc. This is not to say that the nursery school and the nonhuman primate play group are completely equivalent, nor that findings from one are transferable to the other, but from an evolutionary viewpoint the nursery school is not so culturally unique and "artificial" as might first be supposed.

Number of Participants

Most interactions were *diadic* (i.e., involved only two children) as far as could be determined, and this was true for both agonistic-quasiagonistic (81%) and nonagonistic (91%) interactions. The remaining interactions were *triadic* (i.e., involved three children) except for a minor fraction (1.3%) which involved four or more children. The triadic interactions often appeared to consist of two children acting in concert against one, but many occurred within large, loosely-organized groups which numbered as many as eight children.

The number of children participating was not related to sex composition of the interacting group, to presence of objects in the interaction, or to the overall distribution of types of interaction endings (see definitions previously given in Chapter 2). However, larger groups were more likely to engage in "rough-and-tumble" interaction; considering only agonistic-quasiagonistic interactions, diadic encounters were significantly less likely to have *other*-endings than encounters involving three or more children (see Fig. 5.1, $\chi^2 = 5.08$, $df = 1$, $p < .025$). *Other*-ending interactions included considerable locomotion which resulted in children moving off-camera during an interaction. Quasiagonistic ("rough-and-tumble") interaction is characterized by much locomotion while genuinely agonistic interaction is not (Blurton Jones, 1967).

Schaller (1963) noted that 81% of social play interactions among mountain gorilla infants were diadic. Wild rhesus monkey infant play groups usually number two or three individuals (Southwick, Beg, & Siddiqi, 1965). Over 75% of social play interactions among young zoo-living crab-eating macaques are diadic; triadic interactions are fairly common, and interactions involving four or more are rare (Fady, 1969).

Durations

The mean elapsed time of all recorded interactions (excluding *other*-ending interactions which could not be accurately timed) was 12.9 seconds (agonistic-quasiagonistic: 12.7 sec; nonagonistic: 13.1 sec). Elapsed times were also examined by grouping observations into seven categories: 0 to 5, 5 to 10, 10 to 15, 15 to 20, 20 to 25, 25 to 30, and 30+ seconds (see Fig. 5.2). Both agonistic-quasiagonistic and nonagonistic interactions showed medians of 10 to 15 seconds and modes of 5 to 10 seconds. Mean number of behavior patterns exhibited per interaction, a possible measure of time involved, did not differ between the two types (agonistic-quasiagonistic: $\bar{x} = 25.4$; nonagonistic: $\bar{x} = 22.4$). No duration differences existed between diadic and triadic (or more) interactions or between male-male and male-female interactions. So, duration does not appear to be an important factor in differentiating types of children's social interactions, at least in terms of the factors covered here.

		Interaction Ending	
		Other	Not-other
Number of participants in male-male interactions	2	27	142
	3+	13	26

Fig. 5.1. Number of participants in a social interaction as related to the interaction's ending, Slade Nursery School, Oxford.

115

Duration of play interactions between young crab-eating macaques rarely exceeds 10 seconds (Fady, 1969).

Sex Differences

Males constituted 70% of the observed group of children. They participated in 96% of the observed interactions, which did not differ from chance for either diadic (92%) or triadic (98%) interactions. However, all-male interactions occurred significantly ($\chi^2 = 148.4$, $df = 1$, $p < .001$) more often than chance expectancy; the actual frequency of occurrence almost doubled the expected frequency of occurrence in diadic and triadic, agonistic-quasiagonistic and nonagonistic interactions.

Much evidence exists which links an interaction's nature with the sexes of its participants: all-male interactions tended to be agonistic or quasiagonistic in

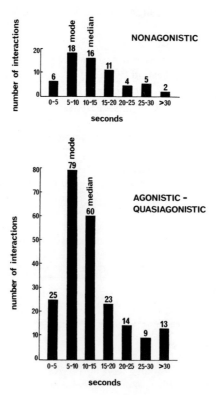

Fig. 5.2. Distributions of duration of children's interactions in Slade Nursery School, Oxford: nonagonistic (top) and agonistic-quasiagonistic (bottom).

nature, mixed-sex interactions were "genuinely" agonistic, and all-female inter-actions were usually nonagonistic. For example, considering diads, female-female interactions were significantly most often nonagonistic (χ^2 = 15.38, df = 2, $p < .001$). Mixed-sex interactions ended in separation of the participants more often than all other endings combined, and this was statistically significant (χ^2 = 19.79, df = 3, $p < .001$).

Sex differences in nonsexual behavior exist in many young primates. Young male crab-eating macaques initiate rough-and-tumble play more often than females, who prefer less violent play, for example, approach-withdrawal play (Fady, 1969). In the rhesus macaque, infant males initiate more social play than females (Hinde & Spencer-Booth, 1967), and play initiated by males is more often rough-and-tumble than that initiated by females (Harlow & Harlow, 1965). In studies of children, teachers usually rate boys as more aggressive than girls (Garai & Scheinfeld, 1968), and Thompson (1967) reported that the most intense fights of preschool children always involve boys.

Objects

Thirty-one percent of the interactions observed involved an inanimate object (i.e., the object, usually a toy, was either touched by both interacting children or was the focus of their attention). No differences in the frequency of object involvement existed between agonistic-quasiagonistic and nonagonistic interactions. This was somewhat surprising as Blurton Jones (1967) reported of nursery school children that "...fights occur over property and little else." Perhaps the object category used here did not include all "property" situations, for example, quarrels over "spaces" such as position in a line.

However, other differences in object involvement existed between agon-istic-quasiagonistic and nonagonistic interactions. When objects were involved, the mean number of physical contacts per interaction was over six times greater in the agonistic-quasiagonistic interactions than in the nonagonistic ones (ratio of 6.75:1). When objects were not involved, the amount of physical contact was not significantly different in these interaction types (ratio of 1.25:1).

Among *separate-*, *continuous-*, and *other*-ending interactions, almost all those involving objects were agonistic-quasiagonistic in nature; *together*-ending interactions were just as likely to be nonagonistic as agonistic-quasiagonistic (see Fig. 5.3). The difference is statistically significant (χ^2 = 13.66, df = 3, $p < .01$) and restated, this seems to indicate that in interactions where children remain together, they are often able to use (share?) a toy without conflict, whereas other types of interaction involving toys are characterized by quarrels. Direc-tionality of winning/losing (i.e., likelihood of winning over those lower in a hierarchy and losing to those higher) was similar in those agonistic-quasiagonistic interactions involving objects and those not involving objects.

117

| | Interaction Ending | | | | |
	Together	Separate	Continuous	Other	
Agonistic / Quasiagonistic	7	33	28	10	78
Nonagonistic	7	4	3	1	15

Fig. 5.3. Social interactions involving objects (toys): type of interaction as related to its ending, Slade Nursery School, Oxford.

Adults' Gradings of Children

Ratings of the children's *aggressiveness, activity,* and *sociability* were obtained from all 10 adults working in the Slade Nursery. Also, seven complete sets of rankings of aggressiveness and activity, and six complete sets of rankings of sociability were obtained. (The remaining sets of obtained rankings were discarded due to incompleteness.) The rankings were tested using the Kendall coefficient of concordance (Siegel, 1956), and agreement was significantly higher than chance in all cases: aggressiveness ($W = .57$, $p < .001$), activity ($W = .57$, $p < .001$), sociability ($W = .36$, $p < .001$). This implies that the adults applied significantly similar standards in their rankings of the children.

The composite results from the three types of ratings and the three types of rankings correlated significantly with each other, as measured by the Spearman rank correlation test (Siegel, 1956). The correlations between aggressiveness and activity were particularly high (see Table 5.1). Correlations between ratings and rankings of the same characteristic were the highest found. However, the meaning of the correlations across characteristics is unclear, since the same adults graded the same children. Either (for example) children who behaved aggressively were also likely to be active, or the adults used similar criteria in assessing these characteristics, or both. It is likely that a genuine "connection" existed, as the adults denied having consciously used similar criteria, and later results from behavioral data confirmed at least some of the correlations found. Only rankings will be used in the further analysis, as these contained fewer ties and were amenable to concordance testing.

The subjects' rankings were examined in relation to five other independent variables: age, height, weight, time at school, and I.Q. (Table 5.2). Activity ranking was significantly correlated with weight and time spent in the nursery school. The physically robust children might be expected to have a greater range of activities open to them, and this, added to greater familiarity from longer school experience, might account for greater activity being related to these two

TABLE 5.1   *Adults' Rankings and Ratings of Preschool Children: Intercorrelations between Agressiveness, Activity, and Sociability, Slade Nursery School, Oxford*[a]

	Agg. Ranking	Act. Ranking	Soc. Ranking	Agg. Rating	Act. Rating	Soc. Rating
Aggressiveness ranking	. . .	.86****[b]	.52***	.93****	.81****	.50***
Activity ranking	. . .	. . .	.42**	.85****	.97****	.45**
Sociability ranking	. . .	. . .	. . .	.48***	.43**	.92****
Aggressiveness rating	. . .	. . .	. . .	. . .	.80****	.40*
Activity rating	. . .	. . .	. . .	. . .	. . .	.40*
Sociability rating	. . .	. . .	. . .	. . .	. . .	. . .

[a] Spearman rank correlation coefficient (r_s), df = 28.

[b] * = $p < .05$; ** = $p < .02$; *** = $p < .01$; **** = $p < .001$.

variables. Sociability ranking was significantly correlated with I.Q. score, confirming earlier findings by Parten (1933). The correlation between heavier children and greater aggressiveness ranking approached statistical significance. Social class was unrelated to any of the adults' three ranking scales.

All inter-correlations between age, height, weight, and time at school were statistically significant, as the latter three variables are all age-dependent (see Table 5.3). The non-age-dependent variable, I.Q., was not significantly correlated with any of the four, and nonsignificant negative correlations existed with age and time at school, since three "retarded" children had been kept on at school past their fifth birthdays. Children of upper-middle class backgrounds (II and III, $N=18$) scored higher on I.Q. tests than children of lower class backgrounds (IV and V, $N=10$): Mann Whitney U test, $z = 1.68$, $p = .0465$. Age, height, weight, and time at school did not vary with social class background.

The main reason for obtaining the adults' gradings of the children was to compare their subjective impressions with objective empirical results. For example, two objective measures of a child's "sociability" are the number of social interactions in which he participates and the number of social behavior items he directs to other children during such interactions. (The two measures are highly inter-correlated: $r_s = .975$, $df = 26$, $p < .001$.) To examine this, the author computed Spearman rank correlation coefficients which compared three ranking scales (aggressiveness, activity, and sociability) with three types of interaction totals (agonistic-quasiagonistic, nonagonistic, and total interactions). Tables 5.4 and 5.5 give the results. Both measures showed all interaction types to be significantly correlated with aggressiveness and sociability, but correlation with activity was consistently lower. This suggests that adults' interpretations of sociability are accurate and that they also interpret accurately the high likelihood of aggressive children being more socially inclined than timid children. It

TABLE 5.2 *Relationships between Adults' Gradings of Preschool Children and Other Variables, Slade Nursery School, Oxford[a]*

	Age (mo)	Height (in)	Weight (lbs)	Time at school (mo)	I.Q.
Aggressiveness ranking	.05	.13	.36	.15	.01
Activity ranking	.29	.21	.44**[b]	.38*	-.04
Sociability ranking	.06	-.02	.16	.05	.40*

[a] Spearman rank correlation coefficient (r_s), $df = 28$.
[b] * $= p < .05$; ** $= p < .02$.

also suggests that despite high correlation between activity and sociability rankings, the former cannot significantly predict which children actually will behave more socially.

Adults' gradings were also compared with more specific results of behavior, such as the number of physical contacts between children during agonistic-quasiagonistic social encounters with children ranked by aggressiveness (Fig. 5.4). The most and least aggressive children (from the gradings) showed the least physical contact, probably because the most aggressive found it unnecessary to use physical aggression because of their established high (and presumably feared) status, and the least aggressive avoided physical contacts. Frequency increased as the middle of the aggressiveness ranking was approached, except for a few children in the middle who exhibited few physical contacts. It is thought that these children represented an artifact of the ranking procedure, that is, those children not well-known to the adults because of their inconspicuousness (lack of prominent aggressive or fearful behavior) might have been difficult to rank and therefore got placed arbitrarily in the middle. Adults participating in the grading replied equivocally about this when questioned later. None said that they had done so purposefully but several described grading procedures that would have produced that result.

Position in the aggressiveness ranking was also related to the "directionality" of winning and losing in male diadic interactions over objects. Individual boys tended to win over those ranked below them and lose to those ranked above them; this hierarchical tendency was statistically significant ($\chi^2 = 15.42$, $df = 1$, $p < .001$). This agreement indicates either a valid relationship between aggressiveness and winning-losing of property fights, or use of this criterion by the adults in grading, or both. Number of wins did not correlate with aggressiveness ranking ($r_s = .04$), but the number of losses did ($r_s = .43$, $df = 20$, $p < .025$). This seems to indicate that sheer number of wins is less important than who wins over whom, although number of losses per se *is* important. The six most aggressively-ranked boys won a composite of 77% (33 of 43) of their quarrels over objects, while the six least aggressively-ranked boys won only 38% (14 of

TABLE 5.3 *Characteristics of Preschool Children: Inter-Correlations between Variables, Slade Nursery School, Oxford*[a]

	Age (mo)	Height (in)	Weight (lbs)	Time school (mo)	I. Q.
Age	...	.62**[b]	.52*	.88**	-.12
Height	...	...	.78**	.56*	.01
Weight	...	...	...	.48*	.13
Time in school	...	...	...	...	-.17
I. Q.	...	...	...	...	...

[a]Spearman rank correlation coefficient (r_s), $df = 28$.

[b]* $= p < .01$; ** $= p < .001$.

37) of theirs, mostly over younger part-time children, which is a statistically significant difference $(\chi^2 = 10.87, df = 1, p < .001)$.

Dominance Hierarchy

Attempts to interpret the nonrandom nature of primate interpersonal relationships according to some system of "dominance" (i.e., rank order, social hierarchy) are legion and of long standing (see, e.g., Maslow, 1936). However, for all its persistence, the concept is much misused and usually of questionable validity. Gartlan (1965) pointed out at least four separate usages of "dominance" in the literature as well as numerous contradictions arising from them. Alexander and Bowers (1969) have stated other reservations: that dominance is partially situational, that many aggressive encounters are ambiguous, that other social structures may exist independently and simultaneously. Finally, Berkson and Schusterman (1964) found a simpler explanation for the classic test of relative intra-individual dominance: acquisition of a desired food item. Using juvenile gibbons, they found that the individual finally consuming the banana prize "...was determined more by which animal had the food than by dominance relationships."

However, the questionable nature of the nonhuman empirical work has not prevented the application of the concept of dominance to human affairs (see, e.g., Tiger, 1970a). Such speculation (or "ethologizing," to use Callan's, 1970, term) is not restricted to the popularized works of Ardrey and Lorenz; Maslow, Rand, & Newman (1960) attempted to relate it to the sexual fantasies of psychiatric patients. Quantitative studies of "dominance" in human ongoing social interactions were not pursued, and this author's preliminary report (1969) of such a study seems to represent the first published attempt. More detailed and sophisticated research on the topic is now underway. (K. Krebs, personal communication).

TABLE 5.4 *Relationships between Adults' Rankings of Preschool Children and Ranked Numbers of Social Interactions Participated in by Each Child, Slade Nursery School, Oxford[a]*

	No. of agonistic and quasiagonistic interactions participated in	No. of nonagonistic interactions participated in	Total interactions participated in
Aggressiveness ranking	.49***[b]	.39*	.46**
Activity ranking	.37	.40*	.37
Sociability ranking	.58***	.57***	.58***

[a]Spearman rank correlation coefficient (r_s), $df = 28$.

[b]* = $p < .05$; ** = $p < .02$; *** = $p < .01$.

A "dominance hierarchy" was derived from diadic male agonistic-quasiagonistic encounters which involved winning and losing. Females did not participate in sufficient property fights to construct a female hierarchy. In such encounters, the winning boy gained or retained possession of an object or space, and the losing boy lost or failed to gain possession. Following Rowell (1966b), the observer first constructed an Apparent Ranking of the group's boys; this was based on his subjective impressions before behavioral results were available. This was adjusted until maximal "directionality" was achieved (as in the previous section), the result being statistically significant ($\chi^2 = 23.44$, $df = 18$, $p < .001$). This is graphically represented by the predominance of dots in the upper triangle of Fig. 5.5, while the fewer dots in the lower triangle represent exceptions to "directionality." (Random dispersal of the dots throughout the square would have indicated absence of "directionality" and hierarchy.) Thompson (1967) found significantly similar results in two smaller groups of preschool children.

The usefulness of a dominance hierarchy comes from its power to help explain a group's social behavior or from its power to provide organization to otherwise puzzling behavioral phenomena. For example, division of Fig. 5.5 into four quadrants reveals a concentration of 56% (23 of 41) interactions in the upper-left quadrant. Chance expectancy is only 25%, and this significantly disproportionate dispersal ($\chi^2 = 9.57$, $df = 2$, $p < .01$) indicates that most interactions involve the more dominant males engaging in possession struggles with each other. Jay (1965) showed similar findings for adult male langurs; males in the upper half of the hierarchy accounted among themselves for 49% (59 of 120) of the dominance interactions within the group. Thompson's (1967) data on two nursery groups showed similar trends: 43% (9 of 21) and 34% (10 of 29) of dominance interactions involved only high-ranking boys.

Fig. 5.4. Number of physical contacts between children during agonistic-quasiagonistic interactions in Slade Nursery School, Oxford. Children ranked by aggressiveness.

Dominance ranking was significantly correlated with number of wins $(r_s = .69, df = 16, p < .001)$, but not with number of losses $(r_s = .17, df = 16, p < .5)$; this is the inverse of the comparable correlations found with aggressive ranking. Similar statistically significant findings have been reported by Thompson (1967) for preschool boys, by Jay (1965) for adult male langurs, and by Tokuda and Jensen (1969) for pig-tailed macaques. This indicates that lower-ranking individuals rarely win, but that losses are not so important (presumably) as long as they are to individuals of similar ranking.

Dominance ranking was significantly correlated with all three adult gradings: aggressiveness $(r_s = .73, df = 16, p < .01)$, activity $(r_s = .66, df = 16, p < .01)$, and sociability $(r_s = .585, df = 16, p < .02)$. Thompson (1967) found that in both groups of boys he observed, the most dominant individual from his observations was also ranked highest by the nursery teacher. In the one group he tested, Thompson also found that the most dominant boy ranked first in peer-popularity, as determined from sociometric rating.

In the Slade, dominant males tended to be older ($r_s = .49$, $df = 16$, $p < .025$), heavier ($r_s = .45$, $df = 15$, $p < .05$), and more nursery-experienced ($r_s = .41$, $df = 16$, $p < .025$), but no taller ($r_s = .38$, $df = 15$, $p < .10$), or more intelligent ($r_s = .21$, $df = 16$, p = n.s.) than subordinate males. In two groups of 8 boys each, Thompson found that the most dominant boys ranked first and second in age, and second and fourth in weight. Tokuda and Jensen (1969) found high-ranking pig-tailed macaque males to be older and heavier than subordinates. In her study of leadership in a nursery group, Parten (1933) found that leaders were likely to be older, more intelligent, and more inclined toward social participation than nonleaders.

Esser (1968) found a significant correlation between *contact rank order* and *pecking order* in six- to ten-year-old, behaviorally-disordered boys in a hospital. The former was the average of three rank orders: percentage of observations containing social contacts between children, same for child-adult social contacts, and number of different children socially contacted; the latter was derived from staff rankings using "popular and respected" as criteria. Among normal three- to four-year-old boys we found comparable positive correlations between the derived dominance hierarchy and number of social interactions participated in ($r_s = .65$, $df = 17$, $p < .005$), number of social behavior items directed to other children ($r_s = .58$, $df = 16$, $p < .01$), and number of social behavior items received from other children ($r_s = .52$, $df = 16$, $p < .025$).

Blurton Jones (1967) stated that: "'dominance' says nothing useful or instructive about the social organization of the class of three- to five-year-olds I

TABLE 5.5 *Relationships between Adults' Rankings of Preschool Children and Ranked Individual Totals of Social Behavior Items Directed by Children to Others, Slade Nursery School, Oxford[a]*

	No. of items agonistic and quasiagonistic interactions	No. of items nonagonistic interactions	Total no. of items
Aggresisveness ranking	.60***[b]	.58**	.60***
Activity ranking	.34	.37	.35
Sociability ranking	.49**	.42*	.50**

[a] Spearman rank correlation coefficient (r_s), $df = 28$.

[b] * = $p < .05$; ** = $p < .01$; *** = $p < .001$.

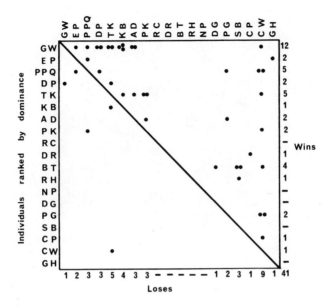

Fig. 5.5. Graphic representation of male dominance hierarchy, Slade Nursery School, Oxford. Each dot represents a diadic fight over toy possession. For a child's wins, read across; for a child's losses, read down.

observed or of the groups within it. Certainly some individuals regularly won fights but these were not all also leaders or peacekeepers or given priority access to objects." But other workers (e.g., Gellert, 1961, 1962) have found dominance-subordinance to be useful in predicting social behavioral consequences. Our findings showed the existence of a well-defined dominance structure on the basis of winning/losing of encounters in naturalistic circumstances. The directionality of those encounters which did or did not involve possession of objects seemed not to differ, although numbers were too small for statistical treatment. The former case would seem to be a subset of Blurton Jones's "priority access to objects." Whether these individuals were also those which frequently acted as "leaders" or "peacekeepers" depends on definitions of these terms, but it may have been so. Parten (1933) examined "leadership" in a nursery school group: the highest ranking individual dominated the group's activity through "brute force," but other types of leadership also occurred. Dominant individuals seemed more often responsible for decisions about changes in the group's activities and the assigning of roles within those activities.

Chance (1967) recently proposed that dominance structure in primate groups is more closely related to "attention structure" than access to desired

Fig. 5.6. An object struggle between two boys (standing) over possession of a wooden trolley. The two other boys attend closely to the interaction.

objects or outcome of competition. "Attention structure" is indicated by the orientations of individuals, which focus on the dominant animal, although Virgo and Waterhouse (1969) have shown that the focused-upon individual may vary with social context. Preliminary findings on nursery children indicate some kind of "attention structure" exists in the nursery group (Hudson, McGrew, & McGrew, 1971). Tiger (1970a) has recently attempted to apply the concept of attention structure to the analysis of human political systems.

Functional Organization of Behavior Patterns

As was discussed in Chapter 2, a behavior pattern's function(s) can be derived from its consequences. For a social behavior pattern, this derivation can be performed at varying levels of specificity: at a general level, the consequences are examined in the whole interaction. For example, Child A's excessive beating may consistently lead to his being avoided by other children. At a more specific level, the consequences may consist of the immediate behavioral response of the other interactant. Such relationships are examined in studies of causation, for example, A's performance of smiling may consistently give rise to B's response of approach. This section concerns the more general level, using behavior patterns of preschool children (Table 2.1 and Chapter 4) exhibited in three types of social interaction (defined in Chapter 2.2): agonistic, quasiagonistic, and nonagonistic. The measure used was the frequency of individual behavior patterns/unit time (the interaction). Analysis cited earlier in this chapter showed that durations of different types of interactions and numbers of behavior patterns per interaction were relatively constant. This section is an attempt to synthesize the detailed, qualitative descriptions of Chapter 4 into a simple framework.

However, these results can only be regarded as tentative, since some commonality of definitional levels exists with the general divisions of agonistic behavior given in Chapter 2. Thus, a possibility of circularity exists in saying that fleeing is classified as an agonistic-quasiagonistic behavior pattern (see Table 5.6), since separation of individuals by flight is included as part of the general definition. The majority of behavior patterns examined are not affected by this stricture, but conclusive derivation of a pattern's function must await the analysis of specific behavioral responses of interactants.

The author first compared 237 agonistic-quasiagonistic with 65 non-agonistic social interactions. (Note definitions previously given in Chapter 2.) Eighteen behaviour patterns occurred significantly more often in agonistic-quasi-agonistic interactions (Table 5.6), and seven behavior patterns occurred significantly more often in nonagonistic interactions (Table 5.7). Statistical significances were computed using the χ^2 one-sample test, $df = 1$, when possible, but the Bionomial test was needed for N's of 20 or less (Siegel, 1956).

TABLE 5.6 *Behavior Patterns Exhibited Significantly More Often in Agonistic-Quasiagonistic Interactions than in Nonagonistic Interactions, Slade Nursery School, Oxford*[a]

Behavior pattern	p
Back	<.001
Beat	= .03*[b]
Beat Up	= .02*
Body Oppose	<.01
Chase	<.001
Fall (involuntary)	<.02
Flee	<.001
Flinch	<.01
Forearm Raise	<.02
Forearm Sweep	<.025
Immobile	<.05
Laugh	= .01
Play Face	<.001
Pull	<.001
Punch	<.01
Push	<.001
Vocal	<.001
Wrestle	<.001

[a] χ^2 one-sample test, $df = 1$, when $N > 20$.
[b] * = Binomial test, when $N \leqslant 20$.

TABLE 5.7 *Behavior Patterns Exhibited Significantly More Often in Nonagonistic Interactions than in Agonistic-Quasiagonistic Interactions, Slade Nursery School, Oxford[a]*

Behavior Pattern	p
Hold Hands	$< .001$*[b]
Normal Face	$= .03$*
Physical Contact	$< .001$
Point	$< .01$
Shoulder Hug	$= .01$*
Walk	$< .02$
Verbalize (polysyllabic)	$< .001$

[a] χ^2 one-sample test, $df=1$, when $N > 20$.
[b] * = Binomial test, when $N \leqslant 20$.

Thirty-nine behavior patterns did not occur significantly more often (at the $< .05$ level) in either type of interaction (Table 5.8). However, several relatively infrequent behavior patterns showed tendencies that would probably have reached significance with higher N's. Nine such patterns occurred more frequently during agonistic-quasiagonistic interactions at the $< .10$ significance level: Back Step, Bared Teeth, Beat Open, Face Thrust, Low Frown, Mouth Open, Pucker Face, Sidle, Verbalize (negative), as did one predominately nonagonistic behavior pattern: Head Shake.

Eight behavior patterns occurred too infrequently for comparison across interactions and are not included in the tables: Hair Pull, Pinch, Rock, Run-Push, Scratch, Spit, Weep, and Yawn.

The author next compared four types of interaction endings within the 237 interactions, in an effort to differentiate agonistic from quasiagonistic behavior patterns. Similarities between the two types made the differentiation difficult (see Chapter 2), and most past investigators of children's social behavior have not separated them. The four types of interaction endings (defined in Chapter 2) and the percentage of interactions ending in them were: separate (36%), continuation (33%), together (10%), and other (21%). Separate-ending interactions were considered as genuinely agonistic, and other-ending interactions were considered as "playful" (quasiagonistic). This division was based on previous primate behavior studies: Blurton Jones (1967) differentiated children's hostile behavior from rough-and-tumble play on the basis of separation of individuals and capture of property; Loizos (1969) differentiated chimpanzees' agonistic behavior from social play on the basis of resulting dispersal or non-dispersal of interactants.

Interpretation of together- and continuation-ending interactions proved more difficult. They seemed to represent intermediates between agonistic and

TABLE 5.8 *Behavior Patterns Exhibited in Both Nonagonistic and Agonistic-Quasiagonistic Interactions (No Significant Differences), Slade Nursery School, Oxford[a]*

Behavior pattern	p
Automanipulate	$< .30$
Back Step	$< .10$
Bared Teeth	$= .09*$ [b]
Beat Open	$= .06*$
Bite	$= .23*$
Crouch	$< .30$
Digit Suck	$= .18*$
Face Thrust	$< .10$
Fall (voluntary)	$< .50$
Gaze Fixate	$< .20$
Grin Face	$= .23*$
Hands Over Head	$= .41*$
Head Shake	$= .06*$
Hug	$< .70$
Jump	$< .80$
Kick	$= .11*$
Lean	$< .20$
Locomote (miscellaneous)	$= .99$
Look	$< .80$
Low Frown	$< .10$
Mouth Open	$< .10$
Pat	$= .15*$
Pucker Face	$= .09*$
Punch Open	$= .11*$
Quick Hop	$< .40$
Reach	$< .40$
Run	$= .30$
Shrug	$= .16*$
Sidle	$< .10$
Sidle Step	$< .80$
Smile	$< .70$
Step	$< .90$
Throw	$= .32*$
Turn	$= .80$
Verbalize	
(monosyllabic)	$< .70$
(negative)	$= .09*$
(non-negative)	$= .21*$
Wide Eyes	$< .25$

[a] X^2 one-sample test, $df = 1$, when $N > 20$.

[b] $* =$ Binomial test, when $N \leqslant 20$.

TABLE 5.9 *Children's Behavior in Agonistic and Quasiagonistic Interactions. Behavior Patterns Exhibited Significantly More Often in Agonistic-Quasiagonistic Interactions with One of Four Types of Endings: Separate, Continuation, Together, and Other, Slade Nursery School, Oxford* [a]

Interaction Ending	Behavior Pattern	p
Separate	Face Thrust	$< .01$
	Flinch	$< .01$
	Point	$< .01$
	Turn	$< .05$
	Verbalize	$< .001$
Continuation	Back	$< .05$
	Body Oppose	$< .001$
	Grin Face	$= .001*$ [b]
	Hug	$< .001*$
	Pull	$< .01$
	Shrug	$= .03*$
	Verbalize (non-negative)	$= .005*$
Together	Wrestle Upright	$< .001$
Other	Chase	$< .001$
	Fall (involuntary)	$< .001$
	Fall (voluntary)	$< .01$
	Flee	$< .001$
	Jump	$< .001$
	Laugh	$< .001$
	Mouth Open	$< .001$
	Physical Contact	$< .05$
	Play Face	$< .001$
	Push	$< .001$
	Quick Hop	$< .001$
	Reach	$< .05$
	Smile	$< .001$
	Vocalize	$< .02$
	Wrestle Prone	$= .006*$

[a] X^2 one-sample test, $df = 1$, when $N > 20$.

[b]
* = Binomial test, when $N \leqslant 20$.

quasiagonistic interactions in which the participants seemed uncertain about the interaction's nature. One individual might behave aggressively while the other responded playfully (see more extensive discussion in Blurton Jones, 1967). In general, continuation-ending interactions seemed to be "more agonistic" than together-ending interactions. Statistical significances were initially figured using

TABLE 5.10 *Children's Behavior in Agonistic and Quasiagonistic Interactions. Behavior Patterns Exhibited Significantly Less Often in Agonistic-Quasiagonistic Interactions with One of Four Types of Endings: Separate, Continuation, Together, and Other, Slade Nursery School, Oxford[a]*

Interaction Ending	Behavior Pattern	p
Separate	Chase	$< .001$
	Fall (voluntary)	$< .01$
	Flee	$< .001$
	Grin Face	$= .03*$[b]
	Hug	$< .05$
	Laugh	$< .025$
	Physical Contact	$< .05$
	Play Face	$< .001$
	Smile	$< .01$
Continuation	Automanipulate	$< .01$
	Point	$< .02$
	Quick Hop	$< .01$
	Wrestle Upright	$< .01$
Together	Back	$< .05$
	Body Oppose	$< .05$
	Look	$< .02$
	Mouth Open	$< .01$
	Push	$< .01$
	Run	$< .01$
	Sidle	$< .02$
	Sidle Step	$< .02$
	Step	$= .025$
	Turn	$< .02$
	Walk	$< .001$
	Vocalize	$< .02$
Other	Face Thrust	$< .05$
	Forearm Sweep	$< .05$
	Pull	$< .05$
	Punch	$< .01$
	Verbalize	$< .001$

[a] X^2 one-sample test, $df = 1$, when $N > 20$.

[b] $* =$ Binomial test, when $N \leqslant 20$.

a χ^2 one-sample test, $df = 3$, for $N > 43$, and Kolmogorov-Smirnov one-sample test for $N \leqslant 43$ (Siegel, 1956). From these, individual endings were tested for significance using the χ^2 one-sample test, $df = 1$, and Binomial test as above. Twenty-nine behavior patterns occurred significantly more often in interactions

TABLE 5.11 *Children's Behavior in Agonistic and Quasiagonistic Social Interactions. Behavior Patterns Not Significantly Present or Absent in Agonistic-Quasiagonistic Interactions with One of Four Types of Endings: Separate, Continuation, Together, and Other, Slade Nursery School, Oxford[a]*

Behavior Pattern	p
Back Step	$< .50$
Bared Teeth	$> .20*$[b]
Beat	$< .90$
Bite	$> .20*$
Crouch	$< .30$
Digit Suck	$> .20*$
Forearm Raise	$> .20*$
Gaze Fixate	$> .20*$
Immobile	n.s.*
Kick	$> .20*$
Lean	$= .80$
Locomote (miscellaneous)	$< .10$
Low Frown	n.s.*
Normal Face	$> .20*$
Pat	$> .20*$
Pucker Face	$> .20*$
Punch Open	$> .20*$
Throw	$> .20*$
Verbalize	
(monosyllabic)	$> .20*$
(negative)	$> .20*$
(polysyllabic)	$< .30$
Wide Eyes	$< .80$

[a] χ^2 one sample test, $df = 3$, when $N > 43$.
[b] * = Kolmogorov-Smirnov one-sample test, when $N \leqslant 43$.

with one type of ending (Table 5.9). Thirty behavior patterns were significantly absent from interactions with one type of ending (Table 5.10). Finally, 22 behavior patterns were of approximately equally probable occurrence in all four types of interaction-endings (Table 5.11).

Other-ending interactions accounted for the majority of the instances of behavior patterns which occurred significantly more frequently in one type of interaction ending. They formed a coherent constellation containing expected combinations: Chase-Flee, Laugh-Smile-Play Face, Jump-Quick Hop, Fall-Wrestle Prone. Blurton Jones (1967) described 10 behavior patterns as constituents of children's rough-and-tumble play: chase, flee, wrestle, jump, open beat, object beat, laugh, fall, push, play face. Nine of the 15 behavior patterns in this study are identical with his, with only beating without contact being absent. The remaining six patterns could probably be included in Blurton Jones's behavioral categories, for example, Physical Contact and Reach may have been subsumed under his wrestling category. From this, Blurton Jones's rough-and-tumble play and our quasiagonistic behavior seem identical.

Patterns significantly absent from quasiagonistic behavior included four genuinely agonistic behavior patterns, and one predominantly nonagonistic pattern, Verbalize, which, when present in agonistic-quasiagonistic interactions, occurred significantly more often in separate-ending interactions.

As Blurton Jones (1967) has pointed out, very similar patterns of social play occur in children and nonhuman primate young. Loizos (1969) listed six behavior patterns exhibited by chimpanzees in social play which closely resembled our findings: play face, pant, chase, flee, grab, wrestle. Only one pattern from her chimpanzee social play constellation was exhibited by the children in another context: Pull in continuation-ending interactions. Bonnet and pig-tail macaque infants display similar behavior patterns during social play: jump, grab, chase, flee, wrestle, maul (Kaufman & Rosenblum, 1966).

Together-ending interactions more closely resembled nonagonistic interactions than any of the other agonistic-quasiagonistic types. Only one behavior pattern, Wrestle Upright, occurred significantly more often in this category (and it also represented the only case of an expected rough-and-tumble pattern occurring in non-other-ending interactions). Together-ending interactions did include 40% of the significant "absences," and these were drawn from both agonistic and quasiagonistic types. This conformed with expectations that together-ending interactions would be the "mildest" of the four interaction endings.

Separate- and continuation-ending interactions contained (as expected) a more diverse constellation of patterns, and the differences between the two appeared to be of degree. Face Thrust, Point, and Pull appeared aggressive, Flinch, Back, Grin Face, and Turn appeared fearful, Body Oppose appeared defensive, and other patterns were less clear. Frequent verbalization probably reflected arguments over toy possession, and walking was the most common means of separation after fighting.

Seven of the nine significant "absences" in separate-ending interactions involved patterns found significantly more often in other-ending interactions. This probably indicates a greater distinction between genuine agonistic and quasiagonistic behavior than between any other two interaction-endings. Only one (Quick Hop) of the four significant "absences" in continuation-ending interactions duplicated a behavior pattern frequent in other-ending interactions.

Four behavior patterns described by Blurton Jones (1967) as agonistic similarly occurred in agonistic contexts in this study—Back, Pull, Verbalize, Walk (from)—but most of this study's comparable patterns did not occur significantly often in any one type of interaction ending. Larger N's would probably have shown many of the behavior patterns in Table 5.11 to be agonistic in nature.

Chapter 6

Nursery Group Formation

Introduction

Compositional modification of nonhuman primate groups has formed the basis for much recent social behavioral research by primatologists. This modification may take several forms, for example, simultaneous assemblage of previously unacquainted individuals (Bernstein & Mason, 1963b), combination of existing groups (Castell, 1967), division of an established group (Morrison & Menzel, 1966), removal of key individuals (Bernstein, 1964a; Sugiyama, 1966), or introduction of outsiders into an established group (Bernstein, 1964b). During modification or immediately afterwards, the investigator records the ongoing behavior of the group members, and this may be compared with the same group's behavior during compositional stability. Comparable research with humans is apparently nonexistent, and the aim of this chapter is to present results of observations of the first type, *group formation*, in a nursery school population. (Preliminary findings have appeared elsewhere: McGrew, 1971; McGrew & McGrew, 1971.)

Before reviewing studies of nonhuman primate group formation, it is important to make a definitional distinction. Following Bernstein (1969), *troop* will be used to denote a natural primate assemblage which remains more or less constantly together. A *group* is defined as an artificial assemblage of two or more primates housed in mutual accessability. Thus, a population of chimpanzees which periodically clusters and disperses in different combinations could not be called a troop, nor could a roomful of cages containing monkeys be called a group. In such terms, the nursery school population observed here constituted a group, and a closer human approximation of the troop situation might be found by observing the infant members of a preliterate hunting and gathering culture, for example, see Konner's (1972) study of African bushmen.

It is assumed that group formation is manifested in the changes in frequency of inter-individual social behavior patterns exhibited by group members. To examine this empirically, a newly forming (or re-forming) group is required. Also required are behavior measures suitable for the free-field situation such as those described in Chapter 4. So, when the majority of places in the Epworth Halls Nursery School in Edinburgh fell vacant simultaneously, the opportunity existed for examining changes in social behavior with nursery experience and, possibly, for studying the development of a group's social structure from its inception. As the majority of the group's children were strangers, i.e., unacquainted with each other or with the older nursery members, it was hypothesized that group formation processes similar to those found in nonhuman primates might occur (although the children were also socially "naive," i.e., not having previously participated in any large, long-term peer-groups, while most nonhuman primate studies involved socially experienced individuals). It seemed likely that the first few hours of group experience would see significant changes in the frequency and direction of certain social behavior patterns which, because of their short-term nature, could not be accounted for simply by maturation.

Nonhuman Primate Studies

Natural group formation, that is, the voluntary synthesis of several previously unacquainted individuals into a structured group, appears to be uniquely human. On the whole, wild nonhuman primates appear to be born into one troop in which they remain throughout their lives. (A few species, e.g., gibbons, establish new groups such as the mated pair, but this is a small and specialized type of grouping.) New nonhuman primate troops usually form through the splitting of larger troops (e.g., Koford, 1963; Sugiyama, 1960), or regional populations may break up and coalesce into various types of subgroupings (Crook, 1967; van Lawick-Goodall, 1968a), but in both cases, the individuals involved are previously acquainted with each other. Also, some nonhuman primate individuals may move between troops (e.g., Lindburg, 1969), but here an existing troop structure is only augmented or modified by the stranger's entry and incorporation. In no known case, do naturally-living nonhuman primate troops spring up from the assemblage of strange individuals.

However uncommon the natural phenomena, detailed examination of the social behavior involved in group formation from the first social contacts onward has been done only with nonhuman primates. These studies have primarily involved macaque species and have been done in captive, experimental conditions. (Apparently logistic inconvenience has so far discouraged workers from attempting such studies in the wild.)

Bernstein and Mason (1963b) introduced 11 rhesus monkeys into an enclosure and recorded social interactions until one hour after the last individual's entry. During that time, 82% of the recorded social interactions consisted of attack, threat, or submission. Using a few general behavior categories, they followed the group's social development over the next 75 days (Bernstein & Mason, 1963a). Status relationships established during the first hour persisted virtually unchanged over the 75-day period. In another study involving the simultaneous release of nine rhesus juveniles into a compound, aggressive behavior was frequent during the first two hours, accounting for 62% of social interactions (Bernstein & Draper, 1964).

Kawai (1960) formed a group of captive Japanese macaques (*Macaca fuscata*) which was later released into the wild. Dominance-subordinance relationships were settled almost immediately upon exposure of strange individuals to each other, but the group remained socially unstable and disintegrated after release into the wild. Several aspects of this study, both theoretical (e.g., how many strange animals are required before their introduction into a group becomes group *re*-formation and not just incorporation of individuals into an established group) and practical (e.g., the paper contains conflicting information about the dates of animal's introductions), make drawing conclusions difficult.

Vandenbergh (1967) released large numbers of rhesus macaques on an island off Puerto Rico and followed band (troop) formation among them. Because of practical difficulties, he was only able to collect long-term, census-type observations and was unable to describe social behavior patterns exhibited during early encounters. In contrast to other studies in which individuals could not leave the group because of cage-size restrictions, Vandenbergh was able to follow relatively unrestricted congregation and dispersal. He found that small groups of females formed quickly but became stable only after integration of adult males.

Bernstein (1969) also reported findings similar to those from the rhesus studies in the group formation of 16 simultaneously released pig-tailed macaques (*M. nemestrina*). Also, Hawkes (1969) recently reported a comparative study of group formation in four species of macaques: rhesus (*M. mulatta*), stump-tailed (*M. arctoides*), crab-eating (*M. fascicularis*), and bonnet (*M. radiata*). He found significant differences in the behavior exhibited by the different species, for example, agonistic behavior comprised 99% of the rhesus group's activity but only 47% of the stump-tailed group's activity; but in all cases the most commonly observed behavior during the first hour was agonistic.

Less is known about group formation in non-macaque species. Bernstein (1971) recently reported a study of compositional modification of a sooty mangabey (*Cerocebus atys*) group in which the age, sex, and numbers of both introduced and resident animals was shown to influence the nature of initial interactions, but in general the patterns closely resembled those of macaques. In a group of 12 capuchin monkeys (*Cebus albifrons*), agonistic interaction level was low during the first hour of group formation, rose to peak levels later in the first day, and decreased to minimal levels on the second day and thereafter (Bernstein, 1965). In a study of gibbon (*Hylobates lar*) group formation, 13 newcomers were added to three residents on a small island. Territorial vocalizations began immediately and only three of the introduced animals were integrated into the group; the others were rejected (Paluck, Lieff, & Esser, 1970). In contrast, chimpanzees may form compatible social groups immediately upon arrival in the laboratory, but prior acquaintance in the wild probably facilitated this (Hummer, May, & Knight, 1969).

Method and Procedure

The nursery school reopened on August 28, 1969, after a summer holiday of six weeks, and experienced returnees and inexperienced newcomers all arrived between 9:15 and 9:35 a.m. Table 6.1 gives individual information about the five nursery-experienced and eight nursery-inexperienced children. (This is not strictly in keeping with the definition given above for group formation since some participants were previously acquainted. However, these five represented a minority remnant from the previous nursery group and were outnumbered by the newcomers.) Because of the observer's unfamiliarity with the children, a white cloth patch bearing the child's initials was safety-pinned on each child's back. The observer marked standardized data-collection sheets containing 11 behavioral categories (see Table 6.2). The number of categories recorded was limited, since the group as a whole and not a single individual was being observed. Experience had shown that use of more categories in group observations resulted in incomplete and therefore biased records. As Bernstein (1970) pointed out, this leads to overestimation of dramatic events at the expense of less conspicuous behavior. The observer recorded the incidence of the behavior patterns within the group during both 45-minute free play periods each morning between August 28 and September 5, 1968. The observer scanned the room, moving when necessary to keep as many children as possible in view.

137

TABLE 6.1 *Information on Individual Children and Attendance Figures for First Seven Days of Epworth Halls Nursery School Term, August 28 to September 5, 1968*

Child	Sex	Age (months)	Time at school (months)	Attendance						
				Day 1	Day 2	Day 3	Day 4	Day 5	Day 6	Day 7
Inexperienced										
Marcia[a]	F	47	0	X	X	X	X	X	X	X
Nora	F	40	0		X	X	X	X	X	X
Ivan	M	45	0	X	X	X	X	X	X	X
Karen	F	49	0	X	X	X	X	X	X	X
Barry	M	39	0	X	X	X	X	X	X	X
Heidi	F	43	0	X	X		X			
Timmy	M	46	0	X	X	X	X	X	X	X
Evan	M	48	0	X	X	X	X	X	X	X
	4-F,4-M	$\overline{44.6}$	$\overline{0}$	7	8	7	8	7	7	7
Experienced										
Cora	F	55	12				X	X	X	X
Neville	M	56	13	X	X	X	X	X	X	X
Jack	M	59	15	X	X	X	X	X	X	X
Homer	M	56	12	X	X	X	X	X	X	X
Ophelia	F	57	14	X	X	X	X	X		
	2-F,3-M	$\overline{56.6}$	$\overline{13.2}$	4	4	4	5	5	4	4
	6-F,7-M	$\overline{49.2}$	—	$\overline{11}$	$\overline{12}$	$\overline{11}$	$\overline{13}$	$\overline{12}$	$\overline{11}$	$\overline{11}$

[a] Names are pseudonyms.

The expected attendance for the initial period was 13, but this was achieved on only one day. This was due to the late arrival of one experienced girl (Cora), the early departure of one experienced girl (Ophelia), and the erratic attendance of one inexperienced girl (Heidi). Observations were meant to continue indefinitely, but unavoidable circumstances forced the termination of observations after completion of Day 7. Three of the five experienced children (Neville, Jack, and Ophelia) unexpectedly found places in primary schools, and their parent withdrew them from the nursery. This move (which occurred on Day 8) radically altered the group's make-up, particularly as one of these children appeared to be the potential dominant male, so that comparison of days preceding the disruption with those following would be unjustifiable. Such unexpected and uncontrollable disruptions, however frustrating to the research worker, are an occupational hazard of choosing a human population in natural surroundings for observation.

TABLE 6.2 *Behavior Categories Used in Group Formation Study, Epworth Halls Nursery School, with Observer Reliability Coefficients*

1. Automanipulate
2. Beat
3. Chase
4. Digit Suck
5. Flee   See definitions in Chapter 4.
6. Immobile
7. Laugh
8. Push
9. Weep
10. Object Struggle — Attempt by two or more children to gain/retain possession of an object, usually a toy.
    Usually involves simultaneous physical contact with object, pulling and evasive body movements (.67).
11. Negative Expletive — Short, explosive verbalization in "negative imperative" form. For example, "Don't!", "Stop it!", "Shut up!" (.70).

Results

Several new children cried (i.e., exhibited Weep, Pucker and Red Face, Vocalization) when separated from their mothers, although this lasted only briefly in all but one case: Marcia cried intermittently throughout the first day. None of the returning nursery-experienced children cried. However, most of this crying occurred while other children were still arriving and before observations began, and little weeping was recorded during the observation period.

The nursery-inexperienced children were easily recognizable. They acted subdued and inhibited, for example, locomotion commonly consisted of slow walking, and jumping and skipping were rare. Verbalizations and loud vocalizations were infrequent. Inexperienced children seemed nervous and anxious, for example, they glanced frequently to other children and adults, manipulated toys only superficially and briefly while switching rapidly from one toy to another. They appeared to spend considerably more time monitoring the adults' activities than did the experienced children. This consisted of initiating more interactions with adults and spending more time in close proximity to them. They allowed themselves to be directed by the experienced children and generally followed their orders without protest.

The nursery-experienced children seemed to readjust quickly to the nursery school situation after their absence of six weeks. They were considerably noisier in their play and were more active in small groups. They demonstrated considerably more skill in using the nursery toys, particularly those involving

139

communal effort, for example, instituting dramatic play at being families in the Wendy House (and often including the inexperienced children in minor roles).

The quantitative results showed that *Object Struggles* gradually increased in frequency over the first seven days of nursery school attendance (Fig. 6.1a). The increase was statistically significant, as tested by the Kolmogorov-Smirnov one-sample test (Siegel, 1956): N=78, D=20, $p < .01$. Composition of object struggles (i.e., experienced-experienced, inexperienced-inexperienced, or mixed) did not differ from chance ($x^2 = 1.35$, $df = 1$, $p < .30$). No difference existed between frequencies of wins throughout the week for the experienced children (N=27, D=.14, n.s.), but inexperienced children won significantly more often as the week progressed (N=38, D=.25, $p < .05$). Twenty-seven diadic object struggles involved winning-losing between experienced and inexperienced children. Though the experienced children constituted the group's minority (38%) they won most (59%) of the mixed encounters ($x^2 = 5.66$, $df = 1$, $p < .02$). Although the newcomers claimed more of the disputed toys as the group formation period progressed, it was still dominated by the returnees.

Push also increased in frequency during the first seven days of nursery school (N=68, D=.24, $p < .01$), roughly paralleling the increase in object struggles (Fig. 6.1b). This constitutes further evidence of increasing agonistic activity over the first seven days, as the observed pushing was usually aggressive. Also, the majority of pushing occurred independently of object struggles, so that the two measures are not biased by association. Frequency of pushing by experienced and inexperienced children did not differ (see Table 6.3), but inexperienced children directed fewer pushes than chance to experienced children (Binomial test, N=34, X=4, Z=3.18, p=.007) while experienced children directed their pushes at chance expectancy ($x^2 = 0$, $df = 1$). Boys did more pushing than girls (Table 6.4).

Beat occurred too infrequently (N=25) over the seven-day period to show any reliable day-to-day trends, but the first and second 3½-day periods were

TABLE 6.3 *Comparison of Frequencies of Behavior Patterns Exhibited by Nursery-Experienced and -Inexperienced Children During the First Seven Days of Nursery Term (x^2 One-Sample Test, df=1)*

Behavior pattern	Experienced children ($N = 5$)	Inexperienced children ($N = 8$)	x^2	p
Push	21	34	.08	$< .80$
Beat	14	11	3.44	$< .10$
Negative Expletive	47	36	15.08	$< .001$
Digit Suck	11	65	14.36	$< .001$
Automanipulate	14	124	40.65	$< .001$
Immobile	12	63	12.99	$< .20$
Flee	11	9	1.88	$< .20$
Laugh	108	53	67.37	$< .001$

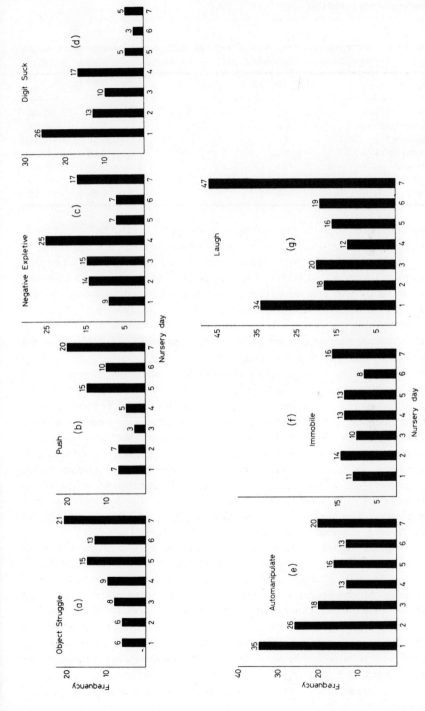

Fig. 6.1 Group frequencies of selected behavior patterns during group formation, Epworth Halls Nursery School. (Daily totals/90 min observation.)

TABLE 6.4 *Comparison of Frequencies of Behavior Patterns Exhibited by Males and Females During the First Seven Days of Nursery Term (χ^2 One-Sample Test, df=1)*

Behavior pattern	Males (N = 6)	Females (N = 4)	χ^2	p
Push	48	14	8.11	< .01
Negative Expletive	56	28	1.78	< .20
Digit Suck	13	62	56.89	< .001
Automanipulate	89	49	1.08	< .30
Immobile	42	33	.50	< .50
Flee	9	11	1.88	< .20
Laugh	101	47	4.06	< .05

compared. Beating occurred more frequently during the second half of the week (χ^2 = 5.76, df = 1, p < .02). The infrequent occurrence was not surprising, as prior observations in the Slade Nursery School had shown pushing to be four times more common than beating. Experienced children beat more often than inexperienced children, but the difference did not quite reach statistical significance (see Table 6.3). Experienced children directed all of their beats to other experienced children (Binomial test, X=0, p=.028), but the direction of inexperienced children's beating was not different from chance (X=3, p=.27). Boys did more beating than girls (Binomial test, X=4, p=.02).

The incidence of *Negative Expletive* did not follow any consistent trend during the first seven days (Fig. 6.1c; N=94, D=.10, n.s.). This was probably due to at least two factors: (1) the category proved more difficult to score than had been anticipated, as brief expletive phrases graduated into longer imperative statements; (2) many agonistic interactions proceeded without verbalization. But differences between subgroups of children existed: although experienced children were in the minority, they exhibited most of the negative expletives (Table 6.3). Experienced children directed more negative expletives to inexperienced than experienced children (χ^2 =6.22, df = 1, p < .02). but inexperienced children directed their negative expletives randomly (χ^2 = 1.28, df = 1, p < .30). No sex differences in incidence of negative expletives existed (Table 6.4).

Negative expletives were usually uttered by a child whose person or possessions were being threatened. Younger, inexperienced children seemed to use them in defense, while older, experienced children seemed to use them offensively. In the former case, negative expletives often accompanied other defensive patterns, for example, Body Opposition or Forearm Raise, but they were also often used alone, especially by females. Defensive negative expletives seemed to be delivered in a characteristic whining tone, and detailed spectrographic analysis would probably isolate this. Offensive negative expletives were more succinct, and they often accompanied threatening gestures, for example, Point, Low Frown. Here they often preceded a physical contact, taking place before the other child had acted, and seeming to function as a warning.

Fig. 6.2 The girl (1.) delivers an object beat with a wooden mallet to the back of the boy's neck.

Digit Suck decreased in frequency during the first seven days of nursery school (Fig. 6.1d; N=79, D=.26, $p < .01$). Non-nutritional sucking has been generally considered a mammalian response to distress and frustration (P. H. Wolff, 1968a), and a soothing ("de-arousing") behavior pattern (Bridger & Birns, 1968). Both functions seem appropriate to the nursery situation: presumably the children's anxiety was highest during initial exposure to the strange nursery and decreased as they became acquainted with the surroundings and the other children.

Following this reasoning, we expected that the inexperienced children would suck more, which they did: while making up 62% of the group, they performed 86% of the digit sucking (Table 6.3). The preponderance of digit sucking by nursery-inexperienced children occurred over six of the seven days (Sign test, p=.062). Newcomers exhibited all extended bouts of digit sucking, some lasting as long as several minutes. Females did seven times as much digit sucking as males (Table 6.4).

Automanipulation also decreased gradually in frequency over the seven-day period (Fig. 6.1e; N=141, D=.15, $p < .01$). Inexperienced children exhibited 90% of the automanipulation observed, significantly more than the experienced children (Table 6.3), and this excess occurred on all seven days (Sign test, p=.008). As was discussed in Chapter 4, automanipulation is a pattern common in "social stress" situations, and this fits with the explanation offered for the parallel decrease in digit sucking. No sex differences in frequency of automanipulation emerged (Table 6.4).

Frequency of *Immobile* remained relatively constant during the nursery's first seven days (Fig. 6.1f; N=85, D=.04, n.s.). This result was surprising, as it had been expected that immobility would decrease throughout the week, being a

143

Fig. 6.3 A girl displays tears and automanipulation after losing a conflict over possession of a toy.

common vertebrate fearful pattern. New, inexperienced children showed significantly more (84%) immobility than did experienced children (Table 6.3), and this preponderance occurred on six days with the seventh tied (Sign test, $p=.016$). No sex differences in frequency of immobility existed (Table 6.4).

Weep occurred infrequently ($N=7$) over the seven-day period, and no difference was found between the week's halves (Binomial test, $x=3$, $p=.50$) or between experienced and inexperienced children ($x=1$, $p=.18$). No sex differences in frequency of weeping existed (binomial test, $x = 3$, $p = .28$).

Of the quasiagonistic behavior patterns recorded, *Flee* occurred too infrequently ($N=21$) over the seven days to show any reliable day-to-day trends, and comparison of the first and second halves of the week yielded no difference ($\chi^2 = 1.19$, $df = 1$, $p < .30$). No differences were found between incidence of fleeing by experienced and inexperienced children (Table 6.3), or between the sexes (Table 6.4).

Chase also occurred infrequently ($N=12$) and was similarly tested, but no difference between the first and second half of the observation period was found ($\chi^2 = .75$, $df = 1$, $p < .40$). Experienced children did more chasing than inexperienced children (Binomial test, $x=4$, $p=.025$), and boys did more chasing than girls ($x=0$, $p=.005$).

Laugh frequencies showed a bimodal distribution over the first seven days, and this was significantly different from chance (Fig. 6.1g; $N=166$, $D=.14$, $p < .01$). Both experienced and inexperienced children exhibited this bimodality. Laughter appears to function differently in two types of situations, that is, "nervous" laughter may occur in conflict situations, and this may explain the high incidence of the first day. Also, laughter could be an indicator of relaxation, of spontaneity and lack of inhibition, which might explain its higher incidence later in the week when all children had become more comfortable in the novel social situation. Ambrose (1963) has discussed the ambivalent nature of laughter in younger children.

This explanation conforms with the occurrence of laughter in "rough-and-tumble" play (see Blurton Jones, 1967), an activity in which social experience and acquaintanceship with other participants appear necessary. Experienced children made up only 38% of the nursery group but exhibited 67% of the laughter (Table 6.3), and much of this took place during rough-and-tumble play episodes. The preponderance of laughter by experienced children was seen on all seven days (Sign test, $p=.008$). Males laughed significantly more often than females (Table 6.4).

Discussion

The nursery school children's overall social response to group formation differed significantly from that seen in groups of nonhuman primates. Almost all the nonhuman primate studies found aggressive behavior to be most frequent immediately after initial exposure of the group members to each other. Following the initial high peak, the level of aggression rapidly decreased and stabilized at a low level within a few days. The overall pattern in the Epworth Halls nursery group was almost the opposite: aggressive behavior was initially low, and it gradually increased throughout the seven-day period.

Bernstein and Mason (1963b) attributed the high level of aggression in their rhesus macaque group formation study to a "high level of arousal induced by the novel situation." It is likely that the nursery also presented a highly arousing (i.e., fearful) social situation to the children, but they seemed to react instead with nervous caution. During the first day or two they seemed to avoid potentially agonistic situations which they would later react to with resistance or counter-aggression. As the first week progressed, this restraint seemed to lessen and children gave the impression of then seeking to define limits of aggression, for example, seeing how far a quarrel could be pushed before tears resulted. This "testing" was not confined to peers, as adults' reactions were also monitored. Presumably many of the conflicts over objects were related to the novel necessity of sharing toys or taking turns. The majority of children had only one sibling, often an infant, and may have lacked such competition over desired objects at home.

It is more difficult to compare the development of fearful and "conflict" behavior during human and nonhuman group formation. Many of the nonhuman

145

primate studies used a broad category of behavior, *agonistic*, which included both aggressive and fearful behavior patterns. Also, most of the fearful behavior patterns recorded in the nonhuman primate studies were socially oriented, for example, submission, while this study used patterns which might be termed nonsocial *indicators* of fearfulness, for example, digit sucking. (Of course, this is not to say that the latter did not also have additional socially communicative function.) In general, changes in frequency of fearful-ambivalent behavior in nonhuman primate studies resembled that described for aggression: high initial frequency followed by stabilization at a lower level. In his study of pigtail macaques, Bernstein (1969) found that the decrease in submission leveled off by the end of the first day of group formation. Changes in the children's fearful behavior followed a similar pattern, although the decrease was more prolonged.

In the nursery, the decrease in children's fearfulness seemed to be a straightforward reaction to accumulated familiarity with the nursery group. Even the increasing aggression level seemed to be of manageable, secondary importance, although it may be that the behavior patterns chosen for recording were more related to the overall fear of social novelty rather than fear of specific agonistic encounters.

Two patterns prominent in rough-and-tumble play, chasing and fleeing, were consistently infrequent throughout the seven days. Only on Days 6 and 7 did reversible quasiagonistic episodes begin to appear. This finding concurs with the view that rough-and-tumble play is a highly "socialized" type of behavior, which one would not expect to find in a newly-formed group of predominantly peer-inexperienced children.

It is more difficult to conclude whether or not a "social structure" was established by the end of the seven days. This is certainly possible in nonhuman primates: wild-born, subadult geladas (*Theropithecus gelada*) formed into species characteristic one-male groups within 10 days of being released into an enclosure (Kummer, 1967). However, this is an area of dispute, for example, Menzel (1968) stated his belief that "social relations among comparative strangers might be months if not years in developing to the state seen in animals that have lived together continuously since infancy." The length of time necessary for a group of children to establish a social hierarchy of the type described in Chapter 5 or by Thompson (1967) is unknown. Both his and our studies dealt with nursery groups which had been already together for at least two months. Type of social structure (e.g., stable versus temporary, rigid versus flexible) established is probably closely tied to speed of establishment. Bernstein's (1969) finding that the inter-individual direction of agonistic responses during the first 20 minutes of group formation produced a hierarchy almost identical to that seen two weeks later ($r_s = .98$) was probably facilitated by the high agonistic level found in macaque group formation. In our study, seven days were insufficient to collect enough data on winning and losing of object struggles to construct a hierarchy.

However, if social structure is defined as *the consistent, nonrandom channeling of socially communicative behavior patterns between types of individuals in a group*, this occurred in our study. That is, although it would be possible for significant changes in the frequencies of specific behavior patterns to occur at the group level while inter-individual frequencies remained random in direction and number, instead significant patterning in inter-individual encounters emerged within the first seven days of group formation. These consisted of (at least) two types: nursery experienced-inexperienced, and male-female.

As might be expected, the older, nursery-experienced children dominated the group during formation. They were more aggressive than the younger, nursery-inexperienced children and won more than their random share of object struggles. In contrast, inexperienced children showed more fearful behavior and only began to win object struggles late in the seven-day period. Experienced children reserved the severest physically aggressive pattern, Beating, for each other, and used a threatening behavior pattern, Negative Expletive, more often toward the inexperienced newcomers. Inexperienced children directed aggressive patterns either randomly or avoided directing them toward experienced children.

Unfortunately, two variables are confounded in this comparison: age and nursery experience. The nursery-experienced children were significantly older than the nursery-inexperienced (Mann-Whitney U test, $U=0, p=.001$), so that any interpretation can only be speculative. (The uniform entrance age of three years was necessitated by other studies going on simultaneously which required long-term comparisons.) From the children's behavior, however, it seemed that the novelty of the nursery situation inhibited the inexperienced children's activities, while the experienced children took up immediately where they had left off six weeks earlier. This is supported by the fact that the experienced children exhibited significantly more laughter, a constituent of rough-and-tumble play, which requires familiarity with the social surroundings but is not restricted to either age group. Thus, it seems likely that social experience through primary contact with a large peer group was responsible more than age for the changes seen, although a control study would be necessary to confirm this.

In general, males seemed to dominate the group's activities during group formation at the expense of the females. Boys displayed more aggressive behavior (Beat, Push) and more quasiagonistic behavior patterns (Chase, Laugh) than girls. Sex differences in fearfulness were more equivocal, but the only significant difference, in Digit Sucking, showed it to be predominantly female. Sex differences in behavior during group formation have been recorded in several non-human primate studies (Bernstein & Mason, 1963b; Hawkes, 1969). The differences probably reflect the general finding that sex differences in social behavior occur in all young primates, and males are always the most aggressive. Recent studies (Goy, 1968; Hamburg & Lunde, 1966) have linked this with higher prenatal androgen levels in males. (As an aside, it is unclear how children

147

recognize a peer's sex. External appearance seems unlikely: many of the girls wore slacks or jeans, some boys wore kilts, and hair lengths overlapped. It may be that associations of sex with common first names is involved; if so, one would expect children to have more trouble identifying children with uncommon names. Identification is not always accurate: one new boy, Gary, was mistaken for, i.e., referred to as, a girl by several children during his first few days in the nursery school.)

Discussion of possible explanations for the behavioral differences between the nursery children and nonhuman primates during group formation is included in the next chapter's discussion of another modification of group composition: introduction of a strange individual into an established group.

Chapter 7

Introduction Into the Group and Social Development

Introduction

The aims of the research described in this chapter were two-fold: first, to investigate the possible occurrence of short-term changes in children's behavior immediately after introduction into an established group, and, second, to examine the behavioral details of long-term social changes in the introduced children. Like the preceding chapter, this involves another type of modification of group composition, but whereas Chapter 6 dealt with group changes, this chapter concentrates on the viewpoint of the introduced individual.

Stimulation for this chapter came from two sources: (1) traditional developmental psychology, and (2) nonhuman primate behavior studies. The first was a "negative" stimulus: it prompted the realization that behavior patterns involved in nursery school "socialization" had never been elucidated. The second type of studies have produced, in the past 10 years, considerable information about processes of group organization and individual development which appear to have important relevance to human social organization (see, e.g., Reynolds, 1968, 1970). Of course, this relevance cannot be demonstrated by superficially transferring conclusions across primate species; instead, ideas resulting from studies of one species must be used if possible as a basis for similar investigation of other species.

Nonhuman Primate Studies

The most common type of compositional modification reported in the nonhuman primate literature is the introduction of outsiders into an established group. Reports have come from various sources: observations of wild-living troops and their relations with solitary individuals (e.g., Southwick & Siddiqi, 1967); attempted experimental introduction of individuals into wild-living troops (e.g., Maxim & Buettner-Janusch, 1963); anecdotal observations of captive groups altered during other research (e.g., Wilson & Wilson, 1968); and experimental introduction or reintroduction of individuals into captive groups (e.g., Bernstein, 1964a).

Some useful distinctions can be made, for example, between *temporary* and *permanent* introductions. In studies involving the former, individuals are usually placed in the group's quarters for a brief period, then withdrawn, and the process is repeated with another individual after an interval. In the latter situation, a skeletal group is usually filled out by successive introductions. Also, *introduction* should be differentiated from *exposure*, the important factor being accessibility. Several studies have examined effects of exposure to strangers, for example, by holding up a strange monkey outside a group's cage (Ploog & MacLean, 1963), or by placing a strange individual in a box in the group's midst (Bernstein, 1966).

Experimental addition of individuals to free-living nonhuman primate troops has proved difficult. The resulting disruption may make subsequent observations impossible because of quickly-acquired, long-lasting troop wariness of humans. But, as several workers have pointed out, it is also difficult and expensive to capture and bring intact natural troops into the laboratory (for an exception, see Alexander & Bowers, 1969), and most investigators have been forced to use artificial groups in laboratory or zoo enclosures.

Using squirrel monkeys, Ploog and MacLean (1963) temporarily introduced single males into predominately male groups and recorded increased subsequent agonistic interaction. Rosenblum, Levy, and Kaufman (1968) temporarily introduced strange, adult females into two squirrel monkey groups and saw only minimal, transient disruption. Castell (1969) stressed the similarity between squirrel and rhesus monkey bisexual groups' reactions to introduced strangers: both respond with "collective aggression" as well as individual displays.

Kawai (1960) formed an initial group of six Japanese macaques, then added 39 others individually or in small groups. He noted that some dominance relationships were settled within seconds of the stranger's entry. Bernstein and Draper (1964) formed a group of 11 juvenile rhesus macaques and later introduced a strange adult male, which was treated as an intruder. Also using rhesus macaques, Bernstein (1964b) introduced variously-aged individuals of both sexes singly into an established group. He recorded the first 20 minutes of the introduction in detail and continued periodic observations for two days. Group members responded aggressively to the outsider's entry, particularly if it offered resistance. Southwick (1967) added four pairs of strangers to the rhesus macaque cage in the Calcutta Zoological Gardens. Each introduction (made only after the group's behavior had resumed baseline levels) produced large increases in agonistic behavior, sometimes as much as ten-fold.

Gartlan and Brain (1968) described the introduction of adult vervet monkeys (*Cercopithecus aethiops*) into large and small captive groups. Both groups treated newcomers agonistically although the reaction was much less severe in the large group; only young monkeys were able to successfully enter the small group. A captive group of crab-eating macaques violently resisted the introduction of two adult males, although they had been caged next to the group for three months (S. L. Washburn, 1966). Bernstein (1969) recently published the most extensive study of group modification, using pigtail macaques. He compared four types of introduction (1) individuals successively into a group, (2) individuals simultaneously to one another, (3) group to group, and (4) trio into group, and found that successive introductions of individuals produced the greatest agonistic disruption.

Less research on modification of group composition in apes has been done. Bernstein and Schusterman (1964) introduced individual gibbons into a part-time group of five juveniles. Introduction produced only temporary excitement, and aggressive behavior when present at all, increased only slowly. Another study compared individual rhesus and gibbon responses during exposure to a strange conspecific; the rhesus macaques reacted with characteristic dominance/subordinance patterns while gibbons showed friendly approach (Bernstein, Schusterman, & Sharpe, 1963). Among situations likely to lead to aggressive chimpanzee interaction, Wilson and Wilson (1968) listed the introduction or reintroduction of individuals into the colony.

None of the above studies included long-term follow-ups of the successfully introduced individuals and their "progress" in the group, but all the authors assumed that the newcomers eventually became incorporated into the group's social structure and developed stable relationships. However, Bernstein and Schusterman (1964) noted that in trying to form another gibbon group a

151

year after their original study, using animals that had been previously acquainted and then separated, the previously peaceful relations between adult male and juvenile male had soured. Apparently the juvenile had matured sufficiently to be considered an adult threat, and the older male responded to his presence agonistically.

The more general problem of the development of peer relationships in the nonhuman primate group has received considerable research attention. In the rhesus macaque alone, this has been studied in strictly controlled laboratory conditions using different combinations of peer and/or maternal deprivation (Harlow, 1969; Harlow & Harlow, 1969), in small semi-natural groups in out-door-indoor enclosures (Hinde, Rowell, & Spencer-Booth, 1964; Hinde & Spencer-Booth, 1967), and in wild-living, provisioned troops (J. H. Kaufmann, 1966). In general, these studies have stressed the importance of peer experience, particularly in social play, as essential for normal socialization and the assumption of appropriate adult roles in later life.

Most field studies have not examined the relative contributions of age and social experience to social development. In wild populations, study of the relative importance of these two variables would presumably require comparable observations of infant development in different-sized troops, assuming all other factors are equal and assuming that troop size is directly proportional to amount of social experience. The hazards of the first assumption are clear, and the second, that bigger troop size means more infants, hence more socially-experienced infants, remains to be justified. Another way of approaching the problem in the field would be to compare the social development of those infants born during the usual birth season with those exceptions born at other times. In species with such a restricted birth season, one would expect the former animals to have maximum peer experience while the latter's would be minimal.

Harlow and his co-workers have varied such factors as age, peer-experience, and maternal-experience in laboratory social development studies of rhesus monkeys. Alexander (1966, cited in Harlow & Harlow, 1969) compared the social interaction of three maternally-reared rhesus infant groups: (1) one peer-experienced from three weeks on, (2) one peer-deprived for their first four months, and (3) one peer-deprived for their first eight months. The two deprived groups showed less body contact, less affectional interchange, more agonistic responses, and were more hostile to strange monkeys than the peer-experienced animals. In all cases the 8-month deprived group was more extreme than the 4-month deprived group in differences from the controls. However, widely varying results have been obtained in similar experiments by Joslyn (1966, cited in Harlow & Harlow, 1969), and another factor, differential mothering in isolated mother-infant pairs as compared with group-living pairs, remains unassessed.

Human Studies

An important point emerging from most nonhuman primate studies is that the first few hours, even minutes, after a new individual's introduction into a group may contain important social behavioral changes. Similar processes may exist in *Homo sapiens*, especially when young children enter a large peer group for the first time. However, examination of the developmental psychology literature yields little information on this. Studies of long-term development, in terms of months or years, abound. But even a lengthy monograph such as that of Jersild and Fite (1939) omits information about dates and times of observations, particularly as these relate to a child's date and time of entry into the nursery. Initial social contacts have been largely ignored in studies of preschool children.

An exception to this is R. W. Washburn's (1932) attempt at grading children's reactions in new social situations. She recorded a child's behavior during its first 15 minutes in a nursery group, using three categories (each for five minutes: number of attentional shifts and social contacts, amount of activity, and amount of vocalization). The children observed ranged in age from 18 months to 4½ years old and were of varying social experience: 11 children had attended a nursery school for eight months. These children's behavior on their first day in the nursery school and their first day in Washburn's nursery group were compared.

The older long-term studies of social development were reviewed by Jersild and Fite (1939), who observed 18 children in the autumn and following spring of a nursery year. Later studies have followed the same vein, usually examining selected aspects of long-term social experience. In a series of studies, nursery children were examined at four consecutive ten-day intervals; relationships were found between sociometric score, teacher judgement of friendship, and observations of free play (McCandless & Marshall, 1957a). Stott and Ball (1957) used cross-sectional samples of children from under 3 to over 12 years old in studying the development of ascendance-submission in social interaction. Emmerich (1964) examined 34 social behavior categories in 38 children over four terms of nursery school. One of the few studies to separate age and length of time in nursery was that of Raph, Thomas, Chess, and Korn (1968) who observed social interaction in 97 three- to five-year-olds.

All these studies agree with the general conclusions reached by Jersild and Fite in 1939: "It appears that nursery school experience aids in the development of 'positive' personality traits, promotes social skills, prepares the child to adjust somewhat more effectively to future group situations which he may be called upon to meet [p. 10]."

But although 30 years have elapsed, the detailed study of the behavior patterns involved in this development remains largely undone. What are the overt

153

behavioral correlates of the "positive personality traits"? What are the vocalizations, facial expressions, gestures, postures and locomotion which constitute the "social skills"? How does the preparation for adjustment take place on a day-to-day interactional basis in the nursery?

The cited studies used general, inferential, or undefined behavioral categories which cannot be used to answer these questions. For example, R. W. Washburn (1932) recorded "activity," which she defined as motion of the trunk or limbs; such a category is objectively defined but is too general to be socially useful. Emmerich (1964) used 34 behavior categories, but his items, for example, "maintain and enhance own status" are too inferential to be accurately replicable. Finally, Raph, Thomas, Chess, & Korn (1968) used a seven-category system, for example, "negative behavior" defined as "interactions in which the S's behavior was predominantly negative, destructive, argumentative, and the like." This behavior classification may provide useful general knowledge about the children's sociability, but it cannot be used in seeking to understand the development and inter-relationships of detailed behavior patterns.

Methods and Procedures

The study was conducted in the Epworth Halls Nursery School described in Chapter 3.

Twenty-nine children (15 girls, 14 boys) between three and five years old participated in the study. Group size varied between 13 and 19 as introductions of new individuals were made. Individual information is given in Tables 7.1 and 7.2.

Twelve children (six girls, six boys) joined the nursery group as vacancies naturally occurred. Most had just turned three years old, and only one had previous experience with large peer groups. Five of the 12 attended the nursery while older siblings were also attending. All children were behaviorally "normal," although one child, Calvin, exhibited prolonged "anxious" behavior in connection with maternal separation.

Twelve of the remaining 17 children (nine girls, eight boys) were nursery members before introductions began, and five children were introduced without systematic observation during the study, due to scheduling difficulties or observer illness. The nonobserved sub-group of 17 (Table 7.2) were older (mean age = 42 months), but of similar social experience: only three had participated in large peer groups before entry. Six of the children had younger siblings present with them in the nursery.

Newcomers were introduced singly into the established group at a minimum of seven days apart, as soon after their third birthdays as possible. Each was observed from the moment he entered the play room on his first day. These

TABLE 7.1 *Individual Information on "New" Children Observed During Introduction Into the Epworth Halls Nursery School*

Child	Sex	Age at entry (months)	No. of siblings	Siblings in nursery	Previous peer groups	Social class
Isabel[a]	F	39	2	—	—	III
Moira	F	36	1	older sister	—	II
Kathie	F	36	1	—	—	II
Hazel	F	36	1	—	—	III
Carrie	F	36	1	older brother	—	III
Teresa	F	39	1	—	—	III
Tommy	M	36	1	older sister	—	III
Ian	M	37	2	older brother	Sunday school	IV
Norman	M	49	3	younger brother	—	II
Sammy	M	36	3	older brother	—	II
Kenneth	M	36	0	—	—	—
Calvin	M	36	1	—	—	—
TOTALS	6 - F 6 - M	median = 36	median = 1	6+, 6-	1+, 11-	4 - II 5 - III 1 - IV

[a]Names are pseudonyms.

observations lasted an average of 82 minutes per day over the child's first five mornings in the nursery. Only one mother (Calvin's) stayed longer than ten minutes with her child; she remained for half the morning on his second day in the nursery, and recording was suspended during that period.

The observer wrote in longhand an abbreviated, running account of the incoming child's behavior, emphasizing social interactions and using the glossary of behavior patterns given in Chapter 4. Every time a pattern appeared, it was scored once, regardless of its elapsed time, and scores given in the tables represent mean daily number of these bouts per child. The behavior of group members toward the newcomer was noted when possible. Only patterns of sufficiently frequent occurrence were analyzed quantitatively, and qualitative impressions are given for others.

Children who had been observed at introduction were reobserved for five mornings approximately 65 nursery days later. The follow-up observation series was done by the same observer under the same conditions.

Nursery Entry

A "new" child usually walked into the nursery with his mother (although Tommy, Carrie, and Ian were exceptions who entered with older siblings). The

155

TABLE 7.2 *Individual Information on Group Members of the Epworth Halls Nursery School*

Child	Sex	Age at entry (months)	No. of siblings	Siblings in nursery	Previous peer groups	Social class
Karen	F	49	1	—	—	IV
Heidi	F	43	1	Moira	—	II
Marcia	F	47	1	Edward	Sunday school	II
Nora	F	40	3	—	—	II
Cora	F	40	1	Tommy	—	III
Ellen	F	36	1	—	—	I
Kristine	F	36	0	—	—	—
Gladys	F	56	1	—	—	I
Bertha	F	36	1	—	—	—
Evan	M	48	2	—	—	I
Ivan	M	45	2	Ian	Sunday school	IV
Barry	M	39	1	—	—	—
Timmy	M	46	1	—	—	III
Oliver	M	42	2	—	—	III
Homer	M	40	1	Carrie	—	III
Gary	M	36	1	—	—	III
Edward	M	37	1	Marcia	Sunday school	II
9-F, 8-M		mean = 42.1	median = 1	6+, 11-	3+, 14-	3 - I
						4 - II
						5 - III
						2 - IV

^aNames are pseudonyms.

child usually walked with short, slow steps, held his mother's hand with one hand, and either carried a snack in the other or sucked his thumb or fingers. After being greeted by the nursery nurse and handing his snack to her, the child often clung to his mother, leaned away from the nursery nurse, and avoided her gaze.

The mother then usually stooped beside her child to caress and verbally encourage him. Several mothers took their children in hand and walked about the play room pointing out toys and handing them to the children. Sometimes the nursery nurse did this while the mother looked on. As soon as the child was involved in some play activity or was interacting with the nursery nurse, the mother usually said good-bye and left quietly. A mother's failure to take leave properly initiated the worst disruption seen on a child's first day: Teresa's mother sneaked away while her daughter's attention was diverted, but within seconds Teresa glanced toward her mother's former location. A few seconds of

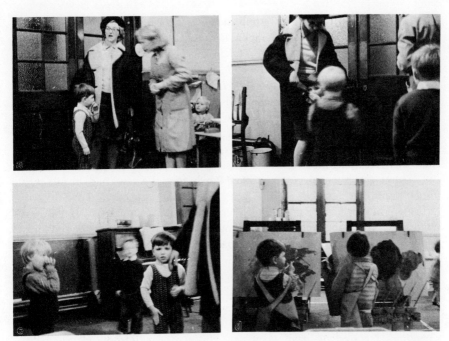

Fig. 7.1. A nursery-inexperienced child's first day in the Epworth Halls Nursery School. a. The nursery nurse (right) meets FV and his mother at the play room door. b. At the approach of two nursery members, FV retreats into contact with his mother. c. As FV and his mother tour the nursery, other children follow. d. Later, while painting, FV glances at the child beside him.

agitated searching followed, and then Teresa ran from the play room screaming for her mother.

New children's reactions at entry varied greatly. Four of 16 cried when their mothers said goodbye or soon after they left, and two had to be restrained by the nurse from running after them. However, other new children quickly entered into play activities and ignored their mothers, who usually left within two or three minutes of arrival. One new boy, Edward, "walked" on his knees into the nursery with a friend, both singing the "Diddy men" song, on his first morning. His mother didn't bother to enter the playroom. Children with older siblings also attending the nursery seemed less upset with the mother's departure, as did some children who knew nursery members from outside the nursery. The numbers of such children were too small to warrant conclusions, however, and other children, for example, Kathy, who knew none of the nursery children prior to entry, behaved similarly.

The reaction of nursery group members to a newcomer's entry ranged from neutrality to nonagonistic approach; no aggressive responses were seen. Children paid considerable attention to the morning's arrivals between 9:15 and 9:30, and sometimes spontaneously congregated at the play room door to greet arriving children. This insured that a new face was obvious. Upon initially noticing a new child, a group member visually fixated him; the visual inspection ranged from a brief glance (e.g., by a seated child engaged in manipulative activity) to staring while immobile (e.g., by standing children unengaged in activity). The observing child's facial expression usually remained neutral, but some slight frowning (not "low frown," see Blurton Jones, 1967) occurred.

Some group members then walked slowly toward a new child, maintaining visual inspection focused on his face. The visual inspection did not seem "hostile," and aggressive behavior patterns did not accompany it. If the new child were interacting with the nursery nurse, they often glanced back and forth between the two. Although they approached within touching distance, group members usually avoided touching a new child at this point; instead they sidled around him and leaned sideways keeping his face in view. A few group members exhibited patterns resembling those of the newcomers, for example, automanipulation, step, silence. This sometimes involved a "regression": at nursery entry Heidi had shown the peculiar pattern of sucking her two middle fingers, and this sometimes recurred on days when new children were introduced. Similarly, Marcia, an older, "well-adjusted" girl rarely thumb-sucked except when newcomers entered, and the pattern was identical to that exhibited at her entry 18 months before.

A new child with an older sibling already attending the nursery experienced a different entry. Some older siblings took charge from the first moment in the play room: they verbally announced the stranger as their brother or sister; they physically directed the new child's movements by holding his hand or walking with an arm on his shoulders. After instructing the new child to give his snack, toy, etc. to the nursery nurse, the older sibling sometimes steered him directly into a play activity. This could mean that he was not as readily available for inspection as an unaccompanied child, who might hang about or follow the nursery nurse for a few minutes before becoming involved in a play activity.

First Day in the Nursery

The nursery nurse often spent the first few minutes with a child after his mother left. Crying lasted only briefly, and she wiped the child's eyes before introducing him to a play activity, usually the toy zoo or a table toy, for example, jigsaw puzzle, bead-stringing. Non-crying children generally went directly into play activities or exploration of the room. In either case, the child was left on his own within five or ten minutes. Thereafter, the nursery nurse checked on him throughout the morning, especially if he appeared to be wandering aimlessly or remained immobile and inactive. She sometimes introduced a newcomer to other children at a table, but this was not stressed (as children were not given any special instructions about newcomers), and the stranger was usually left to meet group members on his own. In general, the nursery nurse's behavior allowed the new child freedom to explore and encounter the others, with intervention only if he seemed "lost" or excessively troubled.

In response to attention from the group members and the nursery nurse, the new child seemed inhibited and shy. All incoming children displayed much automanipulation and all but one showed periods of immobility during the first minutes. Four of 15 sucked or mouthed objects or digits and one child rocked briefly. Other conspicuous behavior patterns were chewing or rolling the lips and repeatedly shrugging the shoulders. In response to eye contact, the new child glanced or looked away and usually down, and sometimes this amounted to a permanent "Chin In." The "Slope" posture was common, as were sidling locomotion and shuffling. The ratio of backing and walking to back-step and step was less than normal, giving the effect of hesitant locomotion. Running was infrequent, and three of 13 new children did no running on the first day.

New children spent much time in "passive" exploration, e.g., sitting or standing in one location and slowly surveying the room. They also intently observed children engaged in play activities but entered into few themselves. A few children remained most of the first morning at the toy first given them by the teacher. Engagement in new activities was usually superficial and brief, but older siblings aided new children considerably by giving instruction on a toy's workings. Newcomers usually avoided gross, boisterous activities and often sought out quiet locations, for example, the book corner or the empty Wendy House, which they vacated if group members approached. They usually declined requests such as "You pick up that big block!" and invitations such as "Do you want to be the baby?" by moving silently away.

Newcomers exhibited few agonistic and quasiagonistic behavior patterns. Usually their actions were the antithesis of aggressive: arms kept down and close to the trunk, face and eyes averted, movements slow, silent. They appeared to avoid competitive (e.g., lining up for the slide) and potentially quarrelsome situations (e.g., several children active at one toy). If he had unwittingly blundered, for example, by picking toy parts being used by another child, the new child usually gave way. However, exceptions to this occurred, apparently because of the stranger's ignorance of "status" and "protocol," for example, on her first day Ellen contested Timmy, an older experienced male, over the slide and won.

The newcomers' amount of verbalization varied. Most were conspicuously silent at first or spoke softly; they answered many questions with nonverbal head nods and shakes. None yelled or squealed as was common during quasiagonistic bouts, nor did they make loud, nonvocal noises even when children around them were producing a din. Again, a child with an older sibling present behaved more "normally" and verbalized more; most of it was directed to the sibling and did not generalize immediately to unknown group members. Three new children (Hazel, Moira, Carrie) exhibited the opposite extreme: they verbalized excessively on the first day, and their verbalization decreased during the second through fifth days. This "nervous" garrulousness was directed equally to adults and other children, and its content was not concentrated on maternal absence or complaints.

Sex differences emerged on the first day in those behavior patterns quantitatively analyzed (see Table 7.3). In general, the six boys observed were more fearful and inhibited than the six girls. They showed significantly fewer instances of five behavior patterns: *laughing, walking,* total *looking,* child-oriented *looking,* and other *looking.* Nonsignificant differences in other behavior categories, for example, immobility, smiling, running, reinforced this conclusion.

Interactions between the group members and the new child continued largely nonagonistically during the first day. After initial inspection, some children ceased to pay the newcomer special attention, although they might look

TABLE 7.3 *Sex Differences in Mean Frequencies/Child of Behavior Patterns Exhibited on the First Day in the Epworth Halls Nursery School*

Behavior Pattern	Males (N=6)	Females (N=6)	p[a]
Automanipulate	12.7	13.8	n. s.
Glance	65.3	52.7	n. s.
Immobile	15.3	12.8	n. s.
Laugh	1.5	4.8	.052
Lean (to child)	3.5	2.8	n. s.
Look (total)	36.7	56.2	.047
Adult-oriented	8.8	8.3	n. s.
Child-oriented	28.5	40.5	.017
Other	0.8	3.5	.027
Run	5.5	19.7	n. s.
Smile	12.3	19.2	n. s.
Verbalize (total)	33.8	40.7	n. s.
Adult-oriented	9.8	9.8	n. s.
Child-oriented	19.2	21.5	n. s.
Other	5.0	9.3	n. s.
Walk	41.7	79.7	.008

[a]Mann-Whitney *U* test.

at him instead of glance if he walked by later. Others initiated friendly approach: asking him questions (e.g., "What's *your* name?"), including him in play activities (e.g., "You can sit *there*"), offering explanations of nursery procedure (e.g., "The clay goes on the shelf"), or even offering toys (e.g., holding out a sand tool to a newcomer watching sand play) as described by Blurton Jones (1967). Such approaches included smiles, head tilting to the side, light touching of the newcomer's arms or trunk, and "pleasant" vocal modulation. Not all group members approached new children, some did so only tentatively and others questioned adults about newcomers instead.

Girls seemed to attend more to newcomers than boys, and several girls (especially Cora, Nora, Teresa, Marcia) displayed a remarkable degree of maternalistic attentiveness. (Nonhuman primates display similar differential attentiveness, for example, juvenile rhesus females direct over four times more positive social behavior to infants than do juvenile males. Chamove, Harlow, & Mitchell, 1967.) This included verbalizations intended to comfort, often in response to a new child's specifically-expressed fears, for example, "All the Mummies come back after milk. . . .when the bell rings" in response to Calvin's question "When's my mummy coming back?" The soothing tones (sometimes recognizably similar to their mother's inflections) were accompanied by tactile comforting: holding hands, hugging, hand on child's back, arm around shoulders, patting, kissing. These "Little Mothers," one as young as three, would smile frequently at the new child and even "joke" with him, for example, point out incongruities in a painting while laughing and glancing back and forth between it and the child's face, apparently in an effort to cheer him up. They often diligently reported a new child's difficulties to the nursery nurse.

Boys could be friendly to newcomers but most seemed indifferent. Newcomers did not often participate in predominantly-male activities on the first day, for example, building with big blocks, marching with "guns," etc., and this may account for the lack of interaction. The three male older siblings observed (Ivan, Norman, Homer) did not spend as much time with their younger newly-introduced siblings as did the female older siblings. Homer and Ivan virtually ignored them unless the younger sibling initiated the interaction, and Norman alternated between seeming "protectiveness" and "annoyance" at being followed about.

One older sibling, Cora, completely dominated her younger brother Tommy's first day. They entered the nursery holding hands, and throughout the morning's first play period she steered him from activity to activity, monopolizing his attention. This included "defending" him from the other children's advances, which she did with verbal threatening, low frowns, and pushing. The defence was especially directed to Kenneth, the new child's best friend outside the nursery, who was repeatedly repulsed. When Kenneth joined the sibling pair at a table, they would leave, often with Cora pulling Tommy away. Later in the morning she left him alone for spells but returned if he were joined by others. Tommy usually responded passively to this herding, but he joined his older sister in some threatening. This was an extreme case, but another older group member, Moira, followed her younger sibling more than vice versa on the latter's first day.

First Five Nursery Days

Conspicuous changes in the new children's behavior occurred during their first five days in the nursery. Changes in the incidence of specific behavior patterns are given in Table 7.4. Four patterns showed statistically significant decreases: *automanipulation, glancing, immobility,* and total *looking.*

Nonagonistic social interaction involving new children occurred from the first day and increased steadily between the first and fifth days for most of them. Both number of activities and number of children with whom they interacted increased while interaction with adults remained unchanged. New children expanded their play activities to include more "gross" pastimes, for example, see-saw, slide, and more social intercourse, for example, group play in the Wendy House and block corner, which had been initially avoided. The increase in number of children successively interacted with was fastest in those children previously unacquainted with nursery group members, but children initially dominated by older siblings or friends also increased their spheres of contact.

One new child, Calvin, displayed the most "anxious" behavior of any newcomer, and on his fourth day still exhibited periodic bouts of weeping, red and puckered face, sobbing, automanipulation, digit sucking, etc. He produced a seemingly constant stream of questions about his mother: Where was she?, When would she come?, etc. Yet even Calvin displayed considerable "social adjustment": on his first day he directed three times as many verbalizations to adults as to children; by the fourth day, the ratio was even. On his fourth day he entered into sustained, nonagonistic interactions with eight different children although he still seemed a trying social partner. Several children directed Calvin to the nursery nurse, a hand placed on the small of his back (see Blurton Jones, 1967).

Agonistic interaction involving a new child occurred infrequently, but it also appeared to increase over the first five days. This was manifested in a new child's failure to defer to a group member's threats or attempts at claiming toy possession. Often a new child increasingly ignored situational developments which he earlier had fled from or avoided. "Fearful" behavior patterns (e.g., fleeing, backing away, giving up toy possession) seemed to give way to "defensive" patterns (e.g., raising the forearm, flinching but not turning away, covering with the hands, or hunching over the disputed toy). "Passive resistance" pre-

TABLE 7.4 *Comparison of New Children's First and Fifth Days in the Epworth Halls Nursery School, in Mean Frequencies/Child of Behavior Patterns*

Behavior Pattern	First day (N = 12)	Fifth day (N = 10)	p^a
Automanipulate	13.3	6.6	.025
Glance	59.0	45.9	.033
Immobile	14.1	10.1	.033
Laugh	3.2	3.8	n. s.
Lean (to child)	3.2	4.3	n. s.
Look (total)	46.4	36.2	.025
Adult-oriented	8.6	6.9	n. s.
Child-oriented	34.5	29.2	n. s.
Other	2.2	17.0	n. s.
Run	12.6	16.8	n. s.
Smile	15.8	20.8	n. s.
Verbalize (total)	37.2	42.6	n. s.
Adult-oriented	9.8	5.8	n. s.
Child-oriented	20.3	27.4	n. s.
Other	7.2	9.5	n. s.
Walk	60.7	71.3	n. s.

[a]Sign Test (confirmed by Mann-Whitney U test).

dominated and active aggression by a new child was rare during his first five days. Several of the instances of active aggressive behavior involved new children acting under the protection of an older sibling, for example, Tommy beat and kicked group members soon after entry while his older sister beat, pushed, pinched, and pulled the hair of his attackers.

New children rarely participated in quasiagonistic interactions. New children with older siblings present did so first, sometimes joining them in mobile, rowdy play groups. This occurred mostly in the latter half of the five-day period, and new children seemed to prefer non-contact play. They were the first to drop out if play became rougher, that is, if running, jumping, and laughing turned into pushing, wrestling, and falling. However, most newcomers did not participate in such quasiagonistic interactions during the first week.

All four statistically significant sex differences found on the first day did not persist until the fifth day. The females' greater frequency of looking, both at other children and at the surroundings, gradually decreased while the boys' looking remained unchanged (Figure 7.2a). However, the boys' walking increased dramatically, almost doubling in frequency, while the girls showed a nonsignificant decrease (Figure 7.2b). Laughter remained a predominately female activity on a child's fifth day, but the difference was still nonsignificant ($p = .11$). Only one sex difference emerged on the fifth day: leaning toward other

163

TABLE 7.5 *Sex Differences in Mean Frequencies/Child of Behavior Patterns Exhibited on the Fifth Day in the Epworth Halls Nursery School*

Behavior Pattern	Males (N = 5)	Females (N = 5)	p^a
Automanipulate	6.4	6.8	n. s.
Glance	48.4	43.4	n. s.
Immobile	11.4	8.8	n. s.
Laugh	2.2	5.4	n. s.
Lean (to child)	2.6	6.0	.028
Look (total)	35.8	36.6	n. s.
Adult-oriented	6.4	7.4	n. s.
Child-oriented	28.6	29.8	n. s.
Other	1.4	2.0	n. s.
Run	12.2	21.4	n. s.
Smile	18.0	23.6	n. s.
Verbalize (total)	42.0	43.2	n. s.
Adult-oriented	6.0	5.6	n. s.
Child-oriented	28.4	26.4	n. s.
Other	7.8	11.2	n. s.
Walk	75.0	67.6	n. s.

[a]Mann-Whitney U test.

children (Table 7.5). Girls exhibited more than boys, but this may have been a statistical artifact in view of its inconsistencies.

Behavior of group members toward the new child also changed during his first five days. By the third or fourth day, newcomers received little special visual attention, nor did they evoke digit sucking, automanipulation, etc. in group members. Group members knew the newcomer's name within a few days and recognized his mother. They often gave roles in imaginative play to new children, e.g., "You be the baby and I'll be the mummy, all right?"

However, even on his fifth day the new child was still granted some social latitude by group members. A group member, Tommy, was unsuccessfully constructing a block stack; whenever he had nearly completed it, another child would move the adjacent box or brush against it, causing it to fall. Tommy pushed, verbalized with loud, negative expletives ("Don't!", "Get out!") and otherwise threatened these children, but when a newcomer, Calvin, apparently unwittingly stumbled into the blocks, Tommy treated him differently. Tommy pushed against Calvin's trunk with conspicuously less force and quietly told him to go away, following this soon afterwards with "Now, you go to see Mrs. Bruce" (the nursery nurse) while patting Calvin's back.

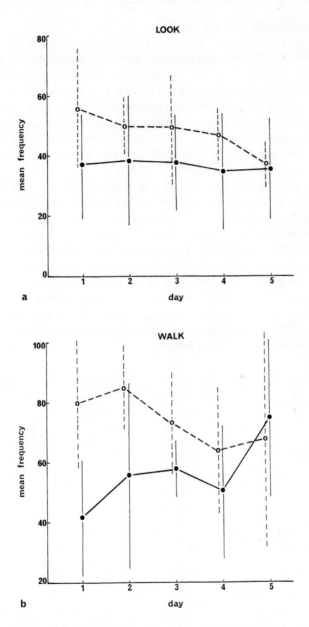

Fig. 7.2. Sex differences in children's behavior over the first five days in the Epworth Halls Nursery School. a. Look. b. Walk. Boys = solid line; Girls = broken line.

Long-Term Behavior Changes

Many statistically significant changes in a child's behavior occurred between his first five nursery days and the five-day follow-up period about 65 days later. Specific behavior pattern frequencies are given in Table 7.6, which compares the first nursery day and the approximate 65th day, and Table 7.7, which compares the two five-day totals. Significant long-term decreases were noted in: *automanipulation, immobility,* and *looking* (total, child-oriented and adult-oriented). *Running* and all but adult-oriented *verbalization* increased significantly over the 65-day interval.

Sex differences in behavior after an average of 65 days of nursery experience were in the same direction as those indicated over the first five days (Table 7.8). Only three significant sex differences emerged: the female predominance of total looking and peer-related looking resembled similar significant differences found on the first day. One reversal emerged: boys exhibited significantly more undirected verbalizations, and this predominance extended over the whole reobservation period (Males' $\bar{x} = 87.2$, females' $\bar{x} = 54.8$, $U = 1, p = .016$).

By the time re-observations began, the new children were completely integrated into the group and indistinguishable behaviorally from other group members. No significant day-to-day changes were found in the second observations, an indication of behavioral stability.

TABLE 7.6 *Comparison of New Children's First and Approximately 65th Days in the Epworth Halls Nursery School, in Mean Frequencies/Child of Behavior Pattern*

Behavior pattern	First day (N = 12)	Approx. 65th day (N = 9)	p^a
Automanipulate	13.2	4.9	.002
Glance	59.0	54.9	n. s.
Immobile	14.1	7.8	.02
Laugh	3.2	5.4	n. s.
Lean (to child)	3.2	5.4	n. s.
Look (total)	46.4	38.1	n. s.
Adult-oriented	8.6	5.9	n. s.
Child-oriented	34.5	32.1	n. s.
Other	2.2	1.9	n. s.
Run	12.6	19.7	< .05
Smile	15.8	17.9	n. s.
Verbalize (total)	37.2	62.1	.02
Adult-oriented	9.8	7.4	n. s.
Child-oriented	20.3	41.4	.035
Other	7.2	13.2	n. s.
Walk	60.7	64.4	n. s.

[a]Sign test (confirmed by Mann-Whitney U test).

TABLE 7.7 *Comparison of Group Totals from Two Five-Day Observation Periods Approximately 65 Days Apart, Epworth Halls Nursery School, Mean Frequencies/Child of Behavior Patterns*

Behavior Pattern	First period (N = 10)	Second period (N = 9)	p[a]
Automanipulate	48.0	21.8	.008
Glance	259.2	269.1	n. s.
Immobile	61.3	39.9	.01
Laugh	19.7	32.6	n.s.
Lean (to child)	22.7	30.2	n. s.
Look (total)	215.3	178.6	.039
Adult-oriented	42.7	29.8	.027
Child-oriented	171.5	146.9	.05
Other	10.5	10.2	n. s.
Run	76.2	109.8	< .05
Smile	97.3	98.8	n. s.
Verbalize (total)	206.5	351.4	.01
Adult-oriented	35.1	48.3	n. s.
Child-oriented	128.2	234.0	.01
Other	43.3	69.2	n. s.
Walk	331.6	325.2	n. s.

[a]Sign test (confirmed by Mann-Whitney U test).

Chapter 5 reported that winners and losers of struggles over objects could be ranked in a "dominance" hierarchy which correlated, among other things, significantly with adults' ratings of aggression. Although no quantitaive records were kept on this nursery group's object struggles, observers felt that Tommy won most consistently over other males as of September, 1969. If so, he achieved this "dominant male" status in less than 8 months of nursery experience, in spite of being only fourth oldest among the group's males. Two factors may have aided his rise: his older sister's aggressive presence in the nursery initially, and his acquaintanceship with more group members outside the nursery than any other child.

Discussion

The occurrence of short-term behavioral changes immediately after nursery entry appears to have been underestimated in previous studies of children's social development. Such changes are not accounted for by maturation alone, as the time scale is too short, for example, as few as five days. Nor does rapid learning of the behavior patterns explain the changes: children in practically all cases displayed ability to perform the behavior patterns from the first day, and

TABLE 7.8 *Sex Differences in Mean Frequencies/Child of Behavior Patterns Exhibited on the Approximately 65th Day in the Epworth Halls Nursery School*

Behavior pattern	Male (N = 4)	Female (N = 5)	p^a
Automanipulate	5.5	4.4	n. s.
Glance	56.5	53.6	n. s.
Immobile	8.7	7.0	n. s.
Laugh	4.0	6.6	n. s.
Lean (to child)	5.2	5.6	n. s.
Look (total)	27.7	46.4	.056
Adult-oriented	5.5	6.2	n. s.
Child-oriented	22.5	39.8	.024
Other	1.0	2.6	n. s.
Run	16.5	22.0	n. s.
Smile	16.0	19.4	n. s.
Verbalize (total)	69.5	56.2	n. s.
Adult-oriented	7.2	7.6	n. s.
Child-oriented	42.2	40.8	n. s.
Other	20.0	7.8	.044
Walk	77.7	52.2	n. s.

[a]Mann-Whitney U test.

no changes were seen in the patterns' form over the child's first five days. It is likely that the nursery situation, which for all but one of the introduced children constituted his first regular contact with a large peer group, presented a radically novel impact sufficient to force readjustment of a child's established social communicatory habits. That is, although each new child's behavioral "repertoire" already contained efficient running, laughter, smiling, etc., his existing systems of deployment based on experience with siblings and neighborhood friends, were inadequate to deal with the nursery situation. This inadequacy may have resulted from an inability to respond with appropriate patterns to another's advances, or failure to do so because of fear, or both.

It is possible that the nursery's novel impact was unrelated to peer-social factors but instead resulted from other situational factors, for example, a strange building, strange toys, strange adults. This seems unlikely as at least nine of the 12 new children had encountered the play room at least once before, and six of them had visited it many times, usually accompanying their mothers bringing and picking up older siblings. Such brief visits, usually regular and twice-daily, enabled preliminary nursery exploration, although social contact with nursery group members was minimal since they were either arriving or leaving. The visits also included interaction with the same nursery nurse, who worked in the nursery before, during and after the research described here, and at least visual familiarity with other associated adults, including the observer. The nursery school building, a converted church annex, was a typical Victorian structure in design and appearance. Most of the nursery toys were of familiar commercial origin, although some large objects were custom-made. From this, it seems likely that the nursery's social novelty and not other novel factors produced the greatest impact on the new child. This is underscored by another socially-significant fact: several of the children had never been separated from their mothers and left with a strange group before.

The relative contributions of maturity and social experience to the short-term and long-term behavioral differences found cannot be delineated in the present study. All but one child were within three months of their third birthdays at entry and most had turned three less than a week before entry. To separate the two variables, observations of at least two control groups entering the nursery would be required: a group of peer-group-inexperienced older children, for example, four-year-olds, and a group of three-year-olds who were socially experienced through previous peer contact in play groups or other nurseries, but who were unacquainted with the Epworth Halls group. Whether such children would show similar behavioral changes is problematical, but such studies should be pursued. Raph and her colleagues (1968) found that amount of child-child "negative interactions" at age 5 was highest in children with one year of nursery experience, lower in children with two year's nursery experience, and lowest in children with three year's nursery experience. (However, two variables are still confounded: age at nursery entry and amount of social experience.) Alexander (Harlow & Harlow, 1969) found similar differences between rhesus monkeys which were peer-deprived or peer-experienced. It is likely that the longer peer-group contact is withheld, the more difficulty the socially inexperienced primate will have in redeploying appropriate behavior patterns to fit the new situation.

The absence of aggression by nursery group members toward a new child introduced into the group was most surprising, particularly since this ran counter to the rule among nonhuman primate studies cited earlier. In most of the nonhuman primate studies, incidence of aggression was greatest during the first few minutes or hours, and this persisted until the animal was killed, left the group, or was withdrawn by experimenters. If the animal succeeded in remaining in the group, agonistic interaction gradually subsided.

Several possible explanations exist for the differences found between human and nonhuman primate responses to group composition modification as presented in this and the previous chapter: one relates to temporary versus permanent introduction. All children introduced became "permanent" nursery members, usually until moving on to primary school at age five. (Although, in another sense, the children's introductions were temporary, since most, but not all, seemed to realize that they would be going home at noon.) Several non-

169

human primate experiments involved repeated temporary introductions and removals (e.g., Southwick, 1967); such alterations of group membership may have disrupted social stability, producing chronic frustration and consequent increased aggression. Frustration-aggression may also have been involved in those studies using exposure to strangers instead of their introduction (e.g., Ploog & MacLean, 1963). Efforts by zoo primates to interact and make physical contact with adjacently-housed animals are well-known, and it seems probable that potency of frustration is related to "intelligence" level, so that exposure of strange individuals to caged nonhuman primate groups might produce extreme frustration and attendant aggression. Also, the strangers may have been prevented by the exposure techniques from displaying appropriate submission and appeasement patterns, and this may have prolonged or exacerbated aggression. In the nursery, new children went immediately into group free play and were accessible to all group members.

Age of group members may influence a group's reaction to newcomers. Only Alexander (cited in Harlow & Harlow, 1969) used infant groups for nonhuman primate introduction studies—most workers observed adult groups or groups assembled to approximate the natural troop's age-sex structure. In the nursery, only two adults interacted to any extent with children during free play, and almost all child-child interactions proceeded without adult interference. Group "permeability" may decrease with age in primate groups as dominance and sexual activities assume increasing importance. This certainly appears to be true at a gross level, for example, an adult male vervet's differential treatment of juvenile and adult male intruders (Gartlan & Brain, 1968), a male gibbon's altered response to a maturing juvenile male (Bernstein & Schusterman, 1964). In Bernstein and Draper's (1964) study of a juvenile rhesus group, the first animals to approach and make friendly contact with the introduced adult male were the smallest (youngest?), while the largest juveniles reacted aggressively toward him.

Also, some form of "territoriality" may have been operating in the nonhuman primate studies, as most were observed in home cages which they occupied all the time. The children (and the gibbons Bernstein and Schusterman studied) spent only a fraction of the day in the observation situation and most of the rest at home.

Any or all of these factors may have contributed to the differences seen between human and nonhuman primate group's reactions to introduced strangers, but other less obvious factors may have been involved, for example, phylogentic ones. The gibbon group's response to strangers more closely approximated the human one than any of the lower species studied. Some studies (but not all) of captive chimpanzee groups have shown high "permeability" to introduced individuals (Hummer, May, & Knight, 1969). The "open" structure described in free-living chimpanzees (van Lawick-Goodall, 1968a) contrasts strongly with the "closed" troops found in many monkey populations. However, Lindburg's recent (1969) study of wild rhesus macaque troops in India has shown them to be more "open" than previously supposed, that is, during breeding season incidence of males changing troops increases markedly. Even more surprising in view of previous reports in Rowell's (1969) finding that interchange of baboons between troops is common among both sexes and occurs throughout the year. In human evolutionary terms, protohominid "open" groups, that is, those which allowed easy entry and exit to members of neighboring groups, presumably facilitated gene dispersal and therefore accelerated evolutionary rate. Reynolds (1966) has discussed the probable importance of such "open groups."

Other observational studies of human response to strangers also found a lack of aggression but signs of fearfulness. Blurton Jones (1967) found that if shortly after he entered a nursery school, he returned the gazes of nursery children, they looked away and avoided him. Adult chronic mental patients responded to the presence of strange adults in their ward room by increasing "way station" behavior, that is, making non-functional stops at certain objects in the room (e.g., water fountain), before walking away from the nearest stranger. This behavior decreased significantly after six days' exposure to the strangers (Hershkowitz, 1962).

It is difficult to compare the introduced individual's behavior in the human and nonhuman studies because of the radically different group responses. Castell (1969) emphasized the group's "collective aggression" toward an introduced stranger in both squirrel monkeys and rhesus macaques. In pigtail macaques, Bernstein (1969) observed three newcomer response types: strong defense against attack, attempts to initiate play and/or grooming with residents, and avoidance-escape attempts. The last most closely approximates the new child's behavior, but a big difference still exists: the older children initiated no attacks, unlike the pigtail macaque residents. Again, the closest nonhuman approximate was supplied by the gibbon: newcomers avoided most animals for the first few minutes but engaged in the usual types of social interaction within about 15 minutes (Bernstein & Schusterman, 1964).

If the new child is characterized as "fearful" and "uncertain" at nursery entry, many changes in frequency of specific patterns are explainable. For example, looking and glancing represent examples of visually exploring and monitoring the new environment and its inhabitants. An "uncertain" child might be expected to do more visual shifting than usual because he can take nothing for granted: the potentially unpleasant unexpected is everywhere. In fact, looking and glancing significantly decreased in frequency over the first week, presumably as familiarity with the nursery increased. Seventy-four percent of looking was child-oriented, and this probably represents another indication of the importance of social as opposed to nonsocial novelty. R. W. Washburn

171

(1932) recorded attention shifts (both social and nonsocial) during 3–3½ year-olds' first five minutes in the nursery: all 14 subjects exhibited observant behavior. Observations within the morning support the idea that amount of visual exploration decreases as "uncertainty" decreases. On the child's first day in the nursery, mean frequencies for looking and glancing were high throughout all four quarters; from the second day onwards they decreased as the morning progressed.

Both immobility and automanipulation are indicators of "fearfulness," for example, R. W. Washburn (1932) described as an extreme of newcomer behavior a "period of 'frozen' observation" which some children exhibited for the first five minutes. Both behavior patterns occur in "social stress" situations: after losing a conflict, when crowded into a small space, while another child is being scolded. Grant (1965b) described children's automanipulation as a displacement activity occurring in ambivalent situations. As reported in Chapter 5, subordinate preschoolers display significantly more automanipulation than dominant individuals, these labels being based on win-loss records in object struggles. Immobility and automanipulation decreased significantly in frequency as the first five-day period progressed, presumably reflecting decreasing fearfulness as familiarity with the nursery developed. The same trend existed within mornings: incidence decreased throughout the morning, especially during the first five-day period. The highest single mean frequency per quarter of both automanipulation and immobility occurred in the average child's first 20 minutes of nursery school experience.

The significance of sex differences is difficult to judge, for example, apparent sex differences may result from differential maturation rates. In general boys seemed more fearful than girls at nursery introduction. They showed significantly more laughter and less walking on the first day. Other nonsignificant differences between the sexes (Table 7.3) supported this conclusion, for example, in glancing, running, smiling, verbalization. However, girls exhibited significantly more looking of all but one type, also a possible fearfulness measure. The predominance of female total and child-oriented looking throughout both observation periods was the only consistent long-term sex difference found (Table 7.8). Finally, the only significant sex difference reversal, in verbalizations not oriented to adults or children, probably reflected the frequent quasiagonistic play shown by experienced boys but not girls. This involved considerable yelling back and forth across the room, much of which seemed undirected at any individual or was considered unassignable by the observer.

Long-term behavioral changes continued in the same direction as short-term and intra-daily ones, with one exception (glance), which is at present inexplicable. Most specific changes seem to fit well into the general picture of increased "socialization."

In summary, the socially "naive" child entering the nursery was shown to exhibit significant behavioral changes over his first five days and over a longer period of nursery experience. The direction of such changes was shown to be consistent. These preliminary findings underline the importance of examining the "socialization" process in detail; they emphasize that while "socialization" is a time-consuming process it also appears to have important short-term facets.

Chapter 8

Density and Social Behavior

Introduction

Until recently, discussion of the effects of high human population density concentrated on food supply, living space, and economic factors, and ignored the behavioral implications. An early collection of essays on density problems, *The Population Dilemma* (Hauser, 1963), contained no references to possible social behavioral effects. But with the popularization of such terms as "population explosion" and "biological time bomb," and accompanying horrific visions of future social life, discussion of behavioral implications has increased. Ehrlich's popular book on the subject, *The Population Bomb* (1968) was already in its thirteenth printing by February, 1970. Such discussion by both laymen and "experts" usually concludes negatively, even frantically, and its tone is pessimistic. Coon (1961) stated that "...the problems of food supply and standing room become insignificant and academic compared to the problem of increasing stress and decreasing sanity..." Keyfitz (1966) discussed the possible development of an "etiquette of noninterference" and the building up of a "higher capacity for discretion and reserve" under such crowded circumstances but then rejected this as unlikely in view of past and present societal responses. Carstairs (1969) broached the possibility of an overcrowded society degenerating to the extreme levels of the prison camp and characterized by fanatical, millenial mass movements. On the other hand Ehrlich and Freedman (1971) recently reported findings showing that high density's negative effects on behavior are very selective and that many social problems previously attributed to urban overcrowding are probably due to other factors.

Among animal behaviorists speculating about human overcrowding, Calhoun (1962) discussed increases in varied and fearsome social pathologies, Leyhausen (1965) discussed changes in social organization (from territorial to hierarchical), and McBride (1971) related population pressures to individual social space. Finally, in a series of publications, Russell and Russell (1966, 1968) developed the theme that human violence is a response to social stress, which is part of a complex of responses involved in population size control. They have relied extensively on studies of animals which were exhaustively reviewed in Wynne-Edwards' highly influential book, *Animal Disperson in Relation to Social Behaviour* (1962). But the fact remains that speculations about human behavior and density rest on scant empirical evidence.

In animals, the relationship between density (i.e., amount of space per unit organism) and social behavior has received considerable research attention. The studies fall into two general types: (1) long-term studies of population density, and (2) short-term studies of group density. In the former, the investigator usually follows a population of animals through several generations and seeks to relate cyclical changes in reproduction to physiological aspects of development, particularly endocrine function. Behavior occurring in such conditions is usually treated superficially or indirectly, for example, frequency of fighting scars as evidence of past agonistic behavior. More specific patterns of behavior are usually ignored. Christian and Davis (1964) and Thiessen and Rodgers (1961) reviewed this approach to density-behavior problems.

Group density studies are shorter in length and are more concerned with changes in individual behavior than with reproduction and development. The investigator records the behavior of various-sized groups of animals housed in various-sized enclosures. Behavior categories are usually more specific than those in population studies, but they remain general by ethological standards, for example, "aggressive behavior," "grooming," "sexual behavior."

Almost all laboratory density-behavior studies have involved rodents. The advantages, particularly for population studies, are obvious: small body size (allowing large numbers to be kept in limited accommodation), rapid maturation and year-round breeding (enabling conspicuous, short-term changes in population character), and extensive accumulated physiological knowledge (allowing detailed hormonal analysis). In contrast, the conspicuous absence of similar research on human and nonhuman primates is probably due to several disadvantageous factors: economy, reproductive habits, and ethical considerations. Construction of adequate research facilities is costly, and nonhuman primates are expensive to obtain, so that research workers may be loath to risk fatalities and injury to their subjects. Sexual maturation and length of time between single off-spring is counted in years. Finally, with humans at least, considerable practical and moral restrictions exist on placing individuals in uncomfortable or potentially injurious crowded situations.

Field studies of density-behavior problems have concentrated on rodents, lagomorphs, and birds (see review in Archer, 1970). Long-term population studies of primates remain scarce (Rowell, 1969), although some authors have now begun to present evidence of social organizational changes as possible population regulatory devices, for example, Sugiyama's report (1966) of whole-sale slaughtering of langur infants by invading adult males. Most primatological research is concerned with other aspects of social behavior, and other complicating variables, for example, disproportionate sex ratios, are usually uncontrolled. Southwick (1967) performed the first experimental study of differences in social behavior under different group densities. He reduced by 50% the space available to a caged rhesus monkey group, and a significant increase in total intragroup aggression resulted. Alexander and Roth (1971) drastically reduced the space available to a captive Japanese macaque group and found increases in aggression but no breakdown in social structure.

The long-term human population studies consist of statistical, correlative investigations which are difficult to interpret because of complex interactions between overlapping variables. Juvenile delinquency is more prevalent in overcrowded areas of Edinburgh (Philip & McCulloch, 1966). Many "social malaise" factors, including offenses against the person and child neglect, occur significantly more frequently in the most overcrowded third of Newcastle (Cherry, 1967). Suicide and schizophrenia are more common in high density urban situations (Hays, 1964). But in all cases, these are also likely to be the urban areas with the poorest living accommodations and lowest incomes, both being likely causal factors as well. Such correlations are usually only able to show an association between two phenomena and not any causal relationship between them.

The first short-term group density-behavior study of human beings was done by C. Hutt and Vaizey (1966). They observed three different-sized groups of normal, brain-damaged, and autistic children in a hospital playroom. Normal children spent significantly more time in aggressive-destructive behavior and significantly less time in non-aggressive social interaction at higher densities. Recently, Ehrlich and Freedman (1971) compared groups in small and large rooms and found negligible effects on task performance but complex effects on interpersonal measures.

In comparing studies, it must be remembered that density is *not* a unilateral variable, but the interaction of two variables: number of individuals and amount of space. Thus an experimenter may examine *social* density by observing groups of differing numbers in the same-sized space. Or he may examine *spatial* density by observing same-sized groups in spaces of differing areas or volumes.

Unfortunately, past investigators of density-behavior problems often failed to differentiate these two approaches, or used only one of them in their research. Consequently, behavioral differences found in studies using only varied *social* density conditions might only be due to *group size* differences. The large body of literature devoted to such group size effects testifies to its proven importance (see review in Thomas & Fink, 1963).

Correspondingly, behavioral differences found in studies using only varying *spatial* density conditions might be due to *space* differences alone. Some activities cannot be performed in less than a certain minimum of space and their occurrence may be unrelated to the numbers occupying that space. For example, Draper and Bernstein (1963) showed that single rhesus monkeys exhibited dramatic frequency differences in many behavior patterns, particularly stereotypies, according to the size of cage containing them. However, if both social and spatial differences are investigated using a single group and space variously manipulated, and consistent differences occur, then it is likely that crowding is the influencing factor, and not group size or amount of space alone.

Another method of checking density's role is to observe groups in which number of individuals and amount of space varies in direct proportion. Any differences found cannot be due to density, since the amount of space per unit organism is the same in all conditions. Bailey (1966) demonstrated this in mice: physiological stress reactions previously thought to be density-dependent were elicited by proportionally increasing group size and space simultaneously. Results from this approach alone must remain inconclusive, however, since one cannot tell whether one of the two factors was influential or if they interacted.

Experiment 1

The author first attempted a pilot study of children's behavior using "natural experimental" conditions of differing spatial densities. This took place in the Slade Nursery School, Oxford, between October 31 and December 15, 1966. Depending on weather conditions, the children (mean attendance = 54) present in the school played in three different-sized areas:

High density. During inclement weather, children remained inside the school building and had access to three playrooms, a bathroom, and a hallway. Total area: 1770 ft^2. Mean density: 33 ft^2/child.

Medium density. Following inclement weather when the lawn and garden remained wet, children could play on an outside concrete strip as well as inside. Total area: 2815 ft^2. Mean density: 52 ft^2/child.

Low density. During clear weather children could play on the lawn and garden areas, as well as inside and on the concrete strip. Total area: 8089 ft^2. Mean density: 150 ft^2/child.

This policy was an accepted tradition in the nursery school and seemed to cause no concern or frustration to staff or children. The schedule was not completely weather-dependent, for example, Medium density conditions might be as sunny and clear as Low conditions, being based on standing water present from rains several days before.

Four three-and-one-half-year-old, full-time children were observed during morning free play. All had attended the nursery for several months and were chosen as the two males and two females nearest together in age.

The author observed each child individually over a total of 154 five-minute periods (Total observation time: 12.8 hours). Eight daily periods were spaced regularly throughout weekday mornings (Table 8.1).

The author recorded observations on a portable tape recorder. Observations were later transcribed, timed by stopwatch, and coded onto a standardized sheet. Two percent of the data were rejected because of equipment failure, restriction of a subject through adult intervention, or observer error. The data were punched onto cards and analyzed using conventional electronic data processing methods.

To examine gross activity, behavior was categorized into six types of body movement: hand, arm, leg, gross body, other, and locomotor. Table 8.2 describes these. The author did not ascribe social significance to movements at this stage, which involved only a general survey of motor behavior. This means that the same movement may have been differentially affected by density differences in different social contexts.

The author recorded 11,174 movements which lasted 32,870 seconds, resulting in a mean bout length of slightly less than 3.0 seconds. Tables 8.3 and 8.4, respectively, give mean bout lengths and mean number of movements exhibited during the three density conditions.

Hand movements alone occurred infrequently (approximately 1% of the total movements), as most hand movements were combined with simultaneous arm movements (Arm). No relation to group density was found. Hand movements were used to manipulate small objects, for example, beads, grain, plasti-

TABLE 8.1 *Times of Eight Five-Minute Observation Periods, Slade Nursery School, Oxford*

Observation period	Time (AM)
1	9:30- 9:35
2	9:45- 9:50
3	10:00-10:05
4	10:15-10:20
(Break for Story Time)	
5	10:50-10:55
6	11:05-11:10
7	11:20-11:25
8	11:35-11:40

TABLE 8.2 *Definitions of General Motor Behavior Categories Exhibited by Children in Slade Nursery School*

Hand:	Movements involving only the following joints: wrist, carpo-metacarpal, metacarpo-phalangeal, interphalangeal.
Arm:	Movements involving the following joints: shoulder girdle, shoulder, elbow, plus joints in *Hand.*
Leg:	Movements involving the following joints: knee, upper ankle, lower ankle, transverse tarsal, tarso-metatarsal, metatarso-phalangeal, interphalangeal, hip (partial).
Gross Body:	Movements involving *Arm* and/or *Leg* movements plus movements of other body joints, e.g., inter-vertebral, atlanto-axial.
Other:	Movements of joints other than those included in *Arm* and *Leg*, unaccompanied by limb movements.
Locomotor:	Self-generated movements involving body transfer from one point to another. Direction, unless otherwise stated, is forward in an approximately horizontal plane. It necessarily involves *Gross Body* movements and can rarely be only *Leg.*

cine, and children exhibiting them "worked" with concentration, quiet composure, and lack of social interaction. Hand movements also constituted much of automanipulation.

Arm movements occurred most commonly of all movement types (a reminder of the importance to the hominids of bipedalism's freeing from locomotion of an appendage pair for other uses). The amount of time children spent in arm movements increased significantly with higher group densities, and the corresponding increase in number of movements approached statistical significance. Children manifested arm movements in every phase of daily activity, particularly investigation of and familiarization with the external environment.

Leg movements also occurred infrequently (less than 3% of the total movements), as most occurred in combination with gross body or locomotor movements. No relation to group density was found. Leg movements were associated with standing (e.g., shuffling feet) or sitting postures (e.g., swinging legs).

Gross Body movements varied the most in form, usually involving simultaneous head, trunk, and limb motion. The amount of time spent in gross body movements decreased significantly as group density increased, and a corresponding decrease in number of movements also occurred. Of the nonlocomotory types, gross body movements involved the greatest energy expenditure and often took the form of postural changes.

TABLE 8.3 *Children's Mean Movement Bout Length (seconds)/Observation Period (5 minutes) during Different Group Density Conditions. (Friedman Two-Way Analysis of Variance, N = 4, k = 3.)*

| Movement type | Spatial density condition | | | |
	Low	Medium	High	p
Hand	2.3	5.3	3.1	n. s.
Arm	89.6	120.5	162.2	.005
Leg	6.1	6.0	6.7	n. s.
Gross Body	54.5	31.5	23.0	.042
Other	1.4	0.6	3.3	n. s.
Locomotor	59.0	45.4	19.5	.005
Total activity	215.4	209.3	217.6	n. s.

Other movements occurred the least frequently of all categories, probably because movement of other body parts while keeping all four limbs motionless is a rare kinesic combination. The primary example was of neck movement orienting the face. No relation to group density existed.

Locomotor movement is essentially gross body movement combined with horizontal displacement of the body. Like gross body movement, it decreased significantly at higher group densities in terms of movement time and approached significance in terms of movements.

In a "natural experiment" all the important variables are rarely controlled for, and interpretation must necessarily be cautious. The most obvious co-varying factor, weather, has been discussed above, and it appears relatively unimportant. (In the light of Bernstein and Mason's [1963a] finding that captive rhesus monkeys' social and nonsocial behavior is related to weather conditions, this needs further investigation.) Another possible explanation for density-behavior differences, changes in general overall activity, can be excluded, as total activity remains constant regardless of density condition.

The different "natures" of the density conditions could account for the differences found. Besides differing in amount of space, they had different topographies, contained different numbers and kinds of toys, and were differently enclosed. Yet the author contends that amount of space and not the other features probably constituted the major factor, for the following reasons:

1. The different areas were not mutually exclusive. A child active during low condition was not forced to play outside, and children often remained inside when they could play outdoors.

2. Similarly, children used many of the same toys and activities in different locations (i.e., density conditions) and often transported toys between them. For example, children sometimes took tables and table toys outside.

TABLE 8.4 *Children's Mean Numbers of Movement/Observation Period (5 minutes) during Different Group Density Conditions. (Friedman Two-Way Analysis of Variance, N = 4, k = 3.)*

Movement type	Spatial density condition			
	Low	Medium	High	p
Hand	0.6	1.3	1.3	n. s.
Arm	26.7	42.6	45.7	.069
Leg	2.1	2.2	1.4	n. s.
Gross Body	21.5	16.0	13.3	n. s.
Other	0.7	0.3	0.7	n. s.
Locomotor	16.2	14.8	6.5	.069
Total activity	67.6	77.3	68.8	n. s.

3. Because of the categories' generality, there was no question of a movement type being "tied" to any density condition. For example, opportunities for hand movements existed in all three conditions, and locomotion was not limited to outdoors.

4. Low and Medium density conditions were very similar in nature: both were outdoors and shared most activities. The only significant difference between the two conditions lay in the former's earthen substrate and the latter's concrete one; it seems unlikely that this could account for differences of the magnitude of the Medium-High ones.

If density were the major operative factor producing the behavioral changes, why should these effects emerge? It seems likely that as group density increased, it became more difficult to perform movements which, in their performance, require a certain minimum of space. Locomotor movement provides the most obvious example. Unaltered performance rates under more crowded conditions probably increase "irritating" encounters with others, either through direct physical contact or through interference with their activities. This might explain the locomotor and gross body movement decreases. For the same reasons, those movements which are minimally "space-consuming" and unobtrusive probably increase, which might explain the arm movement increases. In addition to general changes, specific changes in activity seemed to occur, for example rough-and-tumble cowboy play shifted to play with toy cowboys on a table top.

Experiment 2

The second experiment had two aims: (1) to examine the effects of differing group density conditions on selected, specific *behavior patterns*, particularly those seen in agonistic interactions. And, (2) to compare behavioral differences in differing social and spatial density conditions in the same population. It was conducted using the Epworth Halls Nursery School subjects and facilities, which are described in Chapter 3.

The behavior patterns represented examples of aggressive, fearful, and nonagonistic behavior whose importance and reliability had already been established. Eight patterns were previously recorded during group formation observations (Chapter 6), and Chapter 4 gives their inter-observer reliability coefficients. Table 8.5 lists additional or modified patterns and their reliability coefficients.

Figure 8.1 gives the group density conditions. Two group sizes were used: 100% ($\bar{x}$ = 15.8 children) and 50% ($\bar{x}$ = 8.4 children). The latter resulted from randomly splitting the group, so that half played in the playroom and half outside before the milk time break halfway through the morning, and the two groups exchanged places after having milk. Two room sizes were used: 100% and 80%. The latter resulted from erecting a barrier of chairs and benches across the playroom's width. The room's contents were moved into the 80% area, with their relative positions kept constant, and the other 20% of the room was left empty and unused. Mean attendance during the experiment was 16 (range: 14–19), and the most crowded condition (A) easily exceeded the minimum space requirements of 25 ft^2/child in the national nursery regulations.

The author observed the group during two daily 30-minute free play periods and recorded group frequencies of behavior on a modified check list. The density conditions varied daily in approximately random order. One hour's daily observation for six days occurred under each condition, totaling 24 hours of observation for the complete study.

		Room size	
		80% (593 ft^2)	100% (778 ft^2)
Group size	100% (14–19 children)	A 37 ft^2/child	B 52 ft^2/child
	50% (8–10 children)	C 74 ft^2/child	D 86 ft^2/child

Fig. 8.1. Four mean group density conditions (A, B, C, D) formed from two group sizes and two room sizes, Epworth Halls Nursery School.

TABLE 8.5 *Definitions of Social Behavior Categories Used in Group Density Study, Epworth Halls Nursery School*

---

1. *Object Struggle:* Attempt by two or more children to gain or retain possession of an object, usually a toy. Usually involves simultaneous body contact with the object, and pulling and evasive body movements (.67).

2. *Negative Expletive:* Short, explosive verbalization in "negative imperative" form, e. g., "Don't!", "Shut up!", "Stop it!".

3. *Hit:* Beat (four subcategories) plus Punch (four subcategories). See Chapter 4.

4. *Push:* See Chapter 4.

5. *Destructive:* Manipulative behavior directed to objects which results in their damage or destruction; limb or gross body contact with objects so that they are disconnected or disarranged; inappropriate use of an object likely to result in its damage (.70).

6. *Weep:* See Chapter 4.

7. *Immobile:* See Chapter 4.

8. *Digit Suck:* See Chapter 4.

9. *Automanipulate:* See Chapter 4.

10. *Laugh:* See Chapter 4.

11. *Contact:* Combination of Hold Hands, Hand on Back, Hug, Pat, Shoulder Hug. See Chapter 4.

12. *Run:* See Chapter 4.

Following C. Hutt and Vaizey (1966), we expected that agonistic and destructive behavior patterns would be more frequent at higher densities, and nonagonistic behavior less frequent. However, whereas Hutt and Vaizey examined only social density effects, we expected to find differences between social and spatial density comparisons. Since, in the higher social density conditions the number of children present was doubled, one might expect the frequency of behavior patterns used in social interactions to double proportionally. For example, twice as many children competing for the same number of toys might be expected to be involved in twice as many object struggles. In other words, it was predicted that social density differences would be more potent in their effects on the children's behavior than spatial density differences.

The results of a straightforward comparison across the four group densities are given in Table 8.6. Little evidence of an ordered relationship between density per se and frequency of behavior patterns emerged from this analysis, which

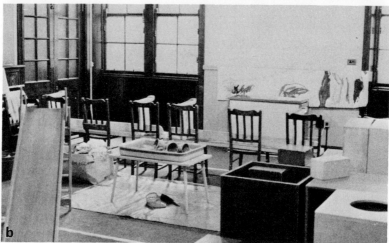

Fig. 8.2. Two room sizes used in a group density experiment. (a) 100% room size (note videotape camera in corner); (b) 80% room size with "natural" barrier of chairs and benches isolating the empty 20% (behind).

does not take account of the various social and spatial manipulations. Only *laugh* varied directly in proportion to density conditions, and the differences did not reach statistical significance. Of the two behavior patterns showing significant differences between conditions, *automanipulate* probably represents an artifact resulting from the as yet inexplicable high frequency during C. Further analysis indicates that *run* is probably spatially-dependent and not related to density (i.e., it was much more common in the two 100% space conditions while the number of individuals occupying that space was irrelevant).

TABLE 8.6 *Children's Behavior Compared Over Four Increasing Group Density Conditions. Mean Individual Totals/30-Minute Observation Period*

Behavior pattern	Density conditions: ft^2/child				p^a
	86 (D)	74 (C)	52 (B)	37 (A)	
Automanipulate	.59	.95	.63	.60	.048
Contact	.50	.64	.42	.65	n. s.
Destructive	.20	.06	.10	.15	n. s.
Digit Suck	.30	.58	.43	.47	n. s.
Hit	.72	.51	.56	.77	n. s.
Immobile	1.05	.93	.73	.80	n. s.
Laugh	2.65	2.13	1.62	1.32	n. s.
Negative Expletive	.56	.47	.26	.32	n. s.
Object Struggle	.35	.40	.23	.27	n. s.
Push	.67	.44	.55	.47	n. s.
Run	4.41	2.82	3.90	2.78	.003
Weep	.08	.06	.05	.08	n. s.

[a]Kruskal-Wallis one-way analysis of variance, $N = 12$.

A more appropriate analytic approach is to compare behavior frequencies along either *social* (i.e., D with B, C with A) or *spatial* (i.e., D with C, B with A) density lines. Spatial and social density effects on the children's behavior (given in Tables 8.7 and 8.8) were different, but in a more complicated manner than the straightforward one predicted. In the spatial density comparisons, six of the seven statistically significant differences found were in the expected direction. One aggressive pattern (*hit*), two fearful patterns (*automanipulate, digit suck*), and one pattern exhibited in response to another's fearfulness (*contact*) occurred more frequently in the more crowded condition. Behavior patterns in the latter category were those shown toward uneasy or distraught individuals, for example, weeping children were sometimes comforted by peers who patted or put an arm around them. Both instances of a nonagonistic pattern (*run*) occurred less frequently at the higher density. Only *destructive* behavior varied in the opposite direction from that found by C. Hutt and Vaizey (1966), but direct comparison with their study is impossible as they used only one general category of "aggressive/destructive behavior." Overall, 16 of the 24 spatial density comparisons were in the predicted direction.

In the social density comparisons, instead of showing greater differences between Low and High density conditions with the High frequencies doubling those of the Low, the results tended toward the opposite direction. No Low-High comparisons involved anything even approaching a doubled frequency, and only a minority of comparisons (11 of 24) varied in the expected direction. Six significant differences emerged, and only two of these (*hit, laugh*) differed as

185

TABLE 8.7 *Spatial Density Effects on Children's Behavior (i.e., Group Size Held Constant and Available Space Varied). Mean Individual Totals/30-Minute Observation Period Under 50% and 100% Group Size Conditions*

	Density conditions					
	50% Group			100% Group		
Behavior pattern	100% space (D) low	50% space (C) high	p^a	100% space (B) low	50% space (A) high	p^a
Automanipulate	.59	.95	< .025	.63	.60	n. s.
Contact	.50	.64	< .05	.42	.65	n. s.
Destructive	.20	.06	= .05	.10	.15	n. s.
Digit Suck	.30	.58	< .025	.43	.47	n. s.
Hit	.72	.51	n. s.	.56	.77	= .05
Immobile	1.05	.93	n. s.	.73	.80	n. s.
Laugh	2.65	2.13	n. s.	1.62	1.32	n. s.
Negative Expletive	.56	.47	n. s.	.26	.32	n. s.
Object Struggle	.35	.40	n. s.	.23	.27	n. s.
Push	.67	.44	n. s.	.55	.47	n. s.
Run	4.41	2.82	< .01	3.90	2.78	< .01
Weep	.08	.06	n. s.	.05	.08	n. s.

[a] Mann-Whitney U test, $N = 12$.

predicted, while four others (*automanipulate, immobile, negative expletive* twice) differed oppositely. It appears as though the children went out of their way to avoid getting involved in agonistic interactions when faced simultaneously with higher group densities and up to twice as many other children. Rather than passively allowing their social interaction frequency to increase in accordance with the higher probability of encounters (*as per* gas molecules), they appear to have actively altered their social behavior so that frequency of encounters did not exceed a certain level. The precise way in which an individual child effects this alteration cannot be derived from group frequency data, but the following discussion section attempts to relate this to interpersonal spacing behavior. C. Hutt and Vaizey (1966) reported a similar reduction in time spent in nonaggressive social interaction at their highest group density condition.

A further qualitative result emphasizes the greater disruptive potential of social density manipulation: splitting the class for the 50% group condition resulted in more than just halved numbers. In some cases, it seemed to affect the social structure of the group by generating novel combinations of individuals, that is, children who rarely played together when the whole group was present were thrown together in interaction.

TABLE 8.8 *Social Density Effects on Children's Behavior (i.e., Space Held Constant and Group Size Varied). Mean Individual Totals/30-Minute Observation Period Under 80% and 100% Space Conditions*

	Density conditions					
	100% space			80% space		
Behavior pattern	50% group (D) low	100% group (B) high	p^a	50% group (C) low	100% group (A) high	p^a
Automanipulate	.59	.63	n. s.	.95	.60	<.025
Contact	.50	.42	n. s.	.64	.65	n. s.
Destructive	.20	.10	n. s.	.06	.15	n. s.
Digit Suck	.30	.43	n. s.	.58	.47	n. s.
Hit	.72	.56	n. s.	.51	.77	<.025
Immobile	1.05	.73	<.025	.93	.80	n. s.
Laugh	2.65	1.62	<.05	2.13	1.32	n. s.
Negative Expletive	.56	.26	<.025	.47	.32	=.05
Object Struggle	.35	.23	n. s.	.40	.27	n. s.
Push	.67	.55	n. s.	.44	.47	n. s.
Run	4.41	3.90	n. s.	2.82	2.78	n. s.
Weep	.08	.05	n. s.	.06	.08	n. s.

[a] Mann-Whitney U test, $N = 12$.

Discussion

In seeking an explanation for the social behavioral differences found, it seems likely that the concept of *personal social space* is involved. Conder (1949) first described an invisible "portable territory" which surrounds a individual's body in many avian species. Hediger (1950) discussed animal social spacing in many species, distinguishing between "contact" species in which many individuals may rest or sleep in physical contact and "distance" species in which inter-individual contact is always avoided. Among nonhuman primates, even closely related species, for example, bonnet and pigtail macaques, may show significant differences in interpersonal spacing (Rosenblum, Kaufman, & Stynes, 1964), and within a single species, spacing may vary according to role, for example, the dominant male in a Japanese macaque troop always maintains a personal space of 1–2 meters while eating (Alexander & Bowers, 1969).

Recent research has shown that human "social space" has a consistent shape which is reflected in physiological measures, for example, galvanic skin response (McBride, King, & James, 1965), and which is altered in behaviorally-disordered states, example, schizophrenia (Esser, Chamberlain, Chapple, & Kline,

1965; Horowitz, Duff, & Stratton, 1964). Maintenance of inter-individual distance has differing communicational significance in different human societies, and this may lead to cross-cultural misunderstandings (E. T. Hall, 1959, 1966). Machotka (1965) distinguished five separate concentric spatial envelopes surrounding the human body.

Little examination of social spacing in children has been done. King (1966) found that average interpersonal approach distance was correlated with earlier scoring of social interactions between preschool children in an experimental playroom. Guardo (1969) and Meisels and Guardo (1969) indirectly examined personal space in primary school children by having them place silhouette figures in various projective situations. The only study of children's spacing behavior during free play appears to be that by P. L. McGrew (1970). She found that preschool children spent more time within three feet of each other and less time in solitary behavior at high group densities; at the same time they avoided physical contact with other children more often when crowded.

Violation of human personal spatial boundaries may produce discomfort and irritation (Felipe & Sommer, 1966; Sommer, 1959). And, as a group becomes more crowded, it is probable that the frequency of violation increases proportionally. (With randomly moving bodies in a container, increased density inevitably causes more collisions between bodies.) In living organisms this may produce a state of persistent discomfort or a social stress condition. In addition to the frustration directly engendered by repeated violations, additional frustration is probably associated with anticipated difficulty in avoiding further violations.

The increased aggressive behavior seen in more crowded groups seems to result from increased violation-produced social stress. There is no a priori reason why reduced space alone should cause increased fighting. In turn, as aggression increases, so, often, does fearful behavior in response to it. Tension within the nursery group seemed to heighten as individuals found it more difficult to avoid involvement in conflicts, whether as aggressors or victims.

Factors other than personal space violation could account for increased incidence of aggression in high density situations. Ewbank and Bryant (1969) showed that increased aggression in high-density pigpens is due to the inability of subordinates to move away from superiors because of simple lack of "manoeuvering space." Similar mechanisms may operate in humans, for example, schizophrenic patients normally respond to intrusions into their personal space with avoidance and not aggression (Esser, Chamberlain, Chapple, & Kline, 1965). Also, crowding produces frustrations other than those related to personal space, e.g., inability to perform certain preferred activities, and these may help produce aggression behavior. The role of personal social space in density-behavior problems can only be fully elucidated when spacing behavior is examined directly and not inferred from other data. (See W. C. McGrew, in preparation.)

Is it possible to relate the results of any of this research to the momentous problems of over-population which introduced this chapter? Unhappily, the findings presented here are at worst equivocal, and at best suggestive. But an examination of the literature and an introduction to the practical problems of density-behavior research has generated some possible ideas for future research.

First, it is clear that "over-crowding" means a great many things to different people. Number of persons per square mile is a next to useless statistic unless one takes into account other relevant architectural, topographical, and climatological factors in addition to the obvious social and biological ones. Mean number of occupancy rooms per person (or more depressingly, mean number of persons per room) may be a more useful measure of high-density stress-producing conditions. An even more sensitive measure might be an index based on group densities encountered during major daily activities: sleep, eating, transport, work (or school), leisure. Finally, the effects of over-crowding may be negatively characterized: under what circumstances, how often, and with what difficulty can an average individual in a society choose to be alone?

The prospect of solitariness or its absence brings in another factor bound to be of importance in over-population problems: *privacy*. Such a viewpoint emphasizes the individual's perception of and ability to adjust to crowding, rather than the group's. How much privacy does a person need? How do such "social tolerance levels" vary according to sensory modality? It would seem that an important factor to be considered in the design of high-density housing developments is extra-efficient sound-proofing of residences, yet this seems to be often neglected. Similar aspects of visual privacy should be considered: rather than large common parks of open ground, perhaps much smaller private plots capable of visual isolation would be more conducive to adjustment to high-density living conditions. A very simple series of experiments, probably using rodents, could be done in which these characteristics and others were systematically varied; for example, two identical, multiple-occupancy enclosures, one with transparent and one with opaque walls, might yield insights into the behavioral effects of the constant visual presence of individual conspecifics.

A comprehensive study of group density effects on human social behavior will require a combined short- and long-term approach. First, the differential effects found in this tentative and limited study indicate that spatial and social density effects should be more thoroughly investigated. A replication using three or four group sizes and available spaces, giving a 9 or 16 cell matrix of density conditions, should be attempted. Limits should be sought for high and low density extremes. Second, some effort should be made to investigate the possible differential effects of two-dimensional (area) versus three-dimensional (volume) spatial variations. High ceilings may be of more than aesthetic utility. Third, cross-cultural studies of societies which have learned to cope with high-density living should be undertaken. As the anthropologist Edward T. Hall has pointed out, the Japanese man in the street who comes from an habitually crowded life style engages in *less* physical contact in daily life than the average Australian coming from much more spacious surroundings. Finally, short-term studies of group density effects using groups of people from different long-term crowding conditions within a single society should be pursued. This might be done by comparing density-behavior in otherwise-matched nursery groups from suburbs and high-rise developments.

Chapter 9

Periodicity in Behavior

Introduction

The problem of possible behavioral periodicity has been largely ignored in studies of children. Most developmental psychologists conducting observational studies have not considered time-of-day or day-of-the-week, apparently feeling that these were not relevant variables. In such studies, Monday's experimental sessions might be lumped with Friday's, and morning and afternoon observations might systematically cancel each other out, distorting or even masking results completely. The author is as guilty of this as anyone else, and the results presented below were derived from other studies only as an afterthought.

The neglect of possible periodicity in behavior is hardly defensible in view of the very extensive animal (see summary in Marler & Hamilton, 1966, pp. 25–72) and human (Aschoff, 1965) literature in the field. More recent studies have emphasized the importance of such phenomena in nonhuman primates (Rohles, 1969). Also, the existence of such periodicities are common knowledge to many experienced nursery personnel. Consequently, the purpose of the research described in this chapter was to investigate possible periodicity in the behavior of freely-interacting nursery school children.

Behavioral periodicity can be defined as recurring rhythmic differences in the frequency of behavior between subunits (e.g., hours) of a "natural" time unit (e.g., day). This particular case, circadian rhythm, has been the most frequently studied, but a week, lunar cycle, month, or year may also constitute the natural unit. Such units are usually based on noncultural referrents for examples, phases of the lunar cycle, but some well-established cultural units such as the five-day school week appear to exert similar influences. Adequate coverage requires that behavior be recorded many times in all sub-units, either with prolonged continuous recording through several natural cycles, or with systematic time sampling of those cycles. As periodicity was not the primary subject of the research, many of the results do not completely fulfill these criteria, for example, in no study was it possible to record a child's behavior throughout an entire year, so any conclusions about annual periodicity must remain tentative.

Method and Procedures

Possible sources of behavioral periodicity were examined in three studies described earlier:

A. Study of children's motor behavior in the Slade Nursery School, Oxford, between October 31 and December 15, 1966. (Chapter 6 gives details.) Potential daily and weekly periodicity were examined.

B. Study of children's social behavior in the Slade Nursery School, Oxford, between December 5, 1967 and March 14, 1968. (Chapter 3 gives details.) Potential weekly, lunar, monthly, and annual periodicity were examined.

C. Study of children's social development in the Epworth Halls Nursery School, Edinburgh, between September 9, 1968 and September 26, 1969. (Chapter 3 gives details.) Potential daily periodicity was examined.

The behavior patterns described earlier were used as the basis for investigating periodicity; Chapter 4 and the Appendix give the definitions. Table 9.1 gives the minimum number of cycles examined for each type of unit. The Kolmogorov-Smirnov one-sample test (Siegel, 1956) was used to test goodness of fit of observed behavior pattern frequencies to frequencies expected by chance. Because of limited and sometimes incomplete data, a rigorous region of rejection was used: only a p of less than .01 was considered sufficient to reject the null hypothesis of chance frequencies of behavior occurrence.

TABLE 9.1 *Minimum Number of Complete Cycles for Each Type of Unit Examined for Behavioral Periodicity*

Nursery School	Periodicity Type				
	Daily	Weekly	Lunar	Monthly	Annual
Slade (A)	12	5	–	–	–
Slade (B)	–	1	4	4	1/3
Epworth Halls	8	–	–	–	–

Daily Periodicity

The most frequently investigated behavioral periodicity has been daily, or circadian, periodicity. This is probably because daily behavioral rhythms are the most obvious and widespread periodicities among living organisms; no animal is continuously active, and consistent activity-rest patterns cause most to be classified as diurnal, nocturnal, or crepuscular. The natural unit is the 24-hour light-dark cycle, and the arbitrary subunit used in studies is usually one hour or less. Studies of human circadian rhythms in vigilance and performance tasks have been made (Aschoff, 1965), but ongoing rhythms in activity and social interaction in naturalistic surroundings remain to be investigated. Much more is known about nonhuman primates, of which most wild-living types so far studied show a characteristic diurnal cycle: sleep throughout the night, feeding and movement during the morning, mid-day rest and grooming period, feeding and movement during afternoon, and another quiet period before nightfall. (Altmann and Altmann [1970] presented the most complete description of a daily cycle, including sleep, in their recent report of a field study of savanna baboons in Kenya.) Within this general outline, more specific periodicities exist, for example, howler monkeys show a distinct early morning peak in inter-troop roaring exchanges (Carpenter, 1965). Studies of captive primates show similar periodicities in behavior although it is rarely possible to ascertain the direct causal mechanisms involved due to the many interrelated variables. Bernstein and Mason (1963a) recorded daily periodicity similar to wild-living forms in a captive rhesus group, as well as grooming frequency changes during the day correlated with air temperature. Wilson and Wilson (1968) reported daily periodicity in chimpanzee aggressive behavior; aggressive bouts were highest immediately before and during mid-morning and mid-afternoon feeding periods. Rosenblum, Kaufman, and Stynes (1969) also found hunger effects on eight categories of social behavior which showed consistent diurnal variation in bonnet and pigtail macaques. Finally, in the best controlled behavioral study yet reported, Thach (1969) found that two captive baboons displayed daily periodicity in "socializing" behavior (i.e., opening a door for access to each other) under continuous illumination. Other nonhuman primate species in which daily behavioral periodicity has been reported are: cebus monkey (Bernstein, 1965); squirrel monkey (Francois, Barratt, & Harris, 1970).

Slade Nursery School

Using motor pattern data from four Slade Nursery School children, group frequencies of six general motor categories and the 20 most commonly occurring motor patterns (movements) were compared over eight observation periods. These five-minute periods were dispersed between 9:30 a.m. and 11:40 a.m. on Monday through Friday mornings (Table 8.1). Ten-minute intervals occurred between all of the observation periods except the interval for Story Time between periods 4 and 5, which lasted 30 minutes. Table 8.2 gives the definitions of general motor categories, and Table 9.2 lists the 20 motor patterns analyzed and the number of times each was seen. The number of individual observation periods comprising each grouped mean varied from 12 to 26. The individual records of the four children's total number of movements and in the six general motor categories closely resembled each other.

The total number of observed movements increased significantly over the eight observation periods from a mean of 66.9 to a mean of 87.7 (Fig. 9.1a, $N = 11174, D = .02, p < .01$). Incidence of movements began to decrease slightly following the longer interval between periods 4 and 5, possibly indicating a hold-over effect from the enforced inactivity of Story Time.

Of the six general motor categories, five showed significant daily periodicity (Fig. 9.1b); only the miscellaneous movements category, *Other*, did not occur at frequencies different from chance ($N = 94, D = .12$, n.s.). *Hand* movements became more frequent at the end of the morning ($N = 135, D = .33, p < .01$). *Arm* movements decreased in frequency throughout the morning ($N = 5808, D = .06, p < .01$). *Leg* movements occurred more frequently during the last two morning observation periods ($N = 282, D = .22, p < .01$). *Gross body* movements increased in frequency over the morning ($N = 2759, D = .09, p < .01$), and the increase was closely paralleled by *Locomotory* movements ($N = 2096, D = .10, p < .01$).

Of the 20 specific motor patterns examined, 12 showed significant daily periodicity (Fig. 9.2). Five (all arm movements) decreased in frequency over the eight observation periods: *Manipulate* ($N = 1552, D = .05, p < .01$), *Pick up* ($N = 1162, D = .08, p < .01$), *Place* ($N = 975, D = .08, p < .01$), *Pour* ($N = 218, D = .18, p < .01$), and *Scoop* ($N = 211, D = .24, p < .01$). A sixth pattern, *Step*, occurred more frequently in the middle of the morning ($N = 173, D = .13$,

TABLE 9.2. *The 20 Most Frequently-Occurring Specific Motor Patterns,*
Slade Nursery School

Motor pattern	Number of times observed
Manipulate	1552
Pick up	1162
Walk	1114
Place	975
Turn	526
Move	383
Stand	377
Reach	325
Run	288
Bend	236
Push	228
Pull	227
Pour	218
Scoop	211
Put down	193
Step	173
Lift	170
Sit down	161
Climb	129
Take out	116

$p < .01$). Six motor patterns (three gross body movements and three locomotory movements) increased in frequency over the eight observation periods: *Walk* ($N = 1114$, D .07, $p < .01$), *Stand* ($N = 377$, $D = .10$, $p < .01$), *Run* ($N = 288$, $D = .18$, $p < .01$), *Bend* ($N = 236$, $D = .18$, $p < .01$), *Lift* ($N = 170$, $D = .24$, $p < .01$), and *Climb* ($N = 129$, $D = .27$, $p < .01$). In all cases, the direction of change agreed with that found for the six general motor categories.

Epworth Halls Nursery School

Daily behavioral periodicity in the Epworth Halls Nursery School was examined by sequentially quartering daily observation periods into four subunits of slightly over 20 minutes each. The data were the same used in Chapter 7: a child's first five days of nursery experience and five-day sample of the same child's behavior 65 nursery days later. Grouped totals were used because individual quarterly totals were often too low for analysis, and inspection indicated that individual trends were similar. Number of individual children contributing to each group mean ranged from 8 to 12. Ten frequently-occurring behavior patterns (defined in Chapter 4) were examined.

Statistically significant differences in behavior pattern frequencies were found between quarters within days (Fig. 9.3), and some differences recurred persistently throughout one or both five-day observation sets.

Looking decreased gradually throughout the morning during both sets of observations. Overall comparison of the 10 days yielded a very regular pattern: the fourth quarter mean frequency/child was always (i.e., on 10 of 10 days) less than the first and second quarter means (Sign Test, $x = 0$, $p = .001$), as was the third quarter mean with only one exception ($x = 1$, $p = .001$). The distribution of looking totals by quarters differed significantly from chance on 5 of 10 days, and the other five days closely approximated the prevalent pattern. The children's first day of nursery experience proved to be the most aberrant from the general pattern: the least difference between first and fourth quarter means occurred on the first day. The first day also provided the only instance of a third or fourth quarter mean exceeding a first or second quarter mean.

In contrast, *Walking* demonstrated the opposite extreme: none of the 10 days showed significant variance from chance between quarters. However, differences between the two five-day observations sets existed. Comparing the first and fourth quarter means: walking decreased over every morning in the first five days, and increased over every morning during the second five-day period 65 days later ($x = 0$, $p = .031$). Likewise, *Smiling* showed no periodicity.

Glance periodicity resembled looking, but only one day's interquartile differences reached significance at less than the .01 level. The first quarter mean exceeded the fourth quarter mean on nine days with only one tie ($x = 0$,

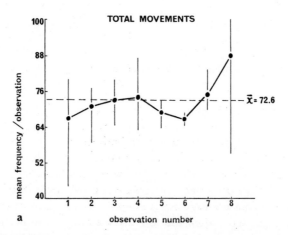

Fig. 9.1a. Daily periodicity in total motor behavior (movement), Slade Nursery School mean frequency per 5-minute observation period. b. Daily periodicity in six general motor behavior (movement) categories, Slade Nursery School, mean frequency per 5-minute observation period.

196

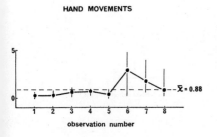

HAND MOVEMENTS

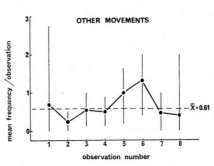

OTHER MOVEMENTS

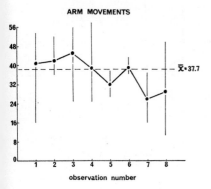

ARM MOVEMENTS

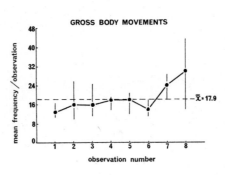

GROSS BODY MOVEMENTS

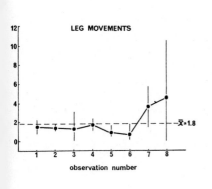

LEG MOVEMENTS

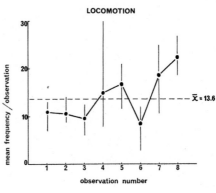

LOCOMOTION

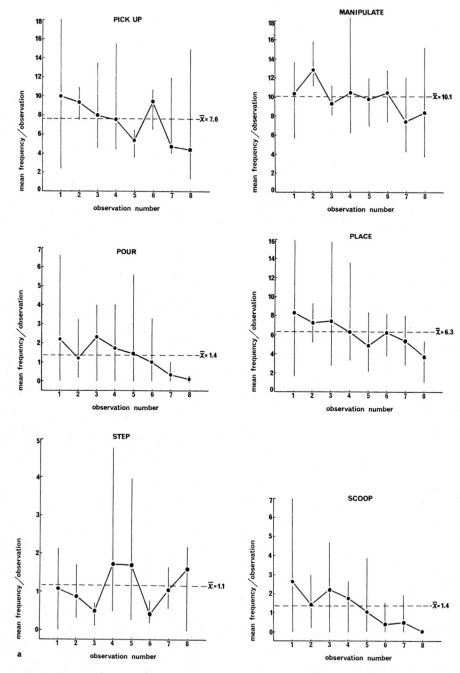

Fig. 9.2a. Daily periodicity in six specific motor patterns, Slade Nursery School, mean frequency per 5-minute observation period. **b.** Daily periodicity in six specific motor patterns, Slade Nursery School, mean frequency per 5-minute observation period.

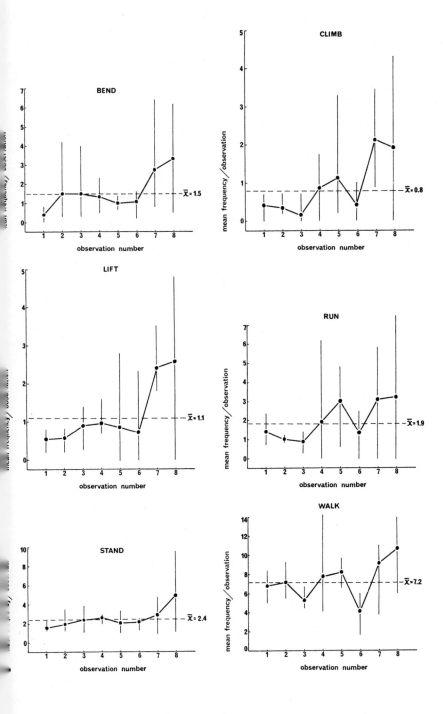

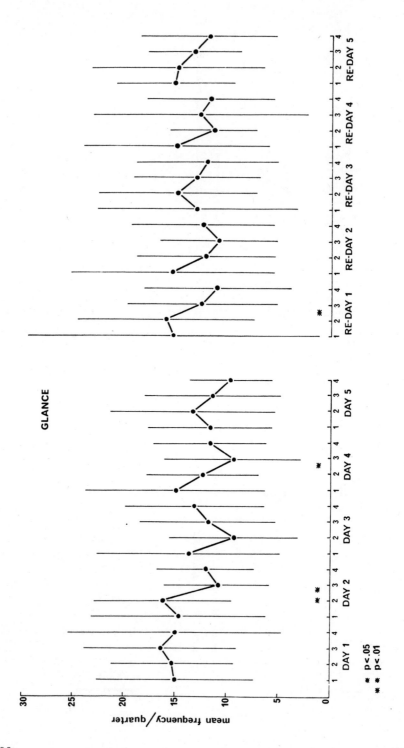

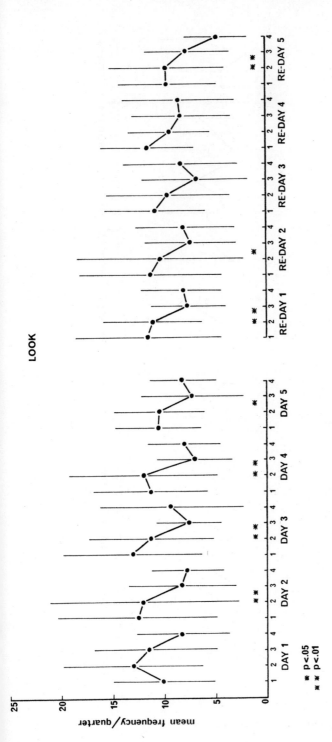

Fig. 9.3a. Daily periodicity in Look and Glance over the first five nursery days and the later five-day period, Epworth Halls Nursery School, mean frequency per 20-minute observation period. **b.** Daily periodicity in Automanipulate and Immobile over the first five nursery days and the later five-day period, Epworth Halls Nursery School, mean frequency per 20-minute observation period. **c.** Daily periodicity in Lean (to Child) and Run over the first five nursery days and the later five-day period, Epworth Halls Nursery School, mean frequency per 20-minute observation period. **d.** Daily periodicity in Laugh and Verbalize over the first five nursery days and the later five-day period, Epworth Halls Nursery School, mean frequency per 20-minute observation period. **e.** Lack of daily periodicity in Walk and Smile over the first five nursery days and the later five-day period, Epworth Halls Nursery School, mean frequency per 20-minute observation period.

201

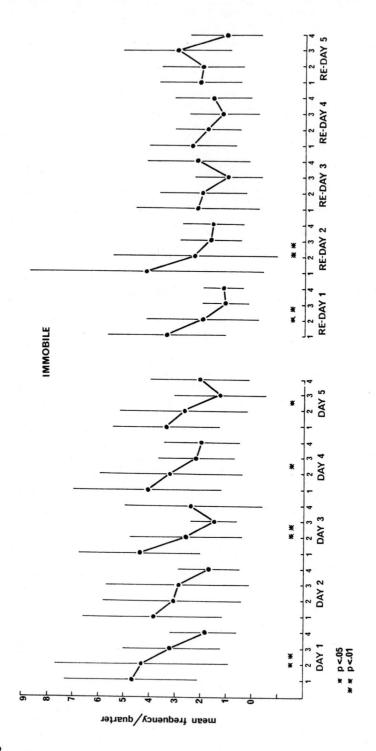

IMMOBILE

mean frequency/quarter

DAY 1   DAY 2   DAY 3   DAY 4   DAY 5

RE-DAY 1   RE-DAY 2   RE-DAY 3   RE-DAY 4   RE-DAY 5

* p<.05
** p<.01

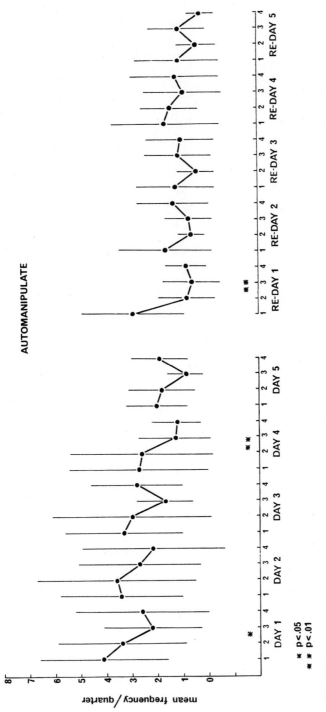

AUTOMANIPULATE

mean frequency / quarter

* p<.05
* * p<.01

Fig. 9.3b.

203

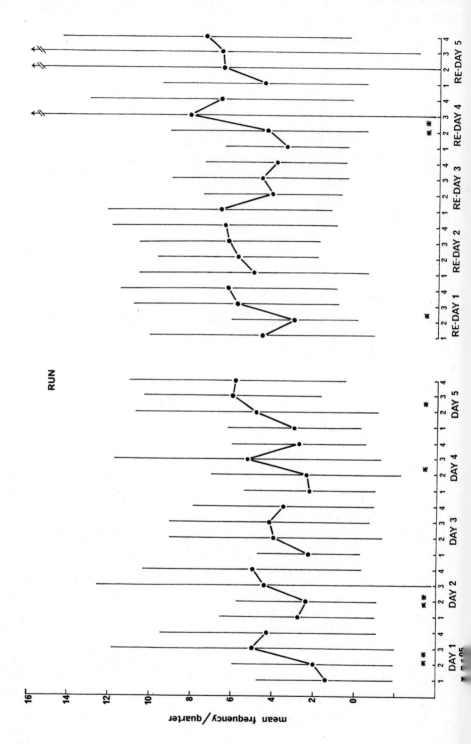

LEAN (TO CHILD)

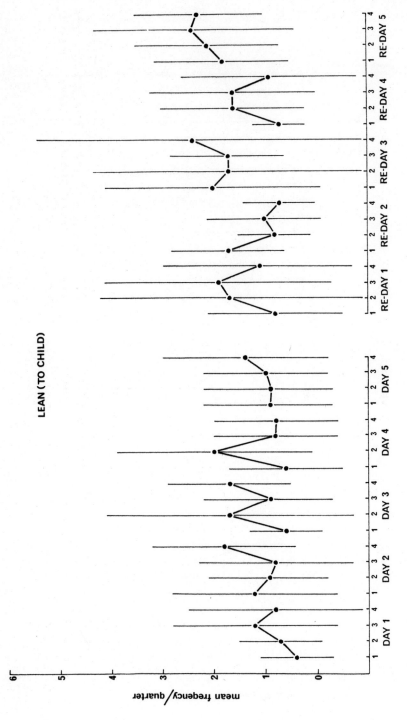

Fig. 9.3c.

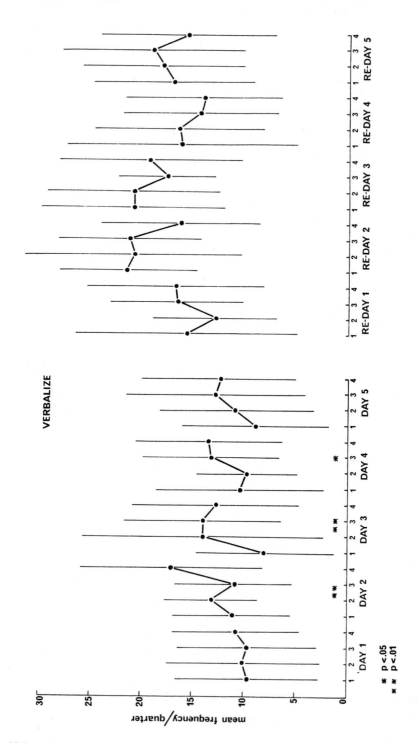

VERBALIZE

mean frequency/quarter

30 — 25 — 20 — 15 — 10 — 5 — 0

1 2 3 4 | 1 2 3 4 | 1 2 3 4 | 1 2 3 4 | 1 2 3 4
DAY 1 | DAY 2 | DAY 3 | DAY 4 | DAY 5

RE-DAY 1 | 1 2 3 4 | 1 2 3 4 | 1 2 3 4 | 1 2 3 4
RE-DAY 2 | RE-DAY 3 | RE-DAY 4 | RE-DAY 5

* p < .05
** p < .01

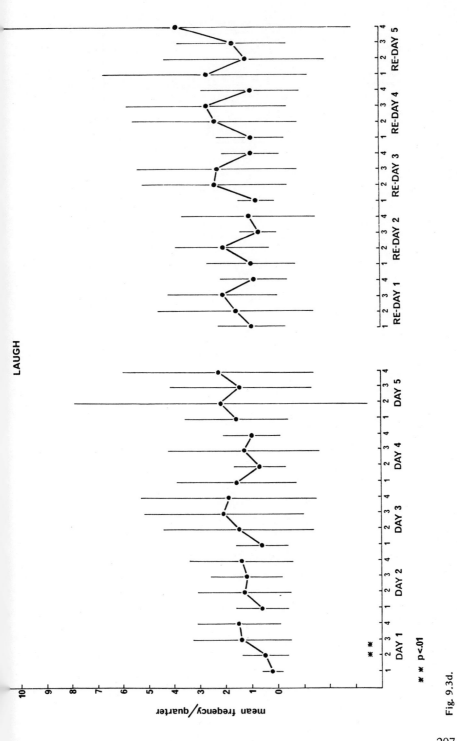

LAUGH

mean frequency/quarter

** p<.01

Fig. 9.3d.

207

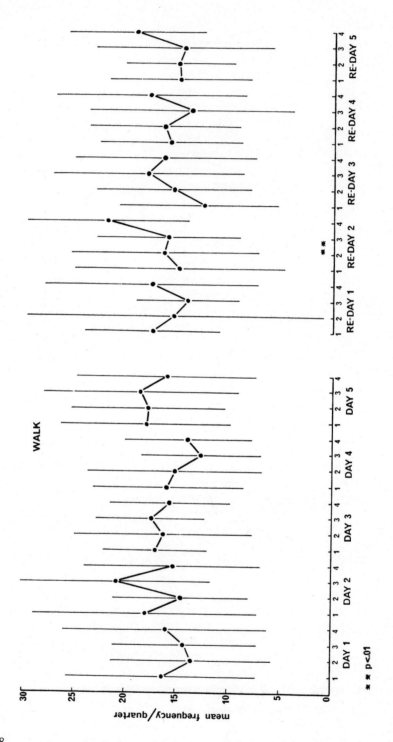

208

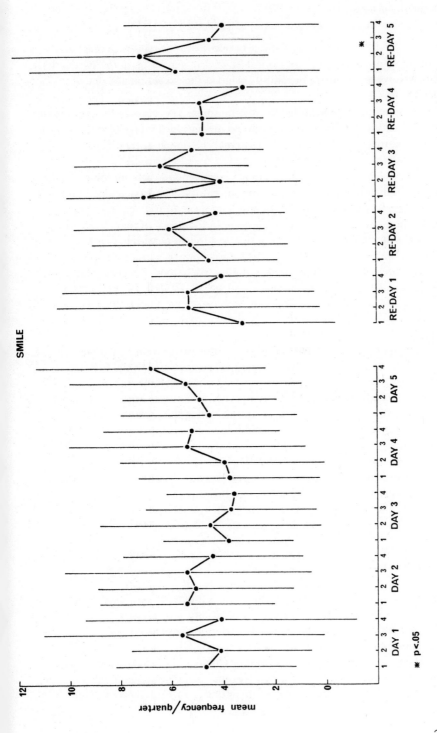

SMILE

mean frequency/quarter

DAY 1   DAY 2   DAY 3   DAY 4   DAY 5

RE-DAY 1   RE-DAY 2   RE-DAY 3   RE-DAY 4   RE-DAY 5

* p<.05

Fig. 9.3e.

209

$p = .002$), and the third quarter mean on eight of nine days with one tie ($x = 1$, $p = .02$). Again, Day 1 deviated most from the general pattern: its quarterly totals were virtually the same, and it included the exception and one of the ties noted above.

Running increased throughout the morning. The third and fourth quarter means exceeded the first quarter means on nine of the 10 days ($x = 1, p = .011$). The first nursery day was the most extreme: the first and second quarter means on Day 1 were the lowest of all 10 days.

Immobility decreased in frequency throughout each morning, and this reached statistical significance on four mornings. The first quarter mean exceeded the second and the fourth quarter means on all 10 days ($x = 0, p = .001$). Day 1's first quarter showed the highest mean frequency of immobility of all 40 quarters, and the difference between first and fourth quarter means was greatest in the first nursery day.

Automanipulation also decreased over each morning. The first quarter mean exceeded the fourth quarter mean on all 10 days of recording ($x = 0$, $p = .001$) and the third quarter mean on nine of ten days with one tie ($x = 0$, $p = .002$). Like Immobility, Day 1's first quarter showed the highest mean frequency of all 40 quarters.

Laughter showed significant periodicity on a child's first day in the nursery, but none thereafter. It increased in frequency from the first quarter of the first day, which had the lowest mean frequency of all 40 quarters.

Verbalization increased over the first five mornings in the nursery school ($x = 0, p = .031$), but no increases occurred during the re-observations. The first day's quarterly means were uniformly low, so that the smallest difference between quarters existed on Day 1.

Smiling showed no significant daily periodicity.

Leaning directed to other children showed consistent periodicity: the fourth quarter mean frequency was higher than the first quarter mean frequency on nine of the ten days ($x = 0, p = .011$). The mean frequency during the first quarter of the child's first day in nursery was the lowest of all 40 quarters.

Weekly Periodicity

Of the time units examined, the week is the most "artificial," that is, tied to cultural instead of natural phenomena. No previous investigation of weekly behavioral periodicity has appeared, although popular reports exist, for example, head-aches are most common after week-ends (Gallup Poll, 1970).

Using the movement data from four children in the Slade Nursery School, frequencies of six general motor categories and the 20 most commonly-occurring motor patterns were compared over the Monday to Friday period. Number of individual observational periods comprising each grouped mean ranges from 27 to 34.

Total number of movements seen was significantly higher during the second half of the week, rising from the Monday mean of 62.5 to the Friday mean of 83.6 (Fig. 9.4a, $N = 11174$, $D = .05$, $p < .01$). The four children's individual records showed similar changes both in total number of movements and in the six general motor categories.

Of the six general motor categories, five showed significant weekly periodicity (Fig. 9.4b); *Leg* movements were not exhibited at frequencies different from chance ($N = 282$, $D = .06$, n.s.). *Hand* movements were significantly more frequent on Tuesdays ($N = 135$, $D = .19$, $p < .01$). *Arm* movements increased in frequency significantly throughout the week ($N = 5808$, $D = .06$, $p < .01$). *Other* movements decreased in frequency significantly over the week ($N = 94$, $D = .19$, $p < .01$). *Gross body* movements were significantly more frequent during the week's second half ($N = 2759$, $D = .07$, $p < .01$) as were *Locomotory* movements ($N = 2096$, $D = .06$, $p < .01$). Some of these results, for example, increased hand movements on Tuesdays, are likely to be spurious.

Of the 20 specific motor patterns examined, five showed significant weekly periodicity (Fig. 9.5). All five increased in frequency over the five days: *Manipulate* ($N = 1552$, $D=.06$, $p < .01$), *Pick up* ($N = 1162$, $D = .11$, $p < .01$), *Walk* ($N = 1114$, $D = .06$, $p < .01$), *Place* ($N = 975$, $D = .10$, $p < .01$), and *Bend* ($N = 236$, $D=.19$, $p < .01$). In all cases, the direction of change agreed with that found for the six general motor categories.

The 30 behavior patterns most frequently occurring in the Slade social behavior study (Table 9.3) were analyzed for possible weekly periodicity. The number of individual observations comprising each grouped mean ranged from 39 to 112. Ten of the 30 patterns showed statistically significant periodicity over the Monday to Friday period (Fig. 9.6). Four behavior patterns increased significantly in frequency during the week: *Walk* ($N = 971$, $D = .085$, $p < .01$), *Smile* ($N = 159$, $D = .14$, $p < .01$), *Crouch* ($N = 113$, $D = .16$, $p < .01$), and *Jump* ($N = 53$, $D = .23$, $p < .01$). Two behavior patterns decreased significantly in frequency over the week: *Look* ($N = 1070$, $D=.06$, $p < .01$) and *Push* ($N = 218$, $D=.17$, $p < .01$). Four behavior patterns showed significantly high or low frequencies on particular weekdays: *Automanipulate* on Thursdays ($N = 110$, $D = .23$, $p < .01$), *Wrestle* on Tuesdays ($N = 68$, $D = .29$, $p < .01$), *Vocalize* on Fridays ($N = 90$, $D = .18$, $p < .01$), and *Verbalize* on Wednesdays ($N = 936$, $D = .08$, $p < .01$). These latter results, that is, extreme frequencies on particular weekdays, are probably chance statistical artifacts.

Lunar, Monthly, and Annual Periodicity

Cowgill, Bishop, Andrews and Hutchinson (1962) reported apparent lunar periodicity in the mating behavior of several prosimian species and based their

211

explanation on moonlight illumination changes directly facilitating nocturnal activities. Altmann and Altmann (1970) found consistent deviation in baboon daily activity during the time of the full moon. Apparently the greater illumination increased the chances of overnight predation on the animals, making them restless; this restlessness carried over to their group movements on the following day. Because of this positive report for other primate species, children's behavior in the Slade Nursery School was examined for lunar periodicity. However, since preschool children sleep 10–12 hours per night apparently regardless of lunar phase, lunar periodicity was not expected in their diurnal behavior.

Behavior patterns given in Table 9.3 were compared over the lunar cycle's approximately 7½-day quarters: (I) Between New moon and First Quarter, (II) Between First Quarter and Full moon, (III) Between Full moon and Second Quarter, and (IV) Between Second Quarter and New moon. Data were analyzed over four consecutive lunar cycles as given in *Astronomical Ephemeris*.

Twenty-seven of the 30 most frequently-occurring behavior patterns showed no lunar periodicity, but three (Verbalize, Pull, and Wrestle) did. No obvious explanation exists for these apparent periodicities, and they are probably spurious chance results.

Behavioral periodicity related to calendar months has not been previously investigated, but it was thought to justify study because of its pervasive influence in Western society. For example, a regular monthly salary payment might influence a household's atmosphere and thus the interpersonal relations of its occupants. However, long-term studies would be required to differentiate this from possible lunar cycle effects.

Data from the Slade Nursery School social behavior study were arbitrarily grouped into six five-day subunits: 1st-5th, 6th-10th, 11th-15th, 16th-20th,

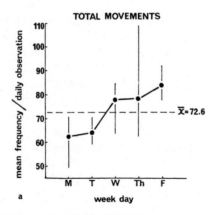

Fig. 9.4. Weekly periodicity in a. total motor behavior and in b. general motor behavior categories, Slade Nursery School, mean frequency per 5-minute observation period.

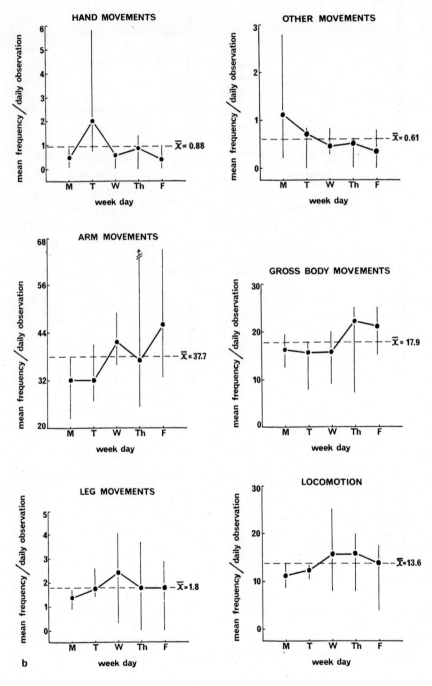

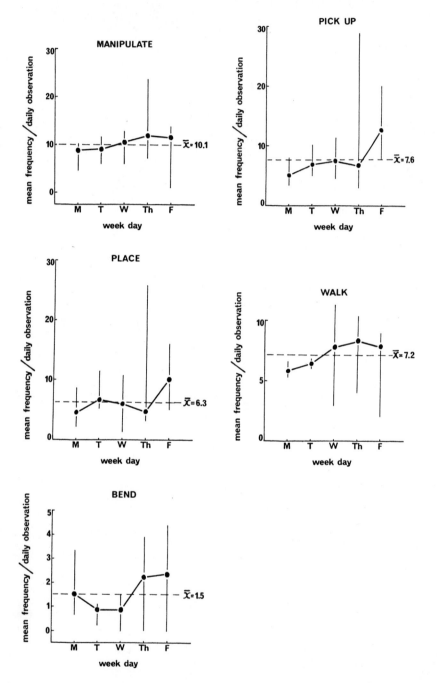

Fig. 9.5. Weekly periodicity in five specific motor patterns, Slade Nursery School, mean frequency per 5-minute observation period.

TABLE 9.3. *Thirty Most Frequently-Occurring Behavior Patterns (Mainly Social), Slade Nursery School*

Behavior pattern	Number of times observed
Look	1075
Walk	976
Verbalize	947
Turn	796
Lean	533
Back	237
Push	218
Run	196
Mouth Open	170
Sidle	165
Smile	160
Physical Contact	126
Automanipulate	114
Crouch	113
Flee	110
Reach	103
Vocalize	92
Pull	91
Point	75
Wide Eyes	75
Wrestle	70
Fall	57
Jump	54
Chase	54
Beat	51
Immobile	47
Low Frown	47
Forearm Sweep	43
Punch	40
Body Oppose	38

21st-25th, and 26th-30th. Frequencies of the 30 most commonly-occurring behavior patterns (Table 9.3) were compared over the six periods. Twenty-nine of the 30 showed ·no intra-monthly variation which might be indicative of monthly periodicity. Again, the explanation for the exception (Verbalization) is probably statistical artifact.

Annual cyclicity in the sexual behavior of nonhuman primates is now well-known (Lancaster & Lee, 1965), and in some cases this can be directly related to physiological cyclicity, for example, testis size changes in free-ranging rhesus monkeys (Sade, 1964). Similar seasonal differences in human sexual behavior exist, but their causation is unclear (Parkes, 1968). In most cases, periodicity in non-sexual social behavior occurs concurrently with sexual behav-

215

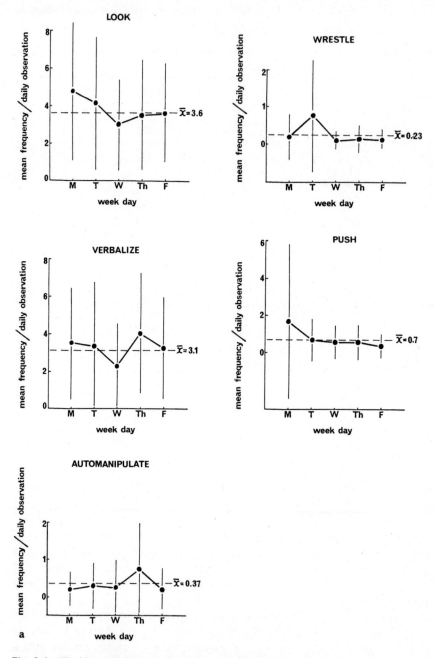

Fig. 9.6a. Weekly periodicity in five behavior patterns, Slade Nursery School, mean frequency per interaction (daily observation). **b.** Weekly periodicity in five behavior patterns, Slade Nursery School, mean frequency per interaction (daily observation).

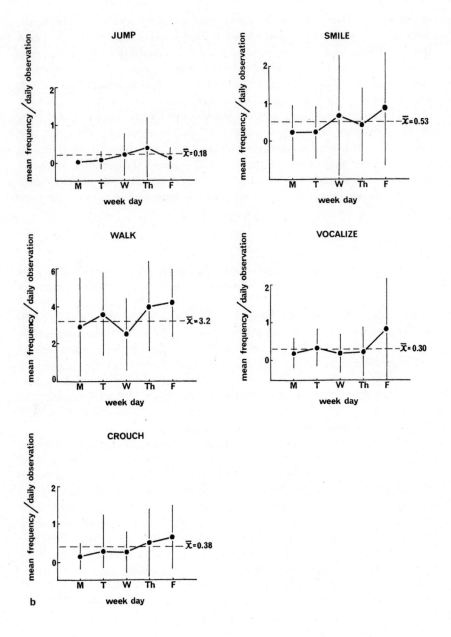

217

ior changes, for example, a female savanna baboon's position in the female dominance hierarchy is enhanced when she is in estrous (K. R. L. Hall & DeVore, 1965). In examining possible annual periodicity in children, one must avoid confusing it with ontogenetic changes and, therefore, cross-sectional (i.e., different groups of different aged children) is preferable to longitudinal (i.e., the same children followed through different ages) data.

The longest and most complete study was the Slade Nursery School study of social behavior which took place over four months: December, January, February, and March. Frequencies of the 30 most commonly-occurring behavior patterns (Table 9.3) were compared over this period. Twenty-nine of the 30 showed no month-to-month variation that might be indicative of annual periodicity. The lone exception, Looking, probably represents a spurious statistical result.

Discussion

From these results, it seems likely that daily and weekly periodicity are factors to be taken into account in understanding preschool children's behavior in the nursery school. This makes the neglect of such variables in past observational studies of young children unfortunate, as simple daily or weekly totals may mask intra-daily or intra-weekly behavioral differences. For example, daily means of leaning toward other children did not show significant short-term or long-term differences (Table 7.3), but significant changes within days occurred consistently throughout both five-day observation periods. Mean totals may also mask short-term and long-term differences, for example, overall frequency of walking did not differ between the two five-day observation periods (Table 7.5), but daily periodicity within each of them differed.

If two children are observed at different times of day, it is possible that any individual differences found are actually due to or enhanced by daily periodicity. Day-of-the-week is even more rarely standardized in developmental studies, yet the same argument applies. An obvious solution is to observe or test an individual at a standardized time and on the same day of the week or to use some counter-balanced design, however tedious and time-consuming this may be.

It seems most unlikely that lunar, monthly, or annual periodicity are important factors in children's free-ranging behavior, although the conclusion for annual periodicity must remain tentative due to incomplete data in this study. Almost all (92%) behavior patterns investigated showed no such periodicity, and the few exceptions were probably statistical artifacts. This is not surprising, as lunar cycle is probably irrelevant for reasons mentioned earlier, and direct monthly effects also seem unlikely. Like a week, a month is a culturally-bound concept unrelated to any natural phenomena, but time-of-the-month, unlike day-of-the-week, was irrelevant to nursery procedure. However, more reason exists for expecting annual behavioral periodicity, for example, Tanner's (1964, p. 347) findings of seasonal differences in children's growth rates, and prolonged observation remains to be done.

In seeking to explain the behavioral periodicity found here, it is possible that periodicity existed only in the observer's behavior and not the children's. This is unlikely because observational procedures remained unchanged during each study, but it could be argued that unconscious observer "warm-up" or "fatigue" effects operated. This is unlikely since in all cases both decreases *and* increases in behavior pattern frequencies occurred consistently over mornings or weeks.

Routine nursery procedures also seemed unlikely to be causes of the behavioral periodicity found. All observations occurred during free play when children interacted almost undirected by adults, and any two observations periods within a day or a week were virtually identical in toys and social companions available, adult-child routines, and observer behavior. However, such influences cannot be ruled out, for example, arrangement and dispersion of the toys changed as the morning progressed, and the nursery nurse's responses to the children may have changed as the week progressed.

Endogenous factors, for example, some physiological activity rhythm, may have been involved in the daily periodicities found, but this is an unlikely explanation for weekly periodicities. Slightly over 80 minutes per day in the Epworth Halls Nursery School or the sampled span of 130 minutes per day in the Slade Nursery School were insufficient samples of the 24-hour day to determine this. Increasing hunger before lunch, boredom, or prolonged confinement may have been involved in the explanation of the increasing gross activity seen as a morning progressed.

The most likely explanation for the behavioral periodicity observed lies in a nursery school's social aspects. As discussed in Chapter 7, the nursery seemed to constitute a powerful, socially novel situation both at entry and afterwards, that is, incoming children usually had no prior experience in large peer groups, and this experience remained limited to the few hours spent each week in the nursery. The social novelty seemed to produce "ambivalence" and "inhibition" in the children which only subsided with increased familiarity with the situation. In this light, it is probably that each morning's arrival constituted a lesser repetition of the original introduction. Fearful behavior patterns which had tailed off the previous morning probably rose again in frequency the next morning in response to the renewal of group contacts after overnight separation. A similar interval of separation existed over the week-end before renewal of group contacts on Monday mornings. A consistent rate of recovery after waning of a pattern's frequency is a common behavioral phenomenon, for example, see Hinde (1966, p. 211). In contrast, the date or the moon's phase were irrelevant to the pattern imposed on a child's life by the nursery school.

The Epworth Halls data support the idea of each day representing a less-extreme repetition of the initial, disturbing introduction. (Some children had to be convinced on their first day in the nursery that their mothers would return at all, and for most children, the time spent in nursery constituted the longest regular period of maternal separation until primary school.) For most behavior patterns, the child's first day was the most aberrant from the usual periodicities seen in the nine remaining days of observation. This aberrancy took two forms: "enhancement" of inter-quartile differences (e.g., run, immobile) or "flattening" of inter-quartile differences (e.g., verbalize, glance). Similarly, for five of the 10 behavior patterns analyzed, the first quarter of Day 1, which one would expect to be the most disturbing, provided the most extreme high or low mean of the 40 quarters. Similarly, Mondays provided the most extreme high or low means in four of the five motor patterns and five of the eight behavior patterns showing weekly periodicity.

In general, direction of *intra-day* differences agreed with the direction of *inter-day* differences. (Chapter 7 showed that inter-day differences during the first five days reflected the direction of differences later found between the two five-day periods 65 days apart.) In the Slade Nursery School study, tendencies for frequencies to increase or decrease similarly over the day and week existed for total movements, gross body movements, locomotion, walking, bending, etc. (However, the one conspicuous exception to this was in arm movements: manipulate, pick up, place, etc.) In Epworth Halls, this consistency held true for increases (run, verbalize) and decreases (e.g., immobile, auto-manipulate), further suggesting stable phenomena.

Comparisons between the two daily and two weekly sets of data, when possible (see Table 9.4) yield high agreement. Two daily patterns were duplicated: both *walking* and *running* increased significantly over the morning in both the Epworth Halls and Slade (A) studies. (Only the Epworth Halls re-observation data from socially-experienced children were directly comparable to data

TABLE 9.4. *Comparison of Behavior Patterns Duplicated in Two Studies of Weekly Periodicity, Slade Nursery School*

Behavior pattern	Slade (A)	p^a	Slade (B)	p^a
Walk	increase	.01	increase	.01
Push	decrease	n. s.	decrease	.01
Run	increase	n. s.	increase	.05
Turn	unclear	n. s.	decrease	.05
Pull	increase	.05	increase	n. s.
Reach	decrease	n. s.	decrease	n. s.

[a]Kolmogorov-Smirnov one-sample test.

from the socially-experienced Slade children.) Six behavior patterns were common to both Slade Nursery School studies, and Table 9.4 gives comparisons of their weekly frequency changes. Five of the six behavior patterns changed in the same direction, but most of the directional trends did not reach the .01 significance level.

Chapter 10

Overview

This chapter represents a brief attempt to comment upon and interrelate some of the findings contained in the preceding nine chapters. Some suggestions for extending the research are also included. It is not an attempt at a "grand synthesis," as considerable discussion has already been presented in the individual chapters. Because human ethology is a new field of inquiry, its research efforts (including this one) remain tentative and inconclusive. But advances are already evident in its short lifetime, and these might be classified into three stages: speculation, description of elements, and investigation of increasingly specific research problems. In other words, one first becomes aware that unanswered questions exist, then one seeks the means to articulate those questions, then one phrases specific questions and attempts to answer them. The answers become increasingly pointed and accurate as knowledge accumulates. This process is not exclusive to the development of human ethology and (ideally) might represent the development of all scientific fields. The three stages provide a useful framework for discussing the research described in this monograph.

Chapters 1 and 2 and some introductory sections of later chapters approximate the speculative stage. Just as man has always sought to delineate a special gulf between himself and the other animals (e.g., see Gregson and Gregson's [1970] historical note on such a fine inter-primate distinction), so he has been just as certain to gaze persistently at his relations on the other side for explanations and inspirations. The cross-disciplinal nature of the research problems dealt with here straddles several established fields, and at least one of these requires brief discussion, that is, the repeated calls for a bringing together of ethology and human behavioral research which have appeared since ethology's origins in the 1930's. These have followed two main lines: first, several research workers have tentatively proposed that the findings of animal ethology might be useful in explaining human behavioral phenomena. Such authorities do not advocate the existence of direct phylogenetic connections between, say, the behavior of rat and human populations, but often the distinction between analogy and homology is left unclear. Foremost of these is Lorenz, whose pioneering descriptive research concentrated mainly on fish and birds, and whose speculations on human behavior reached best-seller status in *On Aggression*. Second, several research workers have suggested that ethological methods and ideas of behavioral analysis might be adapted and applied directly to human behavior problems. Tinbergen has advanced this view in a series of publications, a recent example being the text of his Oxford inaugural lecture published in *Science* (1968). Other workers, for example, Bowlby, have discussed human ethology from both viewpoints. Such speculation has resulted in much stimulating and controversial discussion, and the lay person's enhanced awareness of ethology is demonstrated by the string of recent "pop" ethology best-sellers. (Could Desmond Morris have possibly imagined while completing his Doctor of Philosophy thesis on sticklebacks in 1954 that his future ethological writings would reach the status of *Sunday Mirror* serialization?) Finally, one other type of speculation on animal and human behavior might be mentioned: that which occurs in the final paragraphs of many research grant applications filed by animal behaviorists to medical or health-oriented research-funding bodies. However, all the speculators have some characteristics in common: most have conducted animal behavior research but have declined to attempt empirical investigations of human behavior. Practicing human ethologists have so far been much more cautious about making any pronouncements, a reticence which this author shares.

Chapter 4 exemplifies human ethology's still continuing descriptive phase. Serious attempts at producing an ethogram for the human species have appeared only in the past five years and have usually been restricted to certain human subgroupings: preschool children's social behavior (Blurton Jones, 1967, 1972a; W. C. McGrew, 1969), preschool children's motor behavior (W. C. McGrew, 1970), adult mental patient's behavior (Grant, 1965b, 1968), mother-infant social behavior (Richards & Bernal, 1972). Finally there is Grant's (1969) recent attempt at a comprehensive ethogram for *Homo sapiens*. It is certainly the best effort currently in print, but by its emphasis on facial expressions, it lacks complete coverage of gestural and postural patterns. All behavioral repertoires published so far share certain shortcomings such as the lack of: empirical confirmation in most cases, complete definitions, observer reliability testing. Some of these are alleviated in the fourth chapter, but certain shortcomings remain: the level of description varies in specificity, so that Wrestle is a combination of behavior patterns like Push and Body Oppose. Also, the repertoire is not presented as final but will continue to be enlarged as additional behavior patterns are recognized and described. Finally, the repertoire in Chapter 4 is not suitable for all types of behavioral study. Research workers with access to high quality recording equipment, for example, one-inch videotape or 35 mm cinefilm, and optimal observation situations can probably reduce (if necessary) the categories given here to finer ones, for example, facial expressions into components such as eyebrow, nose, mouth positions. As with behavioral studies of any species, the level of descriptive category chosen for investigation will finally be determined by the particular questions to which the research worker is seeking answers.

The five remaining chapters cover attempts to use the behavioral elements of Chapter 4 as measures in the investigation of selected human behavioral questions. Until recently, such specific investigations have been confined to single infant responses, for example, the directed head-turning response (Prechtl, 1958), and the smiling response (Ambrose, 1961). However, other research workers are currently studying infant behavior using more comprehensive behavioral repertoires (Bernal & Richards, 1970; Richards, 1970). Finally, some investigators are beginning to examine specific behavioral questions concerning older children: reactions of children to a strange observer (P. K. Smith & Connolly, 1972), mother-child separation in parks and open spaces (Anderson, 1972), children's separation and greeting behavior (Blurton Jones & Leach, 1972), mother-child interaction in normal and hyper-anxious children (Leach, 1972). These research workers share several characteristics: they are young, many have limited experience with animal behavior research, and most refrain from speculation in favor of empirical investigation.

Chapter 5 represents a general question: How are children's behavior patterns exhibited in social interactions? This research chronologically preceded the other chapters and comprised in many ways a pilot study. Its specific questions are simple: How many children participate in social interactions? How long do such interactions last? Who participates in the interaction? Are objects or toys often involved? Such normative data, though of obvious and basic interest, were not previously available.

Chapters 6–9 represent four more specific questions: How do children behave during group formation? How does a child's behavior change after introduction into a peer group? How is children's social behavior related to group density? Does children's ongoing behavior show periodicities? Concerning Chapter 6, two interesting control situations would be the observation of group formation in assemblages of completely peer-experienced and peer-inexperienced children, with all children mutually unacquainted. One might expect to find earlier increases and higher levels of aggression in the former type of group. Similar control studies should be conducted on homogenous groups of children differing only in age.

It would also be interesting to conduct studies intermediate between group formation and individual introduction. For example, the introduction of small groups into large established groups, as Bernstein (1969) introduced trios of new animals into larger pigtailed macaque groups. Chapter 6 and 7 especially underline the heuristic value of nonhuman primate studies for human behavioral research. In both cases, the initial experimental research on the topic was done in captive nonhuman primate colonies although observations of children's nursery groups had been going on for decades longer. The comparative results highlight the point that simple extrapolation from nonhuman to human would have been misleading, as important differences as well as similarities were found in group formation and introduction of strangers.

Chapters 8 and 9 represent research on variables usually neglected in studies of children's behavior: group density and periodicity. Both proved to be important influences on behavior which should be taken into account when interpreting past studies or designing future ones. The first examined short-term behavior as opposed to long-term studies of population density, but an obvious extension of the research would be to contrast density-behavior relationships in comparable groups of children growing up in low and high density living areas. Once again, nursery schools could provide convenient settings for such investigations. The second's examination of possible periodicity in children's behavior underlines the importance of scrutinizing data again and again and of reexamining old assumptions in the light of recent findings in related fields. Extension of this analysis with the aim of investigating periodicity of data collected earlier for different reasons was an after-thought, but the phenomenon is of such potential importance that further inquiries into it should be made. More sensible scheduling of school activities and subjects on both daily and weekly bases according to their relative social involvement and activity required might be one practical application of such knowledge.

This monograph had modest aims: it attempted to show that application of ethological ideas and methods to the behavior of preschool children is both possible and potentially useful. Children's ongoing behavior *can* be analyzed in terms of the type of discrete elements hitherto derived by ethologists observing other animals. These behavioral elements *have* proved useful in undertaking new research problems stimulated by nonhuman primate research (e.g., on group formation) and in reexamining neglected aspects of traditional psychological research problems (e.g., social development in nursery school). The question of how useful "human ethology" as here defined will ultimately prove will not be answered until many more studies have been done.

Appendix

Glossary of Selected Motor Patterns

The complete glossary of 133 motor patterns exhibited by four three-and-one-half-year-old children in the Slade Nursery School, Oxford, appears elsewhere (W. C. McGrew, 1970). This excerpted and somewhat refined version contains definitions of the 20 most frequently occurring motor patterns, examined for periodicity in Chapter 9. (See Table 9.3.) Definitions appear alphabetically and include the number of times observed and mean duration. The motor pattern's general movement category is also given: H, Hand; A, Arm; L, Leg; GB, Gross body; O, Other; and Lo, Locomotory.

Bend To flex the trunk at the hips while in a leaning, standing, sitting, or kneeling posture.
  GB, N = 236, $\bar{x}$ dur. = 1.3 sec.
Climb To move upwards on an object, usually by alternately raising the arm and leg of one side, then the arm and leg of the other side; face usually directed upward.
  Lo, N = 129, $\bar{x}$ dur. = 4.2 sec.

227

Lift To raise an arm or leg by elbow or knee flexion; if a large object is involved, trunk extension also usually occurs.

GB, $N = 170$, $\bar{x}$ dur. = 2.1 sec.

Manipulate To move the hands and fingers with continuous flexion and extension while contacting an object.

H, $N = 1552$, $\bar{x}$ dur. = 5.2 sec.

Move To move the trunk and limbs in an irregular, amorphous manner.

GB, $N = 383$, $\bar{x}$ dur. = 3.6 sec.

Pick up To raise a small object by arm flexion alone, in a continuous motion.

A, $N = 1162$, $\bar{x}$ dur. = 1.8 sec.

Place To move a limb to a particular location with a single, continuous motion, usually horizontal extension.

A, $N = 975$, $\bar{x}$ dur. = 1.9 sec.

Pour To tilt an object held out from the body with arm pronation and wrist rotation.

A, $N = 218$, $\bar{x}$ dur. = 3.2 sec.

Pull To move an object toward the body by arm and trunk flexion.

GB, $N = 227$, $\bar{x}$ dur. = 3.2 sec.

Push To move an object from the body by arm and trunk extension.

GB, $N = 228$, $\bar{x}$ dur. = 3.8 sec.

Put down To move an object to a location below shoulder level in a single continuous arm movement, usually downward extension.

A, $N = 193$, $\bar{x}$ dur. = 2.5 sec.

Reach To move the arm toward an object by arm extension and pronation, finishing palm down with hand open and fingers spread.

A, $N = 325$, $\bar{x}$ dur. = 1.4 sec.

Run To move the body rapidly forward, alternating legs during each stride, so that both feet are simultaneously off the ground during each stride.

Lo, $N = 288$, $\bar{x}$ dur. = 3.7 sec.

Scoop To extend the arm down, then horizontally, then up again in a smooth U-shaped motion.

A, $N = 211$, $\bar{x}$ dur. = 3.0 sec.

Sit down To move the body by hip and knee flexion from a higher position into a lower position in which it rests primarily on the buttocks.

GB, $N = 161$, $\bar{x}$ dur. = 2.1 sec.

Stand To move the body into an upright position by extension of knees, hips, and intervertebral joints, with feet not exceeding shoulder's width apart.

GB, $N = 377$, $\bar{x}$ dur. = 1.7 sec.

Step To move one leg forward, placing it on the ground while partially shifting the body's weight onto it.

GB, $N = 173$, $\bar{x}$ dur. = 1.6 sec.

Take out To move the arm toward the body (out of a container) by elbow flexion.

A, $N = 116, \bar{x}$ dur. = 1.9 sec.

Turn To rotate the trunk face-first about the body's longitudinal axis.

GB, $N = 526, \bar{x}$ dur. = 1.4 sec.

Walk To move the body forward, alternating legs during each stride, placing one foot firmly on the ground before lifting the other.

Lo, $N = 1114, \bar{x}$ dur. = 3.2 sec.

References

Ainsworth, M. D. The development of infant-mother interaction among the Ganda. In B. M. Foss (Ed.), *Determinants of infant behaviour*, Vol. 2. London: Methuen, 1963. Pp. 67-112.

Alexander, B. K., & Bowers, J. M. Social organization of a troop of Japanese monkeys in a two-acre enclosure. *Folia Primatologica*, 1969, **10**, 230-242.

Alexander, B. K., & Roth, E. M. The effects of acute crowding on aggressive behavior of Japanese monkeys. *Behaviour*, 1971, **39**, 673-690.

Altman, I., & Haythorn, W. The ecology of isolated groups. *Behavioral Science*, 1967, **12**, 169-182.

Altmann, S. A. A field study of the sociobiology of rhesus monkeys, *Macaca mulatta*. *Ann. also of the New York Academy of Sciences*, 1962, **102**, 338-435.

Altmann, S. A. Sociobiology of rhesus monkeys. II. Stochastics of social communication. *Journal of Theoretical Biology*, 1965, **8**, 490-522.

Altmann, S. A. (Ed.) *Social communication among primates*. Chicago, Ill.: Univ. of Chicago Press, 1967.

Altmann, S. A., & Altmann, J. *Baboon ecology. African field research. Bibliotheca Primatologica*, Vol. 12. Basel: Karger, 1970.

Ambrose, J. A. The development of the smiling response in early infancy. In B. M. Foss (Ed.), *Determinants of infant behaviour*, Vol. 1. London: Methuen, 1961. Pp. 179-196.

References

Ambrose, J. A. The age of onset of ambivalence in early infancy: Indications from the study of laughing. *Journal of Child Psychology and Psychiatry*, 1963, **4**, 167-181.

Ambrose, J. A. The comparative approach to early child development: The data of ethology. In E. Miller (Ed.), *Foundations of child psychiatry*. Oxford: Pergamon, 1968. Pp. 183-232.

Anderson, J. W. Attachment behaviour out-of-doors. In N. G. Blurton Jones (Ed.), *Ethological studies of child behaviour*, London & New York: Cambridge Univ. Press, 1972. Pp. 199-215.

Andrew, R. J. The origin and evolution of the calls and facial expressions of the primates. *Behaviour*, 1963, **20**, 1-109.

Anthoney, T. R. Threat activity in wild and captive groups of savannah baboons. In C. R. Carpenter (Ed.), *Proceedings of the second international congress of primatology*, Vol. 1. *Behavior*. Basel: Karger, 1969. Pp. 108-113.

Archer, J. Effects of population density on behaviour in rodents. In J. H. Crook (Ed.), *Social behaviour in birds and mammals*. London & New York: Academic Press, 1970. Pp. 169-210.

Ardrey, R. *African genesis. A personal investigation into the animal origins and nature of man.* London: Fontana, 1961.

Ardrey, R. *The territorial imperative. A personal inquiry into the animal origins of property and nations.* London: Collins, 1967.

Ardrey, R. *The social contract. A personal inquiry into the evolutionary sources of order and disorder.* London: Collins, 1970.

Argyle, M. *The psychology of interpersonal behaviour.* Harmondsworth: Penguin, 1967.

Argyle, M. *Social interaction.* London: Methuen, 1969.

Argyle, M. Eye-contact and distance: A reply to Stephenson and Rutter. *British Journal of Psychology*, 1970, **61**, 395-396.

Argyle, M., & Dean, J. Eye-contact, distance, and affiliation. *Sociometry*, 1965, **28**, 289-304.

Argyle, M., & Kendon, A. The experimental analysis of social performance. In L. Berkowitz (Ed.), *Advances in experimental social psychology*, Vol. 3. London & New York: Academic Press, 1967. Pp. 55-98.

Argyle, M., Lalljee, M., & Cook, M. The effects of visibility on interaction in a dyad. *Human Relations*, 1968, **21**, 3-17.

Aschoff, J. Circadian rhythms in man. *Science*, 1965, **148**, 1427-1432.

Astronomical ephemerus. London: HM Stationery Office, 1967-1968.

Azrin, N. H., Hutchinson, R. R., & Hake, D. Pain-induced fighting in the squirrel monkey. *Journal of the Experimental Analysis of Behavior*, 1963, **6**, 620-621.

Bailey, E. D. Social interaction as a population regulating mechanism in mice. *Canadian Journal of Zoology*, 1966, **44**, 1007-1012.

Bandura, A., & Walters, R. H. *Social learning and personality development.* New York: Holt, 1963.

Barker, R. G., Dembo, T., & Lewin, K. Frustration and regression: An experiment with young children. *University of Iowa Studies in Child Welfare*, 1941, **18**, 1-314.

Barnett, S. A. "Displacement" behaviour and "psychosomatic" disorder. *Lancet*, 1955, **2**, 1203-1208.

Barnett, S. A. Attack and defense in animal societies. In C. D. Clemente & D. B. Lindsley (Eds.), *Aggression and defense, neural mechanisms and social patterns*. Berkeley, Cal.: Univ. of California Press, 1967. Pp. 35-56.

Bastian, J. R. Primate signaling systems and human languages. In I. DeVore (Ed.), *Primate behavior*, New York: Holt, 1965. Pp. 585-606.

232

Beck, B. B. A study of problem solving by gibbons. *Behaviour,* 1967, **28**, 95-109.

Benedict, B. Role analysis in animals and man. *Man,* 1969, **4**, 203-214.

Benjamin, L. S. The effect of bottle and cup feeding on the non-nutritive sucking of the infant rhesus monkey. *Journal of Comparative and Physiological Psychology,* 1961, **54**, 230-237.

Benjamin, L. S. The beginning of thumbsucking. *Child Development,* 1967, **38**, 1065-1078.

Berg, I. A note of observations of young children with their mothers in a child psychiatric clinic. *Journal of Child Psychology and Psychiatry,* 1966, **7**, 69-73.

Berkowitz, L. The concept of aggressive drive: Some additional considerations. In L. Berkowitz (Ed.), *Advances in experimental social psychology,* Vol. 2. New York & London: Academic Press, 1965. Pp. 301-329.

Berkson, G., & Davenport, R. K. Stereotyped movements of mental defectives. I. Initial survey. *American Journal of Mental Deficiency,* 1962, **66**, 849-852.

Berkson, G., & Schusterman, R. J. Reciprocal food sharing of gibbons. *Primates,* 1964, **5**, 1-10.

Bernal, J., & Richards, M. P. M. The effects of bottle and breast feeding on infant development. *Journal of Psychosomatic Research,* 1970, **14**, 247-252.

Bernstein, I. S. Group social patterns as influenced by removal and later reintroduction of the dominant male rhesus. *Psychological Reports,* 1964, **14**, 3-10. (a)

Bernstein, I. S. The integration of rhesus monkeys introduced to a group. *Folia Primatologica,* 1964, **2**, 50-63. (b)

Bernstein, I. S. Activity patterns in a cebus monkey group. *Folia primatologica,* 1965, **3**, 211-224.

Bernstein, I. S. An investigation of the organization of pigtail monkey groups through the use of challenges. *Primates,* 1966, **7**, 471-480.

Bernstein, I. S. Introductory techniques in the formation of pigtail monkey troops. *Folia Primatologica,* 1969, **10**, 1-19.

Bernstein, I. S. Activity patterns in pigtail monkey groups. *Folia Primatologica,* 1970, **12**, 187-198.

Bernstein, I. S. The influence of introductory techniques on the formation of captive mangabey groups. *Primates,* 1971, **12**, 33-44.

Bernstein, I. S., & Draper, W. A. The behaviour of juvenile rhesus monkeys in groups. *Animal Behaviour,* 1964, **12**, 84-91.

Bernstein, I. S., & Mason, W. A. Activity patterns of rhesus monkeys in a social group. *Animal Behaviour,* 1963, **11**, 455-460. (a)

Bernstein, I. S., & Mason, W. A. Group formation by rhesus monkeys. *Animal Behaviour,* 1963, **11**, 28-31. (b)

Bernstein, I. S., & Schusterman, R. J. The activity of gibbons in a social group. *Folia Primatologica,* 1964, **2**, 161-170.

Bernstein, I. S., Schusterman, R. J., & Sharpe, L. G. A comparison of rhesus monkey and gibbon responses to unfamiliar situations. *Journal of Comparative and Physiological Psychology,* 1963, **56**, 914-916.

Bernstein, I. S., & Sharpe, L. Social roles in a rhesus monkey group. *Behaviour,* 1966, **26**, 91-104.

Bertrand, M. *The behavioral repertoire of the stumptail macaque. A descriptive and comparative study. Bibliotheca Primatologica.* Vol. 11. Basel: Karger, 1969.

Birdwhistell, R. Critical moments in the psychiatric interview. In T. T. Tourlentes (Ed.), *Research approaches to psychiatric problems: A symposium.* New York: Grune & Stratton, 1962. Pp. 179-188.

233

References

Blurton Jones, N. G. An ethological study of some aspects of social behaviour of children in nursery school. In D. Morris (Ed.), *Primate ethology*, London: Weidenfeld & Nicolson, 1967. Pp. 347-368.

Blurton Jones, N. G. Categories of child-child interaction. In N. G. Blurton Jones (Ed.), *Ethological studies of child behaviour*, London & New York: Cambridge Univ. Press, 1972. Pp. 97-127. (a)

Blurton Jones, N. G. Criteria used in describing facial expressions of children. *Human Biology*, 1972, in press. (b)

Blurton Jones, N. G. (Ed.) *Ethological studies of child behaviour*. London & New York: Cambridge Univ. Press, 1972. (c)

Blurton Jones, N. G. Non-verbal communication in children. In R. A. Hinde, (Ed.), *Non-verbal communication*, London & New York: Cambridge Univ. Press, 1972. Pp. 271-296. (d)

Blurton Jones, N. G., & Konner, M. An experiment on eyebrow-raising and visual searching in children. *Journal of Child Psychology and Psychiatry*, 1970, **11**, 233-240.

Blurton Jones, N. G., & Leach, G. M. Behaviour of children and their mothers at separation and greeting. In N. G. Blurton Jones (Ed.), *Ethological studies of child behaviour*, London & New York: Cambridge Univ. Press, 1972. Pp. 217-247.

Blurton Jones, N. G., & Trollope, J. Social behavior of stump-tailed macaques in captivity. *Primates*, 1968, **9**, 365-393.

Bobbitt, R. A., Gourevitch, V. P., Miller, L. E., & Jensen, G. D. Dynamics of social interactive behavior: A computerized procedure for analyzing trends, patterns, and sequences. *Psychological Bulletin*, 1969, **71**, 110-121.

Bobbitt, R. A., Jensen, G. D., & Gordon, B. N. Behavioral elements (taxonomy) for observing mother-infant-peer interaction in *Macaca nemestrina*. *Primates*, 1964, **5**, 71-80.

Boll, E. S. The role of preschool playmates—a situational approach. *Child Development*, 1957, **28**, 327-342.

Bolwig, N. Facial expressions in primates with remarks on a parallel development in certain carnivores (a preliminary report on work in progress). *Behaviour*, 1963, **22**, 167-192.

Bower, T. G. R., Broughton, J. M., & Moore, M. K. Demonstration of intention in the reaching behaviour of neonate humans. *Nature*, 1970, **228**, 679-681.

Bowlby, J. An ethological approach to research in child development. *British Journal of Medical Psychology*, 1957, **30**, 230-240.

Bowlby, J. The nature of the child's tie to his mother. *International Journal of Psycho-analysis*, 1958, **39**, 350-373.

Bowlby, J. *Child care and the growth of love*. Harmondsworth: Penquin, 1965.

Bowlby, J. *Attachment and loss*. Vol. 1. *Attachment*. London: Hogarth, 1969.

Brackbill, Y. Extinction of the smiling response in infants as a function of reinforcement schedule. *Child Development*, 1958, **29**, 115-124.

Brain, C. K. New finds at the Swartkrans australopithecine site. *Nature*, 1970, **225**, 1112-1119.

Brannigan, C. R., & Humphries, D. A. Human non-verbal behaviour, a means of communication. In N. G. Blurton Jones, (Ed.), *Ethological studies of child behaviour*, London & New York: Cambridge Univ. Press, 1972. Pp. 37-64.

Bridger, W. H. Ethological concepts and human development. *Recent Advances in Biological Psychiatry*, 1962, **4**, 95-107.

Bridger, W. H., & Birns, B. M. An analysis of the role of sucking in early infancy. *Science & Psychoanalysis*, 1968, **12**, 156-161.

Brown, J. L. Differential hand usage in three-year-old children. *Journal of Genetic Psychology*, 1962, **100**, 167-175.

234

Burnham, J. C. On the origins of behaviorism. *Journal of the History of the Behavioral Sciences*, 1968, **4**, 143-151.

Buss, A. H. *The psychology of aggression.* New York: Wiley, 1961.

Buss, A. H. Physical aggression in relation to different frustrations. *Journal of Abnormal and Social Psychology*, 1963, **67**, 1-7.

Buss, A. H. Instrumentality of aggression, feedback, and frustration as determinants of physical aggression. *Journal of Personality and Social Psychology*, 1966, **3**, 153-162.

Butler, R. A. Curiosity in monkeys. *Scientific American*, 1954, **190**(2), 70-75.

Calhoun, J. B. Population density and social pathology. *Scientific American*, 1962, **206**, 139-148.

Callan, H. *Ethology and society. Towards an anthropological view.* London & New York: Oxford Univ. Press, 1970.

Candland, D. K. Heart rate and dominance in chicken and squirrel monkey. *American Zoologist*, 1968, **8**, 739-740.

Cannon, W. B. *Bodily changes in pain, hunger, fear, and rage. An account of researches into the function of emotional excitement.* New York: Appleton, 1923.

Carpenter, C. R. A field study in Siam of the behavior and social relations of the gibbon (*Hylobates lar*). *Comparative Psychology Monographs*, 1940, **16**, 1-212.

Carpenter, C. R. Characteristics of social behavior in non-human primates. *Transactions of the New York Academy of Science*, 1942, **4**, 248-258.

Carpenter, C. R. The howlers of Barro Colorado Island. In I. DeVore (Ed.), *Primate behavior.* New York: Holt, 1965. Pp. 250-291.

Carrighar, S. *Wild heritage.* London: Panther, 1965.

Carstairs, G. M. Overcrowding and human aggression. In H. D. Graham & T. R. Gurr (Eds.), *The history of violence in America: historical and comparative perspectives.* New York: Praeger, 1969, Pp. 751-764.

Carthy, J. D., & Ebling, F. J. (Eds.) *The natural history of aggression.* London & New York: Academic Press, 1964.

Castell, R. Die soziale Reorganisation nach der Zusammenfuhrung von Totenkopfaffen-kolonien. In D. Starck, R. Schneider & H.-J. Kuhn (Eds.), *Neue ergebnisse der primato-logie.* Stuttgart: Fischer, 1967. Pp. 272-277.

Castell, R. Communication during initial contact: A comparison of squirrel and rhesus monkeys. *Folia Primatologica*, 1969, **11**, 206-214.

Castell, R. Effect of familiar and unfamiliar environments on proximity behavior of young children. *Journal of Experimental Child Psychology*, 1970, **9**, 342-347.

Chamove, A., Harlow, H., & Mitchell, G. Sex differences in the infant-directed behavior of preadolescent rhesus monkeys. *Child Development*, 1967, **38**, 329-335.

Chance, M. R. A. Social structure of a colony of *Macaca mulatta. British Journal of Animal Behaviour*, 1956, **4**, 1-13.

Chance, M. R. A. An interpretation of some agonistic postures: The role of "cutoff" acts and postures. *Symposia of the Zoological Society of London*, 1962, **8**, 71-89.

Chance, M. R. A. The social bond of the primates. *Primates*, 1963, **4**, 1-22.

Chance, M. R. A. Attention structure as the basis of primate rank orders. *Man*, 1967, **2**, 503-518.

Cherry, G. E. Social malaise and the environment. Paper presented to British Association for the Advancement of Science, Leeds, 1967.

Christian, J. J., & Davis, D. E. Endocrines, behavior, and population. *Science*, 1964, **146**, 1550-1560.

Classe, A. The whistled language of La Gomera. *Scientific American*, 1957, **196**, 111-120.

Comfort, A. *Nature and human nature.* London: Weidenfeld & Nicolson, 1966.

References

Conder, P. J. Individual distance. *Ibis*, 1949, **91**, 649-655.

Condon, W. S., & Ogston, W. D. A method of studying animal behavior. *Journal of Auditory Research*, 1967, **7**, 359-365.

Coon, C. S. Chairman's opening remarks. *Proceedings of the National Academy of Sciences of the United States*, 1961, **47**, 427.

Coss, R. G. *Mood provoking visual stimuli: Their origins and applicability.* Los Angeles: Univ. of California Press, Industrial Design Graduate Program, 1965.

Coss, R. G. The perceptual aspects of eye spot patterns and their relevance to gaze behaviour. In S. J. Hutt & C. Hutt (Eds.), *Behaviour studies in psychiatry.* Oxford: Pergamon, 1970. Pp. 121-147.

Cowgill, U., Bishop, A., Andrew, R. J., & Hutchinson, G. An apparent lunar periodicity in the sexual cycle of certain prosimians. *Proceedings of the National Academy of Sciences of the United States*, 1962, **48**, 238-241.

Cratty, B. J. *Movement behavior and motor learning.* London: Kimpton, 1964.

Crook, J. H. Gelada baboon herd structure and movement: A comparative report. *Symposia of the Zoological Society of London*, 1967, **18**, 237-258.

Crook, J. H. The socio-ecology of primates. In J. H. Crook (Ed.), *Social behaviour in birds and mammals.* London & New York: Academic Press, 1970. Pp. 103-166.

Currie, K. H., & Brannigan, C. R. Behavioural analysis and modification with an autistic child. In S. J. Hutt & C. Hutt (Eds.), *Behaviour studies in psychiatry*, Oxford: Pergamon, 1970. Pp. 77-90.

Dart, R. A. The predatory implemental technique of *Australopithecus. American Journal of Physical Anthropology*, 1949, **7**, 1-38.

Darwin, C. R. *The expression of the emotions in man and animals.* London: Murray, 1872.

Darwin, C. R. A biographical sketch of an infant. *Mind*, 1877, **2**, 286-294.

Davis, D. E. An inquiry into the phylogeny of gangs. In E. Bliss (Ed.), *The roots of behavior*, New York: Harper, 1962. Pp. 316-320.

Davitz, J. R. The effects of previous training on postfrustration behavior. *Journal of Abnormal and Social Psychology*, 1952. **47**, 309-315.

Deag, J. M., & Crook, J. H. Social behaviour and "agonistic buffering" in the wild Barbary macaque *Macaca sylvana* L. *Folia Primatologica*, 1971, **15**, 183-200.

Delgado, J. M. R. Aggressive behavior evoked by radio stimulation in monkey colonies. *American Zoologist*, 1966, **6**, 669-681.

de Monchaux, C. Hostility in small groups. In J. D. Carthy & F. J. Ebling (Eds.), *The natural history of aggression.* London & New York: Academic Press, 1964. Pp. 83-89.

Desmond, M. M., Franklin, R. R., Vallbona, C., Hill, R. M., Plumb, R., Arnold, H., & Watts, J. The clinical behavior of the newly born. I. The term baby. *Journal of Pediatrics*, 1963, **62**, 307-325.

DeVore, I. (Ed.) *Primate behavior. Field studies of monkeys and apes.* New York: Holt, 1965.

Ding, G., & Jersild, A. T. A study of the laughing and smiling of preschool children. *Journal of Genetic Psychology*, 1932, **40**, 452-472.

Dollard, J., Doob, L. W., Miller, N. E., Mowrer, O. H., & Sears, R. R. *Frustration and aggression.* New Haven, Conn.: Yale Univ. Press, 1939.

Draper, W. A., & Bernstein, I. S. Stereotyped behavior and cage size. *Perceptual and Motor Skills*, 1963, **16**, 231-234.

Duncan, S. Nonverbal communication. *Psychological Bulletin*, 1969, **72**, 118-137. (a)

Duncan, S. The pavalanguage of experimenter bias. *Sociometry*, 1969, **32**, 207-219. (b)

Dunnington, M. J. Behavioral differences of sociometric status groups in a nursery school. *Child Development*, 1957, **28**, 103-111.

236

Ehrlich, P. R. *The population bomb.* New York: Ballantine, 1968.

Ehrlich, P. R., & Freedman, J. Population, crowding and human behaviour. *New Scientist and Science Journal,* 1971, **50**(745), 10-14.

Eibl-Eibesfeldt, I. Zur Ethologie des menschlichen Grußverhaltens I. Beobachtungen an Balinsen, Papuas und Samoanern nebst vergleichenden Bemerkungen. *Zeitschrift für Tierpsychologie,* 1968, **25**, 727-744.

Eibl-Eibesfeldt, I. *Ethology. The biology of behavior.* New York: Holt, 1970.

Eibl-Eibesfeldt, I., & Hass, H. Film studies in human ethology. *Current Anthropology,* 1967, **8**, 477-479. (a)

Eibl-Eibesfeldt, I., & Hass, H. Neue Wege der Humanethologie. *Homo,* 1967, **18**, 13-23. (b)

Eimerl, S., & DeVore, I. *The primates.* Nederland: Time-Life International, 1966.

Eisenberg, P., & Reichline, P. B. Judging expressive movement. II. Judgements of dominance-feeling from motion pictures of gait. *Journal of Social Psychology,* 1939, **10**, 345-357.

Ekman, P., Sorenson, E. R., & Frieson, W. V. Pan-cultural elements in facial displays of emotion. *Science,* 1969, **164**, 86-88.

Elkin, A. P. The one-leg resting position in Australia. *Man,* 1953, **53**, 64.

Ellefson, J. O. Territorial behavior in the common white-handed gibbon, *Hylobates lar* Linn. In P. C. Jay (Ed.), *Primates,* New York: Holt, 1968. Pp. 180-199.

Emmerich, W. Continuity and stability in early social development. *Child Development,* 1964, **35**, 311-332.

Esser, A. H. Dominance hierarchy and clinical course of psychiatrically hospitalized boys. *Child Development,* 1968, **39**, 147-157.

Esser, A. H., Chamberlain, R. N., Chapple, E. D., & Kline, N. S. Territoriality of patients on a research ward. *Recent Advances in Biological Psychiatry,* 1965, **7**, 37-44.

Ewbank, R., & Bryant, M. J. Some effects of high stocking rates upon the behaviour of pigs. *British Veterinary Journal,* 1969, **125**, 248.

Eyestone, W. H. Scientific and administrative concepts behind the establishment of the U. S. primate centers. *Symposia of the Zoological Society of London,* 1966, **17**, 1-9.

Fady, J. C. Les jeux sociaux: Le compagnon de jeux chez les jeunes. Observations chez *Macaca irus. Folia Primatologica,* 1969, **11**, 134-143.

Faw, T. T., & Nunnally, J. C. The influence of stimulus complexity, novelty, and affective value on children's visual fixations. *Journal of Experimental Child Psychology,* 1968, **6**, 141-153.

Felipe, N., & Sommer, R. Invasions of personal space. *Social Problems,* 1966, **14**, 206-214.

Fletcher, R. *Instinct in man in the light of recent work in comparative psychology.* (2nd ed.) London: Allen & Unwin, 1968.

Ford, C. S., & Beach, F. A. *Patterns of sexual behaviour.* London: Methuen, 1952.

Francois, G. R., Barratt, E. S., & Harris, C. S. Assessing the spontaneous cage behavior of the squirrel monkey (*Saimiri sciureus*). *Primates,* 1970, **11**, 89-92.

Frank, L. Tactile communication. *Genetic Psychology Monographs,* 1957, **56**, 209-255.

Freedman, D. G. Smiling in blind infants and the issue of innate vs. acquired. *Journal of Child Psychology and Psychiatry,* 1964, **5**, 171-184.

Freedman, D. G. A biological view of man's social behavior. In W. Etkin (Ed.), *Social behavior from fish to man,* Chicago, Ill.: Univ. of Chicago Press, 1967. Pp. 152-188.

Freedman, D. G. Personality development in infancy: A biological approach. In S. L. Washburn & P. C. Jay (Eds.), *Perspectives on human evolutions.* Vol. I. New York: Holt, 1968. Pp. 258-287.

Freedman, D. G. The survival value of the beard. *Psychology Today,* 1969, **3**(5), 36-39.

237

References

Freedman, D. G. An evolutionary approach to research on the life cycle. *Human Development*, 1971, 14, 87-99.

Freeman, D. Social anthropology and the scientific study of human behaviour. *Man*, 1966, 1, 330-342.

Freud, S. *Beyond the pleasure principle.* London: Hogarth, 1948.

Freud, S. *The psychopathology of everyday life.* London: Benn, 1960.

Freud, S. *Two short accounts of psycho-analysis.* Harmondsworth: Penguin, 1962.

Frisch, J. E. Individual behavior and intertroop variability in Japanese macaques. In P. C. Jay (Ed.), *Primates*, New York: Holt, 1968. Pp. 243-252.

Gallup Poll. Most headaches come on a Monday. *The Times (London)*, 1970, Feb. 12.

Garai, J. E., & Scheinfeld, A. Sex differences in mental and behavioral traits. *Genetic Psychology Monographs*, 1968, 77, 169-299.

Gardner, B. T., & Wallach, L. Shapes of figures identified as a baby's head. *Perceptual and Motor Skills*, 1965, 20, 135-142.

Gardner, R. A., & Gardner, B. T. Teaching sign language to a chimpanzee. *Science*, 1969, 165, 664-672.

Gartlan, J. S. Dominance in East African monkeys. *Proceedings of the East African Academy*, 1965, 2, 75-79.

Gartlan, J. S. Structure and function in primate society. *Folia Primatologica*, 1968, 8, 89-120.

Gartlan, J. S., & Brain, C. K. Ecology and social variability in *Cercopithecus aethiops* and *C. mitis.* In P. C. Jay (Ed.), *Primates*, New York: Holt, 1968. Pp. 253-292.

Gellert, E. Stability and fluctuation in the power relationships of young children. *Journal of Abnormal and Social Psychology*, 1961, 62, 8-15.

Gellert, E. The effect of changes in group composition on the behaviour of young children. *British Journal of Social and Clinical Psychology*, 1962, 1, 168-181.

General Register Office. *Classification of occupations.* London: HM Stationery Office, 1968.

Gesell, A. (Ed.) *The first five years of life. A guide to the study of the preschool child.* London: Methuen, 1940.

Giles, H., & Oxford, G. S. Toward a multidimensional theory of laughter causation and its social implications. *Bulletin of the British Psychological Society*, 1970, 23, 97-105.

Goffman, E. *The presentation of self in everyday life.* Garden City, N.Y.: Doubleday, 1959.

Goodall, J. Tool-using and aimed throwing in a community of free-living chimpanzees. *Nature*, 1964, 201, 1264-1266.

Goodhart, C. B. The evolutionary significance of human hair patterns and skin coloring. *Advancement of Science*, 1960, 17, 53-59.

Goy, R. W. Organizing effects of androgen on the behaviour of rhesus monkeys. In R. P. Michael (Ed.), *Endocrinology and human behaviour*, London & New York: Oxford Univ. Press, 1968. Pp. 12-31.

Grant, E. C. The contribution of ethology to child psychiatry. In J. G. Howells (Ed.), *Modern perspectives in child psychiatry*, Edinburgh: Oliver & Boyd, 1965. Pp. 20-37. (a)

Grant, E. C. An ethological description of some schizophrenic patterns of behaviour. *Proceedings of the Leeds symposium on behavioral disorders.* Dagenham, Essex: May & Baker, 1965. (b)

Grant, E. C. An ethological description of non-verbal behaviour during interviews. *British Journal of Medical Psychology*, 1968, 41, 177-184.

Grant, E. C. Human facial expression. *Man*, 1969, 4, 525-536.

Gregson, E. D., & Gregson, R. A. M. A note on a seventeenth-century distinction between feral man and man-like apes. *Journal of the History of the Behavioral Sciences*, 1970, 6, 159-161.

238

Grinsell, L. V. Shaving off the eyebrows as a sign of mourning. *Man*, 1950, **50**, 144.

Gruber, A. A functional definition of primate tool-making. *Man*, 1969, **4**, 573-579.

Guardo, C. J. Personal space in children. *Child Development*, 1969, **40**, 143-151.

Guerney, B., Burton, J., Silverberg, D., & Shapiro, E. Use of adult responses to codify children's behavior in a play situation. *Perceptual and Motor Skills*, 1965, **20**, 614-616.

Gutteridge, M. V. A study of motor achievements of young children. *Archives of Psychology, New York*, 1939, **53**, No. 244.

Haaf, R. A., & Bell, R. Q. A facial dimension in visual discrimination by human infants. *Child Development*, 1967, **38**, 893-899.

Hall, E. T. *The silent language*. Greenwich, Conn.: Fawcett, 1959.

Hall, E. T. *The hidden dimension*. Garden City, N.Y.: Doubleday, 1966.

Hall, K. R. L. Behaviour of monkeys toward mirror-images. *Nature*, 1962, **196**, 1258-1261.

Hall, K. R. L. Tool-using performances as indicators of behavioral adaptability. *Current Anthropology*, 1963, **4**, 479-494.

Hall, K. R. L. Aggression in monkey and ape societies. In J. D. Carthy & F. J. Ebling (Eds.), *The natural history of aggression*. London & New York: Academic Press, 1964. Pp. 51-64.

Hall, K. R. L. Behaviour and ecology of the wild patas monkey, *Erythrocebus patas*, in Uganda. *Journal of Zoology*, 1965, **148**, 15-87.

Hall, K. R. L., & DeVore, I. Baboon social behavior. In I. DeVore (Ed.), *Primate behavior*. New York: Holt, 1965. Pp. 53-110.

Hamburg, D. A. Evolution of emotional responses: Evidence from recent research on nonhuman primates. *Science and Psychoanalysis*, 1968, **12**, 39-54.

Hamburg, D. A. & Lunde, D. T. Sex hormones in the development of sex differences in human behavior. In E. Maccoby (Ed.), *The development of sex differences*. London: Tavistock, 1966. Pp. 1-24.

Haner, C. F., & Brown, P. A. Clarification of the instigation to action concept in the frustration-aggression hypothesis. *Journal of Abnormal and Social Psychology*, 1955, **51**, 204-206.

Hansen, E. C. The development of maternal and infant behaviour in the rhesus monkey. *Behaviour*, 1966, **27**, 107-149.

Hare, P., & Bales, R. F. Seating position and small group interaction. *Sociometry*, 1963, **26**, 480-486.

Harlow, H. F. Love in infant monkeys. *Scientific American*, 1959, **200**, 68-74.

Harlow, H. F. Age-mate or peer affectional system. In D. S. Lehrman, R. A. Hinde & E. Shaw (Eds.), *Advances in the study of behavior*, Vol. 2. London & New York: Academic Press, 1970. Pp. 333-383.

Harlow, H. F., & Harlow, M. K. The affectional systems. In A. M. Schrier, H. F. Harlow & F. Stollnitz (Eds.), *Behavior of nonhuman primates*. Vol. 2. London & New York: Academic Press, 1965. Pp. 287-334.

Harlow, H. F., & Harlow, M. K. Effects of various mother-infant relationships on rhesus monkey behaviours. In B. M. Foss (Ed.), *Determinants of infant behaviour*. Vol. 4. London: Methuen, 1969. Pp. 15-36.

Hartup, W. W., & Himeno, Y. Social isolation vs. interaction with adults in relation to aggression in preschool children. *Journal of Abnormal and Social Psychology*, 1959, **59**, 17-22.

Hass, H. *The human animal. The mystery of man's behaviour*. London: Hodder & Stoughton, 1970.

Hauser, P. M. (Ed.) *The population dilemma*. Englewood Cliffs, N.J.: Prentice-Hall, 1963.

Hawkes, P. N. Group formation in four species of macaques. *American Journal of Physical Anthropology*, 1969, **31**, 261.

References

Hayes, C. *The ape in our house.* New York: Harper, 1951.

Hays, P. *New horizons in psychiatry.* Harmondsworth: Penguin, 1964.

Hediger, H. *Wild animals in captivity. An outline of the biology of zoological gardens.* New York: Dover, 1950.

Hershkovitz, P. The decorative chin. *Bulletin of the Field Museum of Natural History,* 1970, **41**, 7-11.

Hershkowitz, A. Naturalistic observations on chronically hospitalized patients: I. The effects of "strangers." *Journal of Nervous and Mental Disease,* 1962, **135**, 258-264.

Hess, E. H. Attitude and pupil size. *Scientific American,* 1965, **212**, 46-54.

Hewes, G. W. World distribution of certain postural habits. *American Anthropologist,* 1955, **57**, 231-244.

Hewes, G. W. The anthropology of posture. *Scientific American,* 1957, **196**, 122-132.

Hewes, G. W. Hominid bipedalism. Independent evidence for the food carrying theory. *Science,* 1964, **146**, 416-418.

Hill, W. C. O. On muscles of expression in gelada—*Theropithecus gelada* (Ruppell) (Primates, Cercopithecidae). *Zeitschrift fur Morphologie und Oekologie der Tiere,* 1969, **65**, 274-286.

Hinde, R. A. Ethological models and the concept of drive. *British Journal for the Philosophy of Science,* 1956, **6**, 321-331.

Hinde, R. A. *Animal behaviour, a synthesis of ethology and comparative psychology.* New York: McGraw-Hill, 1966.

Hinde, R. A., & Rowell, T. E. Communication by postures and facial expressions in the rhesus monkey (*Macaca mulatta*). *Proceedings of the Zoological Society of London,* 1962, **138**, 1-21.

Hinde, R. A., & Spencer-Booth, Y. The behaviour of socially living rhesus monkeys in their first two and a half years. *Animal Behaviour,* 1967, **15**, 169-196.

Hinde, R. A., Rowell, T. E. & Spencer-Booth, Y. Behaviour of socially living rhesus monkeys in their first six months. *Proceedings of the Zoological Society of London,* 1964, **143**, 609-649.

Hindley, C. B., Filliozat, A. M., Klackenberg, G., Nicolet-Meister, D., & Sand, E. A. Differences in age of walking in five European longitudinal samples. *Human Biology,* 1966, **38**, 364-379.

Hockett, C. F. The origin of speech. *Scientific American,* 1960, **203**, 89-96.

Hollis, J. H., & Gunnell, P. Social dominance behavior of profoundly retarded children. *American Journal of Mental Deficiency,* 1965, **70**, 363-372.

Holt, E. B. *Animal drive and the learning process. An essay toward radical empiricism.* London: Williams & Northgate, 1931.

Horowitz, M. J., Duff, D. F., & Stratton, L. O. Body-buffer zone. *Archives of General Psychiatry,* 1964, **11**, 651-656.

Hudson, P. T. W., McGrew, W. C., & McGrew, P. L. Attention structure in a group of preschool infants. *Proceedings of the CIE architectural psychology conference,* Kingston-on-Thames, 1972, in press.

Hummer, R. L., May, H. C., & Knight, W. F. Observations during first year of operation of a chimpanzee breeding colony. *Zeitschrift fur Versuchstierkunde,* 1969, **11**, 207-221.

Hutt, C. Effects of stimulus novelty on manipulatory exploration in an infant. *Journal of Child Psychology and Psychiatry,* 1967, **8**, 247-251.

Hutt, C., & Coxon, M. W. Systematic observation in clinical psychology. *Archives of General Psychiatry,* 1965, **12**, 374-378.

Hutt, C., & Hutt, S. J. Effects of environmental complexity on stereotyped behaviours of children. *Animal Behavior,* 1965, **13**, 1-4.

Hutt, C., Hutt, S. J., & Ounsted, C. A method for the study of children's behaviour. *Developmental Medicine and Child Neurology,* 1963, **5**, 233-245.

Hutt, C., Hutt, S. J., & Ounsted, C. The behaviour of children with and without upper CNS lesions. *Behaviour,* 1965, **24**, 246-268.

Hutt, C., & Ounsted, C. The biological significance of gaze aversion with particular reference to the syndrome of infantile autism. *Behavioral Science,* 1966, **11**, 346-356.

Hutt, C., & Vaizey, M. J. Differential effects of group density on social behaviour. *Nature,* 1966, **209**, 1371-1372.

Hutt, S. J., & Hutt, C. *Direct observation and measurement of behavior.* Springfield, Ill.: Thomas, 1970.

Hutt, S. J., Hutt, C., Lee, D., & Ounsted, C. A behavioural and electroencephalographic study of autistic children. *Journal of Psychiatric Research,* 1965, **3**, 181-197.

Imanishi, K. Social behavior in Japanese monkeys, *Macaca fuscata.* In C. H. Southwick (Ed.), *Primate social behavior,* Princeton, N.J.: Van Nostrand, 1963. Pp. 68-81.

Isaacs, S. *Social development in young children. A study of beginnings.* London: Routledge, 1933.

James, W. T. A study of the expression of bodily posture. *Journal of General Psychology,* 1932, **7**, 405-437.

Jay, P. C. The Indian langur monkey (*Presbytis entellus*). In C. H. Southwick (Ed.), *Primate social behavior,* Princeton, N.J.: Van Nostrand, 1963. Pp. 114-123.

Jay, P. C. The common langur of north India. In I. DeVore (Ed.), *Primate behavior,* New York, Holt, 1965. Pp. 197-249.

Jay, P. C. (Ed.) *Primates. Studies in adaptation and variability.* New York: Holt, 1968.

Jensen, G. D., & Bobbitt, R. A. Implications of primate research for understanding infant development. *Science and Psychoanalysis,* 1968, **12**, 55-81.

Jensen, G. D., Bobbitt, R. A., & Gordon, B. N. Patterns and sequences of hitting behaviour in mother and infant monkeys (*Macaca nemestrina*). 1969, *Journal of Psychiatric Research,* **7**, 55-61.

Jensen, G. D., & Gordon, B. N. Sequences of mother-infant behavior following a facial communicative gesture of pigtail monkeys. *Biological Psychiatry,* 1970, **2**, 267-272.

Jersild, A. T., & Fite, M. D. The influence of nursery school social experience on children's social adjustments. *Child Development Monographs,* 1939, **25**, 1-112.

Jones, C., & Sabater Pi, J. Sticks used by chimpanzees in Rio Muni, West Africa. *Nature,* 1969, **223**, 100-101.

Jones, I. Stereotyped aggression in a group of Australian western desert aborigines. *Journal of Child Psychology and Psychiatry,* 1971, **44**, 259-265.

Jourard, S. M. An exploratory study of body-accessibility. *British Journal of Social and Clinical Psychology,* 1966, **5**, 221-231.

Kahn, M. W., & Kirk, W. F. The concepts of aggression: A review and reformulation. *Psychological Record,* 1968, **18**, 559-573.

Kaufman, I. C. Some ethological theories of social relationships and conflict situations. *Journal of the American Psychoanalytic Association,* 1960, **8**, 671-685. (a)

Kaufman, I. C. Some theoretical implications from animal behaviour studies for the psychoanalytic concepts of instinct, energy and drive. *International Journal of Psycho-analysis,* 1960, **41**, 318-326. (b)

Kaufman, I. C., & Rosenblum, L. A. A behavioral taxonomy for *Macaca nemestrina* and *Macaca radiata:* Based on longitudinal observations of family groups in the laboratory. *Primates,* 1966, **7**, 205-258.

Kaufmann, H. Definitions and methodology in the study of aggression. *Psychological Bulletin,* 1965, **64**, 351-364.

241

References

Kaufmann, J. H. Behavior of infant rhesus monkeys and their mothers in a free-ranging band. *Zoologica*, 1966, **51**, 17-28.

Kaufmann, J. H. Social relations of adult males in a free-ranging band of rhesus monkeys. In S. A. Altmann (Ed.), *Social communication among primates*, Chicago, Ill.: Univ. of Chicago Press, 1967. Pp. 73-98.

Kawai, M. A field experiment on the process of group formation in the Japanese monkey (*Macaca fuscata*) and the releasing of the group at Ohirayama. *Primates*, 1960, **2**, 181-253.

Kellogg, W. N., & Kellogg, L. A. *The ape and the child. A study of environmental influence upon early behavior.* New York: McGraw-Hill, 1933.

Kendon, A. Some functions of gaze-direction in social interaction. *Acta Psychologica*, 1967, **26**, 22-63.

Kendon, A., & Cook, M. M. The consistency of gaze patterns in social interactions. *British Journal of Psychology*, 1969, **60**, 481-494.

Keyfitz, N. Population density and the style of social life. *BioScience*, 1966, **16**, 868-873.

King, M. G. Interpersonal relations in preschool children and average approach distance. *Journal of Genetic Psychology*, 1966, **109**, 109-116.

Kirchshofer, R., Weisse, K., Berentz, K., Klose, H., & Klose, I. A preliminary account of the physical and behavioural development during the first 10 weeks of the hand-reared gorilla twins born at the Frankfurt Zoo. *International Zoo Yearbook*, 1968, **8**, 121-128.

Kleck, R., Ono, H., & Hastorf, A. H. The effects of physical deviance upon face-to-face interaction. *Human Relations*, 1966, **19**, 425-436.

Klopfer, P. H. From Ardrey to altruism: A discourse on the biological basis of human behavior. *Behavioral Science*, 1968, **13**, 399-401.

Koford, C. B. Group relations in an island colony of rhesus monkeys. In C. H. Southwick (Ed.), *Primate social behavior*, Princeton, N. J.: Van Nostrand, 1963. Pp. 136-152.

Kohler, W. *The mentality of apes.* Harmondsworth: Penguin, 1925.

Konner, M. Aspects of the developmental ethology of a foraging people. In N. G. Blurton Jones (Ed.), *Ethological studies of child behavior.* London & New York: Cambridge Univ. Press, 1972. Pp. 285-304.

Kortlandt, A., & Kooij, M. Protohominid behaviour in primates. *Symposia of the Zoological Society of London*, 1963, **10**, 61-88.

Kraus, R. F. Implications of recent developments in primate research for psychiatry. *Comprehensive Psychiatry*, 1970, **11**, 328-335.

Kummer, H. Dimensions of a comparative biology of primate groups. *American Journal of Physical Anthropology*, 1967, **27**, 357-366.

Kummer, H. *Social organization of hamadryas baboons. Bibliotheca Primatologica.* Vol. 6. Basel: Karger, 1968.

LaBarre, W. The cultural basis of emotions and gestures. *Journal of Personality*, 1947, **16**, 49-68.

Lancaster, J. B. On the evolution of tool-using behavior. *American Anthropologist*, 1968, **70**, 56-66.

Lancaster, J. B., & Lee, R. B. The annual reproductive cycle in monkeys and apes. In I. DeVore (Ed.), *Primate behavior*, New York: Holt, 1965. Pp. 486-513.

Leach, G. M. A comparison of the social behaviour of some normal and problem children. In N. G. Blurton Jones (Ed.), *Ethological studies of child behaviour*, London & New York: Cambridge Univ. Press, 1972. Pp. 249-281.

Lebo, D. Aggressiveness and expansiveness in children. *Journal of Genetic Psychology*, 1962, **100**, 227-240.

Lehrman, D. S. A critique of Konrad Lorenz's theory of instinctive behavior. *Quarterly Review of Biology*, 1953, **28**, 337-363.

Leyhausen, P. The communal organization of solitary animals. *Symposia of the Zoological Society of London*, 1965, **14**, 249-263.

Lieberman, P. H., Kratt, D. H., & Wilson, W. H. Vocal tract limitations on the vowel repertoires of rhesus monkey and other nonhuman primates. *Science*, 1969, **164**, 1185-1187.

Lindburg, D. G. Rhesus monkeys: Mating season mobility of adult males. *Science*, 1969, **166**, 1176-1178.

Loizos, C. Play behaviour in higher primates: A review. In D. Morris (Ed.), *Primate ethology*. London: Weidenfeld & Nicolson, 1967. Pp. 176-218.

Loizos, C. An ethological study of chimpanzee play. In C. R. Carpenter (Ed.), *Proceedings of the second international congress of primatology*, Vol. 1. *Behavior*. Basel: Karger, 1969. Pp. 87-93.

Lorenz, K. *King Solomon's ring. New light on animal ways.* New York: Crowell-Collier, 1952.

Lorenz, K. *On aggression.* London: Methuen, 1966.

Lorenz, K. The enmity between generations and its probable ethological causes. In A. Tiselius & S. Nilsson (Eds.), *The place of value in a world of facts*, Nobel Symp. 14, Stockholm: Almqvist & Wiksell, 1970. Pp. 385-418.

Lowther, F. A study of the activities of a pair of *Galago senegalensis moholi* in captivity, including the birth and postnatal development of twins. *Zoologica*, 1940, **25**, 433-440.

McBride, G. Theories of animal spacing: The role of flight, fight and social distance. In A. H. Esser (Ed.), *Behavior and environment. The use of space by animals and man.* New York: Plenum, 1971. Pp. 53-68.

McBride, G., King, M. G., & James, J. W. Social proximity effects on galvanic skin responses in adult humans. *Journal of Psychology*, 1965, **61**, 153-157.

McCandless, B. R., & Marshall, H. R. A picture sociometric technique for preschool children and its relation to teacher judgments of friendship. *Child Development*, 1957, **28**, 139-147. (a)

McCandless, B. R., & Marshall, H. R. Sex differences in social acceptance and participation of preschool children. *Child Development*, 1957, **28**, 421-425. (b)

McGrew, P. L. Social and spatial density effects on spacing behaviour in preschool children. *Journal of Child Psychology and Psychiatry*, 1970, **11**, 197-205.

McGrew, W. C. An ethological study of agonistic behaviour in preschool children. In C. R. Carpenter (Ed.), *Proceedings of the second international congress of primatology.* Vol. 1. *Behavior*, Basel: Karger, 1969. Pp. 149-159.

McGrew, W. C. Glossary of motor patterns of four-year-old nursery school children. In S. J. Hutt & C. Hutt, *Direct observation and measurement of behavior.* Springfield, Ill.: Thomas, 1970. Pp. 210-218. (Appendix)

McGrew, W. C. Aggression und Gruppenbildung im Kindergarten. *Umschau im Wissenschaft und Technik*, 1971, **21**, 785.

McGrew, W. C. Aspects of social development in nursery school children with emphasis on introduction to the group. In N. G. Blurton Jones (Ed.), *Ethological studies of child behavior.* London & New York: Cambridge Univ. Press, 1972. Pp. 129-156.

McGrew, W. C. Interpersonal spacing behaviour of preschool children. In K. S. Connelly & J. S. Bruner (Eds.), *Development of competancy in infancy and early childhood.* London: Academic Press, in preparation.

McGrew, W. C., & McGrew, P. L. Group formation in preschool children. In *Proceedings of the third international congress of primatology.* Basel: Karger, 1971, in press.

McNeil, E. B. Patterns of aggression. *Journal of Child Psychology and Psychiatry*, 1962, **3**, 65-77.

References

Machotka, P. Body movement as communication. *Dialogues, Behavioral Science Research,* 1965, **2,** 33-66.

Mann, L. The social psychology of waiting lines. *American Scientist,* 1970, **58,** 390-398.

Marler, P. Communication in monkeys and apes. In I. DeVore (Ed.), *Primate behavior,* New York: Holt, 1965. Pp. 544-584.

Marler, P., & Hamilton, W. J. *Mechanisms of animal behavior.* New York: Wiley, 1966.

Marshall, H. R., & McCandless, B. R. A study of prediction of social behavior of preschool children. *Child Development,* 1957, **28,** 149-159.

Maslow, A. H. The role of dominance in the social and sexual behavior of infra-human primates: IV. The determination of hierarchy in pairs and in a group. *Journal of Genetic Psychology,* 1936, **49,** 161-198.

Maslow, A. H., Rand, H., & Newman, S. Some parallels between sexual and dominance behavior of infra-human primates and fantasies of patients in psychotherapy. *Journal of Nervous and Mental Disease,* 1960, **131,** 202-212.

Mason, W. A. Sociability and social organization in monkeys and apes. In L. Berkowitz (Ed.), *Advances in experimental social psychology,* Vol. 1. London & New York: Academic Press, 1964. Pp. 277-305.

Mason, W. A. The social development of monkeys and apes. In I. DeVore (Ed.), *Primate behavior.* New York: Holt, 1965. Pp. 514-543.

Masserman, J. H. (Ed.) *Animal and human. Science and Psychoanalysis,* Vol. 12. New York: Grune & Stratton, 1968.

Masserman, J. H., Wechkin, S., & Woolf, M. Alliances and aggressions among rhesus monkeys. *Science & Psychoanalysis,* 1968, **12,** 95-100.

Masters, W. H., & Johnson, V. E. *Human sexual response.* London: Churchill, 1966.

Maurus, M., & Ploog, D. Social signals in squirrel monkeys: analysis by cerebral radio stimulation. *Experimental Brain Research,* 1971, **12,** 171-183.

Maxim, P. E., & Buettner-Janusch, J. A field study of the Kenya baboon. *American Journal of Physical Anthropology,* 1963, **21,** 165-180.

Mead, M. *Coming of age in Samoa. A study of adolescence and sex in primitive societies.* Harmondsworth: Penguin, 1928.

Mehrabian, A. Some referents and measures of nonverbal behavior. *Behavior Research Methods and Instrumentation,* 1969, **1,** 203-207.

Meisels, M., & Guardo, C. J. Development of personal space schemata. *Child Development,* 1969, **40,** 1167-1178.

Menzel, E. W. Primate naturalistic research and problems of early experience. *Developmental Psychobiology,* 1968, **1,** 175-184.

Menzel, E. W., Davenport, R. K., & Rogers, C. M. The development of tool using in wild-born and restriction-reared chimpanzees. *Folia Primatologica,* 1970, **12,** 273-283.

Michael, G., & Willis, F. N. The development of gestures as a function of social class, education, and sex. *Psychological Record,* 1968, **18,** 515-519.

Michael, G., & Willis, F. N. The development of gestures in three sub-cultural groups. *Journal of Social Psychology,* 1969, **79,** 35-41.

Miller, N. E. The frustration-aggression hypothesis. *Psychological Review,* 1941, **48,** 337-342.

Montagu, M. F. A. (Ed.) *Man and aggression.* London & New York: Oxford Univ. Press, 1968.

Morris, D. *The naked ape. A zoologist's study of the human animal.* London: Jonathan Cape, 1967.

Morris, D. *The human zoo.* London: Jonathan Cape, 1969.

Morris, D. *Intimate behaviour.* London: Jonathan Cape, 1971.

Morrison, J. A., & Menzel, E. W. Adaptation of a rhesus monkey group to artificial group fission and transplantation to a new environment. *American Zoologist*, 1966, 6, 121.

Murphy, L. B. Social behavior and child personality. In R. G. Barker, J. S. Kounin & H. F. Wright (Eds.), *Child behavior and development*. New York: McGraw-Hill, 1943. Pp. 345-362.

Nachshon, I., & Wapner, S. Effect of eye contact and physiognonmy on perceived location of other person. *Journal of Personality and Social Psychology*, 1967, 7, 82-89.

Northway, M. L. *A primer of sociometry*. Toronto: Univ. of Toronto Press, 1952.

Norum, G. A., Russo, N. J., & Sommer, R. Seating patterns and group task. *Psychology in the Schools*, 1967, 4, 276-280.

Oakley, K. P. *Man the tool-maker*. London: British Museum Natural History), 1965.

Oliver, S. C. Ecology and cultural continuity as contributing factors in the social organization of the plains Indian. *University of California, Publications in American Archaeology and Ethnology*, 1962, 48, 1-90.

Oppenheimer, J. R. Changes in forehead patterns and group composition of the white-faced monkey (*Cebus capucinus*). In C. R. Carpenter (Ed.), *Proceedings of the second international congress of primatology*. Vol. 1. *Behavior*. Basel: Karger, 1969. Pp. 36-42.

Paluck, R. J., Lieff, J. D., & Esser, A. H. Formation and development of a group of juvenile *Hylobates lar*. *Primates*, 1970, 11, 185-194.

Parker, C. E. Responsiveness, manipulation, and implementation behavior in chimpanzees, gorillas, and orang-utans. In C. R. Carpenter (Ed.), *Proceedings of the second international congress of primatology*. Vol. 1. *Behavior*. Basel: Karger, 1969. Pp. 160-166.

Parkes, A. S. Seasonal variation in human sexual activity. In J. M. Thoday & A. S. Parkes (Eds.), *Genetic and environmental influences on behaviour*. Edinburgh: Oliver & Boyd, 1968. Pp. 128-145.

Parten, M. Social play among preschool children. *Journal of Abnormal and Social Psychology*, 1933, 28, 136-147.

Parten, M., & Newhall, S. M. Social behavior of preschool children. In R. G. Barker, J. S. Kounin, & H. F. Wright (Eds.), *Child behavior and development*. New York: McGraw-Hill, 1943. Pp. 509-525.

Patterson, G. R., Littman, R. A., & Bricker, W. Assertive behavior in children: A step toward a theory of aggression. *Monographs of the Society for Research in Child Development*, 1967, 32, 1-43.

Peter, HRH Prince. Peculiar sleeping postures of the Tibetans. *Man*, 1953, 53, 145.

Philip, A. E., & McCulloch, J. W. Use of social indices in psychiatric epidemiology. *British Journal of Preventive and Social Medicine*, 1966, 20, 122-126.

Ploog, D. W., & MacLean, P. D. Display of penile erection in squirrel monkey (*Saimiri sciureus*). *Animal Behaviour*, 1963, 11, 32-39.

Ploog, D. W., & Melnechuk, T. (Eds.) Primate communication: A report of an NRP work session held January 30-February 1. *Neurosciences Research Program, Bulletin*, 1969, 7, 419-510.

Poirier, F. E. The communication matrix of the Nilgiri langur (*Presbytis johnii*) of south India. *Folia Primatologica*, 1970, 13, 92-136.

Prechtl, H. F. R. Die Entwicklung und Eigenart frunkindlicher Bewegungsweisen. *Klinische Wachenshrift*, 1956, 34, 281-284.

Prechtl, H. F. R. The directed head turning response and allied movements of the human baby. *Behaviour*, 1958, 13, 212-242.

Prechtl, H. F. R. Problems of behavioral studies in the newborn infant. In D. S. Lehrman, R. A. Hinde & E. Shaw (Eds.), *Advances in the study of behavior*. Vol. 1. London & New York: Academic Press, 1965. Pp. 75-98.

245

References

Premack, D. A functional analysis of language. *Journal of the Experimental Analysis of Behavior*, 1970, **14**, 107-125.

Premack, D. Language in a chimpanzee. *Science*, 1971, **172**, 808-822.

Price, J. The dominance hierarchy and the evolution of mental illness. *Lancet*, 1967, **2**, 243-246.

Rafferty, J. E., Tyler, B. B., & Tyler, F. B. Personality assessment from free play observations. *Child Development*, 1960, **31**, 691-702.

Randolph, M. C., & Brooks, B. A. Conditioning of a vocal response in a chimpanzee through social reinforcement. *Folia Primatologica*, 1967, **5**, 70-79.

Randolph, M. C., & Mason, W. A. Effects of rearing conditions on distress vocalization in chimpanzees. *Folia Primatologica*, 1969, **10**, 103-112.

Raph, J. B., Thomas, A., Chess, S., & Korn, S. J. The influence of nursery school on social interactions. *American Journal of Orthopsychiatry*, 1968, **38**, 144-152.

Rausch, H. L., Dittmann, A. T., & Taylor, T. The interpersonal behavior of children in residential treatment. *Journal of Abnormal and Social Psychology*, 1959, **58**, 9-26.

Reynolds, V. Open groups in hominid evolution. *Man*, 1966, **1**, 441-452.

Reynolds, V. Kinship and the family in monkeys, apes, and man. *Man*, 1968, **3**, 209-223.

Reynolds, V. Roles and role change in monkey society: The consort relationship of rhesus monkeys. *Man*, 1970, **5**, 449-465.

Reynolds, V., & Reynolds, F. Chimpanzees of the Budongo Forest. In I. DeVore (Ed.), *Primate behavior*. New York: Holt, 1965. Pp. 368-424.

Rheingold, H. L. The effect of environmental stimulation upon social and exploratory behaviour in the human infant. In B. M. Foss (Ed.), *Determinants of infant behaviour*, Vol. 1. London: Methuen, 1961. Pp. 143-177.

Richards, M. P. M. Social interaction in the first weeks of human life. *Psychiatria, Neurologia, Neurochirurgia*, 1971, **74**, 35-42.

Richards, M. P. M., & Bernal, J. F. An observational study of mother-infant interaction. In N. G. Blurton Jones (Ed.), *Ethological studies of child behaviour*, London & New York: Cambridge Univ. Press, 1972. Pp. 75-197.

Ripley, S. The leaping of langurs: A problem in the study of locomotor adaptation. *American Journal of Physical Anthropology*, 1967, **26**, 149-170.

Robson, K. S. The role of eye-to-eye contact in maternal-infant attachment. *Journal of Child Psychology and Psychiatry*, 1967, **8**, 13-25.

Robson, K. S., Pederson, F. A., & Moss, H. A. Developmental observations of diadic gazing in relation to the fear of strangers and social approach behavior. *Child Development*, 1969, **40**, 619-627.

Rohles, F. H. (Ed.) *Circadian rhythms in nonhuman primates. Bibliotheca Primatologica*, Vol. 9. Basel: Karger, 1969.

Roos, P. D. Jurisdiction: An ecological concept. *Human Relations*, 1968, **21**, 75-84.

Rosenblum, L. A., Kaufman, I. C., & Stynes, A. J. Individual distance in two species of macaque. *Animal Behaviour*, 1964, **12**, 338-342.

Rosenblum, L. A., Kaufman, I. C., & Stynes, A. J. Interspecific variations in the effects of hunger on diurnally varying behavior elements in macaques. *Brain, Behavior and Evolution*, 1969, **2**, 119-131.

Rosenblum, L. A., Levy, E. J., & Kaufman, I. C. Social behavior of squirrel monkeys and the reaction to strangers. *Animal Behaviour*, 1968, **16**, 288-293.

Rosenthal, R. Weighing the effect of a smile. *New Society*, 1968, **319**, 667-670.

Rowell, T. E. Forest living baboons in Uganda. *Journal of Zoology*, 1966, **149**, 344-364. (a)

Rowell, T. E. Hierarchy in the organization of a captive baboon group. *Animal Behaviour*, 1966, **14**, 430-443. (b)

Rowell, T. E. Variability in the social organization of primates. In D. Morris (Ed.), *Primate ethology*. London: Weidenfeld & Nicolson, 1967. Pp. 219-235.

Rowell, T. E. Long-term changes in a population of Ugandan baboons. *Folia Primatologica*, 1969, **11**, 241-254.

Rowell, T. E., & Hinde, R. A. Responses of rhesus monkeys to mildly stressful situations. *Animal Behaviour*, 1963, **11**, 235-243.

Rowell, T. E., Din, N. A., & Omar, A. The social development of baboons in their first three months. *Journal of Zoology*, 1968, **155**, 461-483.

Rule, C. A theory of human behavior based on studies of non-human primates. *Perspectives in Biology and Medicine*, 1967, **10**, 153-176.

Russell, C., & Russell, W. M. S. An approach to human ethology. *Behavioral Science*, 1957, **2**, 169-200.

Russell, C., & Russell, W. M. S. Population and behavior in animals and man. *Memoirs and Proceedings of the Manchester Literary and Philosophical Society*, 1966, **109**, 1-16.

Russell, C., & Russell, W. M. S. *Violence, monkeys and man*. London: Macmillan, 1968.

Russell, C., & Russell, W. M. S. Primate male behavior and its human analogs. *Impact of Science on Society*, 1971, **21**, 63-74.

Sackett, G. P. Monkeys reared in isolation with pictures as visual input: Evidence for an innate releasing mechanism. *Science*, 1966, **154**, 1468-1473.

Sade, D. S. Seasonal cycle in size of testis in free-ranging *Macaca mulatta*. *Folia Primatologica*, 1964, **2**, 171-180.

Sade, D. S. Some aspects of parent-offspring and sibling relations in a group of rhesus monkeys, with a discussion of grooming. *American Journal of Physical Anthropology*, 1965, **23**, 1-17.

Sade, D. S. Determinants of dominance in a group of free-ranging rhesus monkeys. In S. A. Altmann (Ed.), *Social communication among primates*. Chicago, Ill: Univ. of Chicago Press, 1967. Pp. 99-114.

Sahlins, M. D. The origin of society. *Scientific American*, 1960, **203**, 76-87.

Sainsbury, P. Gestural movement during psychiatric interview. *Psychosomatic Medicine*, 1955, **17**, 458-469.

Schaller, G. B. *The mountain gorilla. Ecology and behavior*. Chicago, Ill.: Univ. of Chicago Press, 1963.

Scheflen, A. E. Communication and regulation in psychotherapy. *Psychiatry*, 1963, **26**, 126-136.

Scheflen, A. E. The significance of posture in communications systems. *Psychiatry*, 1964, **27**, 316-331.

Scheflen, A. E. Quasi-courtship behavior in psychotherapy. *Psychiatry*, 1965, **28**, 245-257.

Scott, J. P. Hostility and aggression in animals. In E. Bliss (Ed.), *The roots of behavior*. New York: Harper, 1962. Pp. 167-178.

Sears, P. S. Doll play aggression in normal young children: Influence of sex, age, sibling status, father's absence. *Psychological Monographs*, 1951, **65**, 1-42.

Sewell, W. H., & Mussen, P. H. Effects of feeding, weaning and scheduling procedure on childhood adjustment and the formation of oral symptoms. *Child Development*, 1952, **23**, 185-191.

Siegel, S. *Nonparametric statistics for the behavioral sciences*. New York: McGraw-Hill, 1956.

Simonds, P. E. The bonnet macaque in south India. In I. DeVore (Ed.), *Primate behavior*, New York: Holt, 1965. Pp. 175-196.

Smith, M. E. An investigation of the development of the sentence and the extent of vocabulary in young children. *University of Iowa Studies in Child Welfare*, 1926, **3**, (5) 1-92.

References

Smith, P. K., & Connolly, K. Patterns of play and social interaction in preschool children. In N. G. Blurton Jones (Ed.), *Ethological studies of child behaviour*. London & New York: Cambridge Univ. Press, 1972. Pp. 65-95.

Sommer, R. Studies in personal space. *Sociometry*, 1959, **22**, 247-260.

Sommer, R. Leadership and group geography. *Sociometry*, 1961, **24**, 99-109.

Sommer, R. Further studies of small group ecology. *Sociometry*, 1965, **28**, 337-348.

Sommer, R. Sociofugal space. *American Journal of Sociology*, 1967, **72**, 654-660.

Sommer, R. Intimacy ratings in five countries. *International Journal of Psychology*, 1968, **3**, 109-114.

Sommer, R. *Personal space: The behavioral basis of design.* Englewood Cliffs, N.J.: Prentice-Hall, 1969.

Sorenson, E. R., & Gajdusek, D. C. The study of child behavior and development in primitive cultures. *Pediatrics (Suppl.)*, 1966, **37**, 149-243.

Southwick, C. H. (Ed). *Primate social behavior.* Princeton, N.J.: Van Nostrand, 1963.

Southwick, C. H. An experimental study of intragroup agonistic behaviour in rhesus monkeys *(Macaca mulatta). Behaviour.* 1967, **28**, 182-209.

Southwick, C. H. Effect of maternal environment on aggressive behavior of inbred mice. *Communications in Behavioral Biology, A*, 1968, **1**, 129-132.

Southwick, C. H., & Siddiqi, M. R. The role of social tradition in the maintenance of dominance in a wild rhesus group. *Primates*, 1967, **8**, 341-353.

Southwick, C. H., Beg, M. A., & Siddiqi, M. R. Rhesus monkeys in north India. In I. DeVore (Ed.), *Primate behavior.* London: Weidenfeld & Nicolson, 1965. Pp. 111-159.

Sparks, J. Allogrooming in primates: A review. In D. Morris (Ed.), *Primate ethology.* New York: Holt, 1967. Pp. 148-175.

Spitz, R. A. A note on the extrapolation of ethological findings. *International Journal of Psychoanalysis*, 1955, **36**, 162-165.

Stephenson, G. M., & Rutter, D. R. Eye contact, distance, and affiliation. *British Journal of Psychology*, 1970, **61**, 385-393.

Storr, A. *Human aggression.* London: Allen Lane, 1968.

Stott, L. H., & Ball, R. S. Consistency and change in ascendance-submission in the social interaction of children. *Child Development*, 1957, **28**, 259-272.

Struhsaker, T. T. Social structure among vervet monkeys *(Cercopithecus aethiops). Behaviour*, 1967, **29**, 83-121.

Sugiyama, Y. On the division of a natural troop of Japanese monkeys at Takasakiyama. *Primates*, 1960, **2**, 109-148.

Sugiyama, Y. An artificial social change in a hanuman langur troop. *(Presbytis entellus). Primates*, 1966, **7**, 41-72.

Sully, J. *An essay on laughter. Its forms, its causes, its development and its value.* London: Longmans, Green, 1902.

Tanner, J. M. Human growth and constitution. In G. A. Harrison, J. S. Weiner, J. M. Tanner, & N. A. Barnicot (Eds.), *Human biology.* London & New York: Oxford Univ. Press, 1964. Pp. 299-397.

Thach, J. S. A bigeminus pattern in social behavior. *Bibliotheca Primatologica*, 1969, **9**, 52-63.

Thiessen, D. D., & Rodgers, D. A. Population density and endocrine function. *Psychological Bulletin*, 1961, **58**, 441-451.

Thomas, E. J., & Fink, C. F. Effects of group size. *Psychological Bulletin*, 1963, **60**, 371-384.

Thompson, D. H. An ethological study of dominance hierarchies in preschool children. Unpublished manuscript, University of Wisconsin, 1967.

248

Tiger, L. *Men in groups.* London: Nelson, 1969.

Tiger, L. Dominance in human societies. *Annual Review of Ecology and Systematics,* 1970, 1, 287-306. (a)

Tiger, L. The possible biological origins of sexual discrimination. *Impact of Science on Society.* 1970, **20**, 29-44. (b)

Tiger, L., & Fox, R. The zoological perspective in social science. *Man,* 1966, **1**, 75-81.

Tinbergen, N. *The study of instinct.* London & New York: Oxford Univ. Press, 1951.

Tinbergen, N. On aims and methods of ethology. *Zeitschrift für Tierpsychologie,* 1963, 20, 410-433.

Tinbergen, N. On war and peace in animals and man. *Science,* 1968, **160**, 1411-1418.

Tinbergen, N., & Moynihan, M. Head flagging in the black-headed gull; its function and origin. *British Birds,* 1952, **45**, 19-22.

Tinklepaugh, O. L., & Hartman, C. G. Behavior and maternal care of the newborn monkey (*Macaca mulatta—"M. rhesus"*). *Journal of Genetic Psychology,* 1932, **40**, 257-286.

Tobias, P. V. Bushmen of the Kalahari. *Man,* 1957, **57** 33-40.

Tokuda, K., & Jensen, G. D. Determinants of dominance hierarchy in a captive group of pigtailed monkeys (*Macaca nemestrina*). *Primates,* 1969, **10**, 227-236.

Tuttle, R. H. Knuckle-walking and the evolution of hominid hands. *American Journal of Physical Anthropology,* 1967, **26**, 171-206.

Ulrich, R. Pain as a cause of aggression. *American Zoologist,* 1966, **6**, 643-662.

Valentine, C. W. *The normal child and some of his abnormalities.* Harmondsworth: Penguin, 1956.

Vandenbergh, J. G. The development of social structure in free-ranging rhesus monkeys. *Behaviour,* 1967, **29**, 177-194.

van der Post, L. *The lost world of the Kalahari.* Harmondsworth: Penguin, 1958.

van Hooff, J. A. R. A. M. Facial expressions in higher primates. *Symposia of the Zoological Society of London,* 1962, **8**, 97-125.

van Hooff, J. A. R. A. M. The facial displays of the catarrhine monkeys and apes. In D. Morris (Ed.), *Primate ethology.* London: Weidenfeld & Nicolson, 1967. Pp. 7-68.

van Hooff, J. A. R. A. M. A component analysis of the structure of the social behaviour of a semi-captive chimpanzee group. *Experientia,* 1970, **26**, 549-550.

van Lawick-Goodall, J. Mother-offspring relationships in free-ranging chimpanzees. In D. Morris (Ed.), *Primate ethology.* London: Weidenfeld & Nicolson, 1967. Pp. 287-346.

van Lawick-Goodall, J. The behaviour of free-ranging chimpanzees in the Gombe Stream Reserve. *Animal behaviour Monographs,* 1968, **1**, 161-311. (a)

van Lawick-Goodall, J. A preliminary report on expressive movements and communication in the Gombe Stream chimpanzees. In P. C. Jay (Ed.), *Primates.* New York: Holt, 1968, Pp. 313-374. (b)

van Lawick-Goodall, J. Tool-using in primates and other vertebrates. In D. S. Lehrman, R. A. Hinde, & E. Shaw (Eds.), *Advances in the study of behavior,* Vol. 3. New York & London: Academic Press, 1970. Pp. 195-249.

Vine, I. Communication by facial-visual signals. In J. H. Crooks (Ed.), *Social behaviour in birds and mammals.* London & New York: Academic Press, 1970. Pp. 279-354.

Vine, I. Judgement of direction of gaze: an interpretation of discrepant results. *British Journal of Social and Clinical Psychology,* 1971, **10**, 320-331.

Virgo, H. B., & Waterhouse, M. J. The emergence of attention structure amongst rhesus macaques. *Man,* 1969, **4**, 85-93.

Vowles, D. M. *The psychobiology of aggression.* Edinburgh: Edinburgh Univ. Press, 1970.

Vowles, D. M., & Clarke, J. The computer analysis of animal behaviour. Unpublished manuscript, University of Edinburgh, 1971.

References

Waldrop, M. F., & Bell, R. Q. Relation of preschool dependency behavior and family size and density. *Child Development*, 1964, **35**, 1187-1195.

Walters, J., Pearce, D., & Dahms, L. Affectional and aggressive behavior of preschool children. *Child Development*, 1957, **28**, 15-26.

Warner, F. Muscular movements in man, and their evolution in the infant: A study of movement in man, and its evolution, together with influences as to the properties of nerve centres and their modes of action in expressing thought. *Journal of Mental Science*, 1889, **35**, 23-44.

Washburn, R. W. A scheme for grading the reactions of children in a new social situation. *Journal of Genetic Psychology*, 1932, **40**, 84-99.

Washburn, S. L. Ischial callosities as sleeping adaptations. *American Journal of Physical Anthropology*, 1957, **15**, 269-276.

Washburn, S. L. Conflict in primate society. In A. de Reuck & J. Knight (Eds.), *Conflict in society*. London: Churchill, 1966. Pp. 3-15.

Washburn, S. L., & DeVore, I. The social life of baboons. *Scientific American*, 1961, **204**, 62-71.

Washburn, S. L., & Hamburg, D. A. Aggressive behavior in Old World monkeys and apes. In P. C. Jay (Ed.), *Primates*. New York: Holt, 1968. Pp. 458-478.

Washburn, S. L., & Howell, F. C. Human evolution and culture. In S. Tax (Ed.), *The evolution of man*. Chicago, Ill.: Univ. of Chicago Press, 1960. Pp. 33-56.

Washburn, S. L., & Lancaster, J. The evolution of hunting. In R. B. Lee & I. DeVore (Eds.), *Man the hunter*. Chicago, Ill.: Aldine, 1968. Pp. 293-303.

Weiskrantz, L. Elliot, J., & Darlington, C. Preliminary observations on tickling oneself. *Nature*, 1971, **230**, 598-599.

White, J. H., Hegarty, J. R., & Beasley, N. A. Eye contact and observer bias: A research note. *British Journal of Psychology*, 1970, **61**, 271-273.

Wilson, W. L., & Wilson, C. C. Aggressive interactions of captive chimpanzees living in a semi-free-ranging environment. 6571st Aeromedical Research Laboratory Technical Report No. ARL-TR-68-9, 1968.

Wolff, P. H. Observations on the early development of smiling. In B. M. Foss (Ed.), *Determinants of infant behaviour*. Vol. 2. London: Methuen, 1963. Pp. 113-138.

Wolff, P. H. Sucking patterns of infant mammals. *Brain, Behavior and Evolution*, 1968, **1**, 354-367. (a)

Wolff, P. H. The serial organization of sucking in the young infant. *Pediatrics*, 1968, **42**, 943-956. (b)

Wolff, S., & Chess, S. A behavioural study of schizophrenic children. *Acta Psychiatrica Scandinavica*, 1964, **40**, 438-466.

Wynne-Edwards, V. C. *Animal dispersion in relation to social behaviour*. Edinburgh: Oliver & Boyd, 1962.

Yablonsky, L. *The violent gang*. Harmondsworth: Penguin, 1962.

Yerkes, R. M. *Chimpanzees, a laboratory colony*. New Haven, Conn.: Yale Univ. Press, 1943.

Zegans, L. S. An appraisal of ethological contributions to psychiatric theory and research. *American Journal of Psychiatry*, 1967, **124**, 729-739.

Zingeser, M. R. Cercopithecoid canine tooth honing mechanisms. *American Journal of Physical Anthropology*, 1969, **31**, 205-213.

Subject Index

Italicized page numbers refer to definitions of the behavior patterns.

V

Verbalize, 42, 54, *65-66*, 206, 210-212, 215, 216
Vervet monkey, 66, 151, 170
Videotape recording, 28, 29, 33-34, 38, 184, 224
Violence, Monkeys and Man, 8
Vocabulary size, 65, 66
Vocalize, 44, *66-67*, 211, 217

W

Walk, 108, *112*, 195, 196, 199, 208, 211, 214, 217, 220, *229*
Washington, 13
Watson, 18
Wave, *87*
Way station behavior, 171
Weapons, 52, 68, 71, 82, 85-86
Weather effects, 180, 193
Weep, 49, 60, *67*, 144, 157, 158
Weight, 29-32, 118-121, 124

West Indian, 29
Whistle, 53, 65
White-faced monkey, 106
Wichita, 67
Wide Eyes, 10, 20, 37, *51-52*, 81, 83, 89
Wild Heritage, 8
Wink, 43
Winner, 48
    definition of, 26
Wisconsin, 13
Wisconsin General Test Apparatus, 9
Witch, 67
Witoto, 62
Wrestle, 60, 99, *105-106*, 111, 211, 212, 216, 224

Y

Yawn, 46, *68*, 76

Z

Zoo, 107, 110, 151, 158

B 6
C 7
D 8
E 9
F 0
G 1
H 2
I 3
J 4